SACRED UNION

Awakening To The Consciousness of Eden

SACRED UNION

Awakening To The Consciousness of Eden

Volume One: The Path of White Tantra
Creating Sacred Union Within

By

Tanishka
author of 'The Inner Goddess Makeover'

ISBN 978-0-9874263-0-7

I Am She
by Tanishka

I am She
Wild, untamed & true

I am She
who reveals that which lies hidden

I am She
betrayed by a million men
who sought to steal the primeval fire
from the core of Gaia's belly
but who tripped on their lies
fleeing from the scene of the crime

In the wasteland of unconscious souls
I cried out to eternity for justice
& heard only my own rage & grief echoing around me

I am She
the Serpent
calling you to awaken

to remember the truth...

'YOU ARE DIVINE!'

Acknowledgments

I would like to thank the Christ, the Magdalene, Ishtar, Gaia, Luna & Sol for pouring their teachings through me as a channel, as well as their patience & faith in me to birth this book. I am also deeply grateful to the couples who have entrusted me with their vulnerability enabling me to midwife this information from Source. I would also like to acknowledge a heartfelt thanks to my parents for teaching me so much about relationships, all my partners who schooled me through my apprenticeship in dancing with my shadow & my daughter, Ariella who continues to be one of my greatest teachers. I would also like to thank my beloved mentors, Kermit the Frog, Stephen Robinson, Jen Powell & Evelynne Joffe. My Red Tent sisterhood circle of support & the village who helped me balance parenthood with service to others: Annie, Deb, Karen, Kitty, Bronwen, Wilma, Charity, Dani, Michelle, Evgenia, Fiona, Kirsten, Echo, China & Lael - thank-you. I would also like to say thanks to my dear friend, Nick for your graphic wizardry & mirth.

Table of Contents

x

⚕ How To Get The Most From This Book

(& My Take On FAQ About Tantra)

The word, Tantra means 'to weave'. So this book series will assist you in creating a deeper & more authentic connection with yourself, with others & with the cosmos by awakening & interweaving all of your inner & outer Divine aspects.

In **'Sacred Union: Volume One'** we awaken & weave together our inner serpents of light by expressing our seven feminine & masculine aspects which govern the chakras (major energy centers). This awakens the totality of ourselves known in mysticism as 'The Holy Hermaphrodite'.

In **'Sacred Union: Volume Two'** we discover how to connect at every level with our partner by sharing the full expression of our inner selves so we feel truly seen & loved. This opening & communion of our total selves elevates our partnerships to that of 'The Holy Couple' as it honors & celebrates all the facets of our multidimensional soul. It is this 'interweaving' of two conscious & whole beings which creates an upward spiral supporting our highest potential rather than a downward spiral of entropy & co-dependence.

In **'Sacred Union: Volume Three'** it is then a natural progression that we weave the fabric of our daily lives in accordance with the graceful ebb & flow of the natural cycles, creating a deep & experiential state of ongoing communion with the Cosmos. The return to Eden. Put simply, these teachings are a map for creating & living Heaven on Earth!

FAQ: Is Tantra About Mastering Sexual Techniques?

There is as much confusion as there is curiosity about Tantra currently in the West as many seek out new inspiration to enhance their relationships. With deep respect to the ancient practices of Tantra & to those bringing them back through books & workshops, I have noted that despite the West's apparent pre-occupation with sex we collectively know little about love which I see as the essence of Tantra. What I believe exacerbates this confusion is that many specialist books on Tantra focus on mastering techniques such as specific breathing practices & sexual postures rather than on first understanding the concept & teachings which inspire one to commit wholeheartedly to a discipline. As a result, I have observed earnest couples caught in a 'head trip' in their effort to perfect certain techniques so they can be 'good' at Tantra, kind of like teenage girls trying to learn & perfect the mechanics of oral sex from glossy mags!

FAQ: Is Tantra For Everyone, Regardless of Sexual Orientation?

Let me state at the outset, my aim is that this book is accessible & usable for all folk, be they heterosexual, bi-sexual, homosexual or transgender. To those of you who don't identify as heterosexual, I offer my sincere apology for the predominant use of heterosexual language when describing couple processes in Volume Two. Although I want to make it clear that ALL of these couple processes are designed for ALL couples. I simply find it easier & more authentic to speak from my personal experience when sharing these as a guide but wholeheartedly celebrate all expressions of Divine love between consenting adults as equally deserving of reverence. I also speak extensively about the significance of acknowledging both genders within us & the need for us to express the multi-faceted aspects that make up both our masculine & feminine psyche if we are to create soul fulfilling & liberating partnerships. This goes far beyond our physical gender or sexual preference, just as love knows no divisive boundaries.

FAQ: Is Tantra Aligned With Any Particular Religion?

My understanding is that most of the ancient Hindu Tantric texts have not survived the passage of time - although many of the teachings were later adopted & adapted by those of the Buddhist faith. That said, what I am presenting is my personal & intuitive view of Tantra. I want to be clear that whilst I refer to Tantra & consider myself a Tantrika (one who practices & facilitates Tantric processes) most of my information is downloaded intuitively. Specifically, this means I channel information as a scribe on behalf of our collective 'Higher Intelligence'. This is information that my soul inwardly receives as inspired thoughts which resonate deep within my being as truth, often coinciding with numerous observations of synchronicity which I then filter through my own experiential wisdom. I have not formally trained under the guidance of a Tantric Master, but on numerous occasions have later seen the intuitive information & processes I have received, facilitated, written about & taught published in Tantric texts & presented in Tantric forums. I simply prefer to work from the inside out, using my intuition to prompt me to seek out relevant quotes & symbols that illustrate what I am being given to share from the inner realms.

I hope that these channelled teachings inspire the creative dance of hearts, minds, bodies with 'The Force' of all creation.

For those of you who noticed an internal flag go up at the word, 'creation' I offer these words for your consideration. We are now in an exciting time of enlightened science, where Darwinism & creationism are no longer in competition. Fundamental thinking, be it of the 'religious' or 'evolutionary' camp is now being superseded as we collectively transcend a dualistic & polarized view of reality which reduced existence to either 'black or white.' This also applies to the futility of arguing over which religious doctrine is 'right'. For a millennia, our relationship to the 'infinite essence of life' has been reduced to the side our rational minds decided had the publishing rights on the 'word of God.' This factional approach to spirituality is akin to picking football teams & then defending to the death what you were told to believe in & support. Fortunately more & more of our species are now developing their subtle senses so they can base their personal truth on their own direct experience.

Tantra is about attuning to the energy body within us, 'The Force' & through acknowledging, understanding & delighting in it, we develop a deep reverence for the life force within us & within everyone & everything - a concept which I believe is the basis of all religion which just got hijacked along the way with political agendas & rules. To that end, I honour 'The Force' by many names such as Source, Universe, Great Mystery & invoke the universal ascended masters who are assisting the conscious unfoldment of humanity. These include energies such as Christ, Shiva, Krishna, Allah, Yahweh, the Magdalene, Isis, Ishtar, Kwan Yin & Shakti but to name a few. :))

FAQ: Is This a Workbook & Is There Homework?

Yeah, I have provided practical processes for you to try in each of the three volumes as applied knowledge is the difference between a head trip & a heart journey. I would urge you to give ALL the practices a try because I've seen them create profound inner shifts within my students & transform frosty marriages into genuinely passionate ones. As always, 'what you put in - you get out' so if you don't want to just read this to boast to some girl in a bar that you've read, 'Tantric books like 'Sacred Union' by Tanishka' which is akin to hurtling through Europe in a bus & saying that you've 'done it' - give them a go. They're simple processes to try & you will feel the positive effects immediately. (And let's be honest, I'm not asking you to do a gallbladder cleanse!) It's not rocket science, so don't get caught up about the 'right way' to do something or you've missed the point. To that end, I will make helpful suggestions en route but as always, listen to your own inner guidance & choose your own adventure!

FAQ: Will This Book Transform My Relationship?

Well, yes if you consider when we transform our view of what is possible in relationship, our relationships will automatically transform. The top selling relationship books over recent decades have focused on the differences between the sexes, which is helpful in developing understanding & compassion for our external opposite. However, this view of relationships is still limited as it defines us by our physical gender which can further entrench an 'us & them' attitude between the sexes. If we are to take our relationships to the next level we must first shift our perception of ourselves & take our awareness to the next level. This means seeing ourselves through the eyes of soul, rather than ego & acknowledging we are both feminine & masculine. When we make this shift, we can then take responsibility for balancing our own feminine & masculine polarities rather than shooting the messenger in the form of our partner who is simply mirroring that which we have been unable to acknowledge in ourselves. This internal imbalance & disempowerment is the ultimate source of all conflict created within partnerships. When we balance the self by creating harmony of opposites within, we can create balanced partnerships & enjoy harmony externally with our opposite. This is the focus of Volume One.

Volume Two in this series is akin to a **'Relationship Revolution'** as it offers a new model of relating as we evolve as a species, reflecting our acceptance & reverence for all forms of love between consenting adults. This model for 'Holy Hermaphrodites' enjoying 'Soul Love' provides a relationship paradigm which is completely inclusive of all gradients along the gender spectrum, reflecting our more evolved status as 'cosmic beings' who recognize we are having a human experience rather reducing our experience of love to that which is limited by the rational mind's reality, based purely upon the identity of our physical gender. In other words, 'love is beyond gender' so if you have categorized yourself as any particular sexual orientation: gay, straight, bi - I invite you to broaden your perception of yourself so your reality may be truly open & inclusive, rather than divisive by basing it upon your previous limited perception of yourself.

FAQ: What Will I Gain From This Adventure of Sacred Union?

'Sacred Union' presents an innovative & groundbreaking approach to relationships by mapping how to create a harmonious inner 'sacred marriage' as a foundation for creating truly fulfilling soul friendships, partnerships & soul clan communities which honor the expression of all of our inner aspects as multi-faceted souls. This reflects an inner calling towards 'oneness' - experiencing ourselves as the 'One World Soul'. This is the consciousness of Eden, returning to a state of innocence & connectedness. We do this by appreciating the necessity & perfection of every moment within our shared co-created matrix of experience. For without every one of our experiences we would not become the 'all knowing' & all accepting heart centered, galactic beings that we are now birthing. Below are the three stages of this metamorphosis:

1. Self Acceptance

The first stage in this homecoming is to create a state of oneness within. First we must seek to understand we are the sum of many parts, by creating a healthy internal relationship with the shadow or rejected parts of our psyche. For it is impossible to transcend duality without first accepting & integrating all of our disparate parts, as this creates wholeness & unification through acceptance & healing.

2. Twin Flame Soul Mate Love

Once we have achieved a certain level of self-awareness through this process of self-acceptance, we then attract our twin flame soul mate. Then through the process of consciously journeying through the solar & lunar cycles as conscious couples we achieve greater harmony & balance with our external opposites, creating oneness on an even greater level. (More about the evolutionary roles of twin flames later!)

3. Soul Clan Communities

The harmonious union of Twin Flames then attracts & creates the formation of conscious communities generated by a common soul frequency being emitted. This intensification of light filled intent draws together like-minded couples & families to gather & reside within the spirit of place which most resonates with their soul.

Ultimately, 'Sacred Union' is about living in a state of connectedness & reverence by attuning to the God/dess force in all of creation by living in a spirit of right relationship with the natural laws & cycles within ourselves, each other & the cosmos. This enables us to maintain harmony & balance with all beings in all dimensions such as the stone, plant, elemental & animal kingdoms.

FAQ: If I'm Already In a Partnership, Can I Skip Volume One?

This book series is divided into three volumes. I strongly recommend reading all three in order, even if you're in a relationship because understanding the masculine & feminine archetypes within both of you is essential to the sharing of those aspects in Volume Two. Any healthy relationship is built on the foundation of two individuals who have a solid understanding of themselves, so as tempting as it may be to skip ahead...DO read the White Path (Volume One) before proceeding on with the Red (Volume Two).

FAQ: If I'm Single, Should I Read the Couples Section?

Personally, I found I had to walk a long way along both the White (Volume One) & Black path (Volume Three) before having the opportunity to walk the Red Path (Volume Two). Similarly, I recommend reading & living the principles explored in the Black path (Volume Three) if you are single, which will in turn amplify your soul resonance, magnetizing your Twin Flame. I would also strongly recommend reading the Red Path (Volume Two) if single, because before we can attract this level of partnership we need to know what it looks like. Further more, by focusing upon this concept you will emit a much clearer intent. In addition, there are helpful chapters on what to look for in a prospective partner & how to create a courtship that lays a solid foundation for Sacred Union.

What You Can Expect

Information that sheds light & with it, a 'light-hearted' viewpoint on our universal shadow traits to assist you in transcending old negative bonding patterns anchored in childhood (& other incarnations) so you can transform your relationship with yourself & your loved ones to uplift each other to your highest potential. There are also practical processes you can easily adopt into your everyday life so you don't have to sit in a cave for seven years wearing a silk kaftan & chanting 'Om' in order to find enlightenment.

What You Will Gain

- A Tantric Tool Kit for both singles & couples to identify & weave together your inner masculine & feminine aspects so you can resolve inner conflict & avoid unconsciously projecting outwardly on others.
- An understanding of the difference between a soul mate & twin flame relationship.
- A clear framework for those of you seeking a twin flame soul mate relationship so you can confidently create a conscious partnership with a step-by-step formula for dating.
- Effective, simple processes for those of you in existing partnerships to resolve conflicts by honoring your partner as your sacred mirror & teacher.

- Simple sacred ceremonies to empower you & your partner with deeply tender & honoring ways to share all the facets of your multi-dimensional souls, creating soul inspired romance like you've never known!

- Awareness into how the heightened times of the natural cycles impact on your ability to relate, such as full moons, storms, solstices & the annual descent of Autumn / Winter.

- How to identify & heal the masculine / feminine gender war within so it may be healed in your relationships, in your community & in the macrocosm between East & West.

- Practical ways to fill your cup by communing with 'The One' in nature & the cosmos through communion with the elements & greater cycles.

- Practical ways to commune with 'the One' in your soul brother / sister connections via conscious community so you don't unconsciously expect 'the one' special person to fill all of your needs.

What This Book Will Not Do

I am not a 'certified clinical expert' who will put you through pop quiz's or tell you how to 'fix' your marriage or your partner! I believe the person you are with is your greatest spiritual teacher who is mirroring your beliefs about what you think you deserve & what you think is possible, so making them the focus of your makeover quest is merely a distraction from your own issues.

When we view our partner through the lens of our soul rather than our ego we become humble, focusing instead on our own lessons which they are reflecting rather than constantly judging our partner. As over time this generates so much residual resentment & tension that it's inevitable our partners become estranged as the mutual pattern of criticism & rejection erodes the love & trust initially shared. Should we then seek someone new without understanding this existing dynamic, the pattern starts again as we fall for our opposite who makes us feel complete but who over time we again reject if we don't own our disowned self. So, transform yourself & everything else will follow.

If you are single, I won't tell you how to 'land a man' or 'a woman' as I see this as a form of seduction that will not ultimately serve you or them.

An Overview of The Three Paths of Sacred Union

White Tantra, Red Tantra & Black Tantra

Are you wanting to create more moments where you really connect soul to soul with others, to the essence of life & the natural elements with the joy & wonderment you once had as a child? Yes...? Does your soul yearn to be truly met in a deeply intimate, mutually honoring & soul fulfilling partnership which enables you to experience greater shared states of ecstasy? 'Yes! Yes! Yes!' You may exclaim wildly, (to quote Meg Ryan in the film, 'When Harry Met Sally') except your mouth is holding a pen, nappy pin or cigarette because you can't figure out how to meet all the commitments of living in the 21st century & stay sane, let alone have time to indulge such flights of self-indulgent fantasy?

Our modern society is structured in a way that reflects how disconnected we have become from ourselves, each other & the greater cycles. For example, do you know what effect the solar cycle has on your mind, body & energy levels? Or what effect the lunar cycle has on your emotional well-being? Or which seasons are the most challenging for relationships & why? When we understand exactly how we are affected by life's natural cycles we can once again enter the dance with them & enjoy greater balance & harmony in every aspect of our lives. As the ancients warned, 'dis-aster' is what befalls those who live a life disconnected from the transits of the stars!

For we enter this physical realm in a state of innocence, full of wonder at the natural world & it's power. Then year by year we become caught up in the illusion of our ego's desires & priorities so we gradually lose our heart connection with Mother Nature & dismiss the magical power of the elemental realms & stars as mere childhood fantasy. As a result our ego driven culture has continued to rebel against Mother Nature by unconsciously trying to prove how grown up & smart we are by endeavoring to show how much we don't need to rely on her like a child trying to individuate from a parent. By ignoring the natural cycles we have inadvertently gone against life itself, (such as trying to appear younger instead of older as we age). This mindset is counter to life itself, illustrated by the reversal of the word 'live' which is 'evil'. The good news is it is only when things get so out of whack that we wake up. And now, as we are humbled by how unsustainable & diseased our modern lives are, we then start our return journey home, back to the Mother, back to a state of innocence rather than an immature mindset of rebellion which has cost us all dearly. So as previously stated, life as we know it is all about to change, there is a global shift taking place which you are an integral part of...

This new consciousness I know as 'Sacred Union' goes far beyond our dualistic notion of just partnering with one other to form a bonded union. It is entering into a state of true connectedness with our multi-dimensional, Divine selves, so that we may connect with & mutually revere that as the true essence in every aspect of creation, including the greater cycles. It is in fact, our natural state, which has been documented as Eden in our myths & legends, when we lived in a state of grace, innocence, harmony & beauty in the bounty of Mother Nature's garden.

Our challenge has been to return home to this way of being, after many lifetimes since we experienced what was known as 'The

Fall.' This was when we sought to know ourselves as the many different facets of 'the One', so we split off & fragmented into individual expressions of 'the One' Divine source. This was not a mistake for which we have been punished but rather part of an unfolding natural cycle, which is now coming to its natural end for those who choose to transcend the wheel of karma or fate. (This simply refers to continuously living through the effects of our unconscious actions.) For those who don't choose to transform at this time, they will continue to cycle on the wheel of cause & effect like the film, 'Groundhog Day' repeating their past lessons until the cycle completes again & so on. Life is eternal.

For those who are actively seeking to understand all their past lessons by looking at the part they have played in creating those experiences, now is a very exciting time! For when we understand how NOT to create the same outcomes by unconsciously living out the same belief patterns, we become truly free to create life anew in every moment according to Highest Will. In other words, when we surrender to our Highest Destiny through daily devotional practices, our ego 'gets out of the way' so we can receive our true birth rite of Divine providence. Then life becomes graceful, effortless & filled with serendipitous events gifted through synchronistic coincidences.

To ascend from a mindset of victim based Hell to creator based Heaven, we simply need to inwardly ascend the Tree of Life & the Tree of Knowledge. These two trees are what Adam & Eve stand in front of in the Tarot card of 'The Lovers'. The Lovers represent both the lessons of our inner feminine & masculine & the lessons we will learn externally in relationship. For example, the feminine must activate her Shakti, (Sacred Feminine essence) up through her chakras to awaken her consciousness if she is to ascend the inner Tree of Life. And the masculine, ruled by the mind must seek to heal the perception of opposites if he is to transcend the inner Tree of Knowledge.

As a tour guide on this journey, I have been guided by one emanation of the Holy Couple, the Christ & the Magdalene to take you on these paths to create Sacred Union within so you may then attract & create external Sacred Union with another. The third & final path I have channelled from Mother Earth & Father Sky, which is how to live in an awakened state of Sacred Union once you've entered into the gates of Eden!

The Three Paths of Tantra.

- The White Path: Creating Sacred Union Within.
- The Red Path: Creating Sacred Union Partnerships.
- The Black Path: Living in Sacred Union with the All.

An Overview of The White Path: Creating Sacred Union Within

Volume One, 'The White Path' introduces you to your inner landscape of feminine & masculine archetypes, known mythically as Gods & Goddesses. By unveiling an awareness of the strengths & vulnerabilities of each of these aspects, you can then express each of their energies consciously. This energetically opens the seven major chakras which these archetypes govern. This enables the 'chi' or life force to flow unimpeded from the base chakra to the crown, activating the inner currents of yin & yang energy known in Tantra as the twin serpents who ascend the inner Tree of Life. This is the image known throughout the world as the symbol for healing, the caduceus, which depicts two serpents spiraling upward on the staff with wings outstretched at the top. This process of self-actualization creates psychological empowerment & increased energetic vitality.

An Overview of The Red Path: Creating Sacred Union Partnerships

Volume Two, 'The Red Path' explains how to create true soul mate partnerships with simple processes to connect soul to soul at each of the seven gates (chakras) with your partner. Starting with practical advice on how to establish a Sacred Union through a conscious courtship, this section assists prospective partners to unveil their true self (soul) at each of the seven gates to avoid the old ego dance of projection & seduction of the lower selves...which ultimately spirals down like a toilet flushing into co-dependency & rejection.

For those in established partnerships, you will receive insights & tools for ongoing partnerships to thrive by learning how to heal the conflict of opposites by transcending the Tree of Knowledge (duality) as well as insight into the cyclic nature of intimate relationships. You will learn why 'the Honeymoon' traditionally lasted a month as well as the true meaning of the 'Seven Year Itch'.

Couples will also receive instruction & experiential processes to survive the annual descent during the darker months of Autumn & Winter, when our shadow or lower self looms larger due to the loss of solar light, making us more prone to project what we reject in ourselves on to our partner, creating increased conflict as depicted by the ancient myths which illustrated this pattern as a six month separation between lovers.

An Overview of the Black Path: Living In Sacred Union with All That Is

In Volume Three, 'The Black Path' you will gain accessible ways to enter into a spirit of true communion with Gaia, our Earth Mother & Sol, our stellar Father as well as the greater cosmic cycles for ongoing balance & harmony. To promote a healthy relationship with the feminine, you will learn simple practices to maintain emotional balance & develop your intuitive wisdom by attuning to the phases of the moon. Similarly, to promote a healthy relationship with the masculine, you will gain practical methods to attune to the seasonal solar wheel & daily solar cycle to assist you in fulfilling your potential. In addition, you will be inspired with simple ways to reconnect with yourself, your loved ones, your community, the natural world & the cosmos to create a deeper sense of meaning to nourish your soul & enhance your way of life.

The Path Of White Tantra

Creating Sacred Union Within

The white Tantric path is the path of the inner maiden or knight, the young teen / twenty-something part of us, (regardless of our current age) whose quest is to individuate from the conditioning we received in childhood, so we can reclaim our unique & authentic personal self-expression.

So in this section you will meet 'All of You.' The aspects of both your inner feminine & masculine halves, which combined make up the blueprint of your multi-faceted soul self. (N.B. The more discordant your parent's relationship, which modeled a blueprint of these inner gender roles, the greater the challenge to harmonize these opposing forces within. Kind of like Lily Tomlin & Steve Martin enacting the discord of two people sharing the same body in the classic comedy, 'All of Me.') To do this, we start by getting to know each of the feminine archetypes (aspects of the psyche) & their counterpart masculine archetypes which collectively represent the inner 'Seven Brides for Seven Brothers' or opposite polarities which must be balanced internally before one can enjoy equal & balanced partnerships externally.

These teachings combine the energetic anatomy of Tantra with the psychological insights offered by classical mythology, to enable you to understand the relationship between each of the masculine & feminine archetypal energies which govern each of the seven major energy centers in the body. These are most commonly referred to as chakras but are also known as stargates or the eyes of God. When we master these seven major lessons we unblock our life force (also known as kundalini in ancient Sanskrit) at each of the seven gates. As these vortexes open we experience ourselves & life as multi-dimensional, enabling us to emanate the frequency of the seven rays of healing & raise the level of both our personal & collective human consciousness.

In Mysticism this energetic process is described as awakening the twin serpent. The masculine & feminine energy meridians together are known pictorially as the caduceus, the symbol for healing which was later adopted by the fraternity of modern medicine. It portrays the two serpents spiraling up a central pillar, (the nervous system) with wings outstretched. (I have included an illustration of this symbol, along with more detailed information in 'The Caduceus' chapter.)

By marrying the seven expressions of your inner yin (feminine) & yang (masculine), you will be freed of the unconscious external search for your 'other half,' which is a recipe for dysfunctional co-dependency, a dynamic which was prevalent in the traditional form of marriage & is now being collectively transcended.

The Significance of Your Foundation Gender

Whilst we are all made up of masculine & feminine energies, just as every part of life is created through the merging of these polar opposites, it is fundamental that before we start the process of trying to heal & reclaim our 'inner opposite,' that we first address the unresolved issues we have with the gender into which we incarnated. For example, you may be a woman who is unconsciously rebelling against your mother by focusing on your career more than relationships to avoid becoming like her or you may be a man who avoids career & the financial responsibility of fatherhood as a way of avoiding becoming like him. It is not a question of whether your choices are right or wrong, it is simply about seeing what underlies any avoidance of gender roles so we can find a balance that works & reflects our authentic self...so we are not unconsciously being a perpetual teenager rebelling against our parents.

For example, many men avoid connecting with & expressing their masculinity if they have never had a heart-centered older man act as a positive role model. This is a man who personally invested their attention, time & genuine care into mentoring them. This is common for men who were primarily raised by their mother with a father who was abusive, absent, submissive or passive-aggressive so was unable to embody the true strengths of the masculine polarity. This is where attending a men's group with emotionally mature men can provide the necessary role models needed for men to embody a whole & healed masculinity that their fathers were often unable to demonstrate.

Similarly, many women may avoid identifying with their feminine self-expression if they grew up with disempowered mothers who embodied more of the shadow feminine traits, behaving in a way that was deceitful, manipulative, emotionally unbalanced or passive aggressive. Ultimately, whichever parent our child self felt more abused or neglected by (be it emotional, psychological or physical), this is the gender we unconsciously disown as we reject them within our own psyche. This obviously affects how we treat both ourselves & others. In other words, if you reject your mother or father on some level it will inhibit your ability to develop & embrace the archetype of mother / father in your own life. This affects not just your ability to parent a child but your inner mother's ability to identify & nurture your needs or your inner father's ability to provide for you & protect you.

The Legacy Of Our Early Gender Conditioning

Whilst I don't want to promote victim consciousness, the majority of us have suffered one or several forms of abuse from our parents, step-parents or family of origin as culturally there was not sufficient awareness or support to promote healthy, conscious relating amongst families. So it's helpful to consider the gender imbalances within each of our parents so our adult self can understand & heal the pattern of abuse to avoid perpetrating it on the next generation. For example, your father may've abused you psychologically by constantly putting you down with unconscious remarks & responses to your self-expression because he had shut down many of his feminine qualities, such as patience, acceptance, compassion & understanding. (This was commonplace amongst many of our dads in an effort to appear more masculine & comply with the traditional gender roles of their time.) This may've then been compounded by a mother who felt so unsupported, that driven by anxiety she operated more out of her masculine - overdoing to the point of burn-out so her feminine expression was always extreme & out of balance. This dynamic has been a common scenario during the patriarchal consciousness as the feminine polarity was not understood, validated or empowered so it was often completely denied or expressed in a very unconscious way. This makes sense when we consider that the feminine energy, (known in mysticism as 'Shakti') represents the aspect of life force which can be chaotic & scattered without the structure of the masculine, ('Shiva') to hold it. This is why when overwhelmed, women tend to spiral into a flood of tears & nervous hysteria & are calmed by the stillness & presence of a man who can simply hold them.

The Hysteria of Our Inner Feminine

Now don't get me wrong, the masculine has made incredible advances through it's ingenuity & practicality over the past five thousand years but it has come at a cost. Consider if you will, how disempowered the expression of the feminine has been in both men & women throughout our patriarchal culture as every aspect of our lives was structured in an anti-feminine way. For example, we lived separately rather than communally. We lived in 'man made' towns & cities surrounded by corporate billboards, ad slogans & commercials telling us what to think, say & do rather than in the support of Mother Nature. We were governed by linear 'man made' time rather than attuning to & living in accordance with the natural cycles. We worked long hours to amass the 'man made' measurement of worth, being the artificial construct of money rather than naturally sharing resources as was done naturally by indigenous peoples. These constructs disempowered our feminine sense of self, creating an inner hysteria we refer to as 'stress' which is now an epidemic in the West. Having endured this as a long-term condition, many older women understandably end up having their feminine physiology (uterus) removed altogether - a procedure aptly named as a 'hysterectomy'.

Ultimately, it is easier to see a symptom rather than look to the cause. So for us growing up in a culture that saw our mothers as often sick, depressed, emotionally unbalanced & financially powerless (because they instinctually shared rather than hoarded what they had) it is understandable that we dismiss them & in doing that dismiss our own inner feminine as having any real worth. For example, I had a client call me in distress because her children were defending her husband who had cheated on her, a response which both hurt & bewildered her. This was because their direct experience of their mother's irrational & overly emotional behavior in direct response to her husband's cheating was personally more confronting in its immediate impact than his. They were also the product of a culture that continually made excuses for men's behavior while being highly critical of women.

It is easy to see & scapegoat a woman who is out of control rather than comprehend the insurmountable odds that are creating her condition. Such as living in a misogynistic society with a husband who has shut down his own feminine, so he mocks everything about her that is feminine from her moods to her curves & her spiritual beliefs. It is no wonder that many grow up perpetuating this scenario by siding with their Dads in cases of family conflict & if female, then finding themselves only understanding the role of family scapegoat when they themselves become mothers. Being someone who is only valued for what they do for others rather than their inherent worth, leads women to become so good at 'overdoing' for acceptance, love & approval that they suffer repeated & chronic energetic burn-out, emotional overwhelm & physical illness.

Ultimately, when we deconstruct & understand the conditions that created our parents' gender imbalance which led to our abuse we can then open our hearts to feel compassion & forgiveness for them, which is the key to our own healing. For when the heart opens, the energy can flow freely up into the throat chakra to release past pain & experience peace, as this is the center for healing.

Identifying Our Own Gender Imbalance

In various cultural segments of society one can observe patterns which reflect gender bias. For example, women who work in rational or masculine polarity fields such as science / IT / industry / business or in a trade often dress in a masculine way, wearing tailored or butch clothes in black, grey or blue. They often de-value feminine concerns such as nurturing others, beauty, socializing, spirituality, nature & art, seeing them as being of lesser interest or value. This is because they want to be taken seriously in a man's world, reflecting their unconscious need to gain approval from society & authority, which is the externalized masculine. Similarly, men who work in feminine gender roles such as fashion / hospitality / community services / childcare or entertainment often wear more flamboyant clothes & colors & de-value masculine concerns such as sports, politics, DIY projects, survival adventures & finance, seeing them as irrelevant or boring. This reflects how they are unconsciously seeking approval from their social circle of friends & lovers, the externalized feminine. The irony is that when we hang out in a dominant gender polarity to avoid experiencing the wounds & insecurities of the polarity which is under-developed, we then crave that under nourished gender externally in our partnerships & friendships as a way of finding balance. For instance, we may crave feminine nurturing to make up for what we lacked from our birth mother so unconsciously we may surround ourselves with girlfriends who are real Earth Mothers & be attracted to men who are more developed in their feminine qualities. Likewise, a man who feels abandoned or rejected by his Father may unconsciously surround himself with friends who are great Dads & be attracted to female partners whose masculine self is dominant.

Gender Imbalance Within Homo-erotic & Transgender Folk

Just as both transgender & homoerotic species exist in the nature kingdom, so too they are a natural part of our human species & are equally as Divine in their own right as any of us by their creative existence. So for those who question why anyone would 'choose' to incarnate into a gender that doesn't resonate with their inner identity - given the suffering this creates personally & socially I offer the following perspective for your consideration. 'Free will' is one of the universal laws that govern our universe, meaning every soul agrees to the circumstances into which they incarnate prior to their birth, on the understanding that whilst the agreed circumstances are going to prove challenging at the level of personality, they are necessary for soul growth. For unless we enter fully into the direct experience of our soul wounds, we cannot transcend them...& graduate from repeating the same lesson lifetime after lifetime. So if a soul has been repeatedly traumatized in numerous lifetimes by a particular gender, it is understandable that they become so polarized that they completely disassociate from one gender, which internally is one half of their soul self. To ensure that they cannot avoid dealing with this gender in their impending incarnation their soul agrees to enter into the physical expression of that gender, knowing they must make their peace with this gender in order to experience wholeness. These gender rejections are found in all of us to varying degrees, so are not the 'cause' of someone having a gender preference either way, although they will influence our choice of partners as we unconsciously re-enact our parents dynamic in order to understand it through adult eyes. Regardless of our sexual gender preference, if we don't seek to heal the gender that is most wounded & fragile within us, we will find relationships very challenging as they will reflect our own inner imbalance. So join me for a stroll down the white path to meet & understand your inner feminine & masculine sides! To do that we must understand the power of the myths that have shaped our inner archetypes.

 The Power of Myth

How Our Role Models Have been Hijacked

'The most dangerous thing in the hands of the oppressor are the minds of the oppressed.'

Steve Biko (apartheid activist)

In every ancient civilization, it was acknowledged that stories held the key to greater understanding of one's self & the meaning of life. So storytellers were highly regarded as spiritual teachers. If we consider the true power of myths as parables that shape our consciousness we realize the ramifications of both their intent & content. For if our cultural fables are enlightened in the lessons they impart, so too will be those who grow up listening to them. Similarly, if the stories within a culture glorify the shadow traits of humanity or askew the natural order, those conditioned by those stories will unconsciously emulate those aberrations. One need only look at the effects from the overwhelming amount of commercial, sexist & violent content shown on television to see how it has shaped our societal values.

History / Herstory

The myths, legends & folk tales we have grown up with are ancient in origin, however their meaning has been significantly altered as the face of religion changed from matriarchy to patriarchy, reflecting the gender bias of each era.

Initially we lived in matriarchal societies where women were considered the dominant gender. Author, Merlin Stone asserts in her book, 'When God Was a Woman' that this was because early civilizations hadn't figured out that men had anything to do with procreation so the feminine was worshipped as the Creator being. Despite some modern male scholars doing their best to refute the existence of matriarchal, matrilineal & matrifocal societies there is overwhelming evidence to the contrary: For example this excerpt from 'The Feminine Universe' by Alice Lucy Trent.

'In a...survey of ancient European civilization between 7000 and 3500 BC, Professor Marija Gimbutas explains how recent archaeology has given us a clear picture of this period, unearthing some 30,000 sculptures of clay, marble, bone, copper and gold from some 3,000 sites. Clearly a vast area and a great period of time are involved (much longer than the whole known 'historical' period), yet certain general statements can be made covering the entire civilization. Prof. Gimbutas shows that the Creator of the world was regarded as a Goddess (like Tiamat, often symbolised as a bird), that the Great Goddess was "the central figure in the pantheon of gods" and that "the pantheon reflects a society dominated by the mother".' Marija Gimbutas, The Gods and Goddesses of Old Europe, 7000–3500 B.C., Thames & Hudson, pp.236–237.

Understandably, after thousands of years of feminine dominated culture, resentment grew amongst the men as the power was not being shared equally. For example, during the first thirteen dynasties in ancient Egypt, men weren't allowed to hold positions of state so it was inevitable that the pendulum should swing in the other direction & hence, monotheistic religions arose which worshipped the 'Father God' instead of the 'Mother Goddess'.

As part of this shift in power from 'herstory' to 'history' many of the feminine qualities were then attributed to the masculine deity. For example, the Holy Sky Father who gives us our 'daily bread' in the Lord's Prayer was once the Earth Mother Goddess who provided her children with grain for bread as the staff of life. So too, each of the earlier myths were distorted so rather than celebrating the feminine as the life giving principle, she was shamed as the source of all destruction.

Pandora

The most flagrant example of this is in the Greek myth of Pandora. In the patriarchal version of this fable about the first woman she is portrayed as a naive young maiden who opens a jar filled with every form of suffering which she inadvertently unleashes upon humanity. Whilst she did not do this intentionally she was blamed for the demise of the human race. Her name means 'all gifted' - which was said to symbolize the individual gifts of ill intent placed in the jar by each of the Olympic Gods. A punishment the Olympiads inflicted because the mortal, Prometheus had dared to access the creative fire from the Gods to empower his fellow man. Some versions of this patriarchal myth say Pandora was his wife, gifted to him as a 'beautiful evil'.

If we look a little further back beyond history to herstory, we discover ancient Greek vases predating the Hesiodic retelling of her myth, which show Pandora with the name, Anesidora - an epithet usually applied to Gaia / Demeter, the Earth Mother Goddess. This name means 'she who sends up gifts' offering the cornucopia of offerings from the bounty of her garden.

'On a fifth century amphora in the Ashmolen Museum, the half figure of Pandora emerges from the ground, her arms upraised in the epiphany gesture, to greet Epimetheus.'

http://en.wikipedia.org/wiki/Pandora

So it was that the Great Goddess, bearing the abundant gifts of nature to lovingly share with humankind was reduced to a naive girl whose brought only suffering. The inherent message being that feminine judgement couldn't be trusted & if women had any power afforded them, the effects would be disastrous. One only need look at the proportion of males to females in positions of worldly power to see the imprint of this insidious inversion of the sacred feminine.

The Power of Word

Once a story is anchored within the collective psyche, it is imbued with accumulative energy as we share evidence of it in our own lives. It is therefore not surprising to learn in ancient Greece, it was an acceptable custom at the 'male only' symposiums to take turns telling derogatory stories about the women in their lives as the 'consumers of men's efforts'. A custom which continues today amongst men & women in single sex groups, fueling the gender war by scapegoating the shadow on the opposite sex under the veil of humor.

Moving Beyond Our Limiting Stories

If knowledge is power, it stands to reason that in order to transcend our unbalanced inversions of natural law, it is intrinsic to our awakening that we reconnect with the true abundance of the earth & revere the feminine as a sacred gift rather than mocking & deriding it as a 'beautiful evil'. The more we make this shift in our collective consciousness, the less mortal women will be feared by men, or cast as scapegoats & dismissed as having nothing of real value to say. This will also allow women to fulfill their potential unimpeded by unconscious negative expectations & perceptions. Equally, it is vital that our epic stories honor the masculine as the fertilizing principle whose heroic efforts are necessary for the creations of the feminine to be birthed & sustained. Both the feminine & masculine are part of the great wheel of death & rebirth. And all of creation is ultimately brought into existence by the joining of both masculine & feminine polarities. The more we embrace a balanced mythology, acknowledging the equally important roles of both feminine & masculine, the easier it will be for men to return to their natural expression of whole & healthy masculinity, unimpeded by the negative patriarchal role models who were ruthless, cruel & vengeful. For example in the pantheon of Greek Gods, their larger than life portrayals of shadow human behavior exemplified those operating out of their reptilian brain. This is the part that governs the most base urges which are driven by selfish gain & are achieved through either force or deception. This is a mode of behavior which is in no way uplifting or inspirational. One must therefore question the validity of these patriarchal ancient Greek overlords as deities. For a true God or Goddess would exemplify & model conscious behavior whereas only a fallen demigod would model unconscious behavior. So the myths & legends of the Greek pantheon of demigods & goddesses are still helpful if we only view them as parables of what not to do. I suspect these deliberately deceptive mythological stories were once introduced as a form of 'Reptilian programming' as they focus on the worst rather than the best of human potential, keeping the collective consciousness focusing on their lowest emanation rather than their highest. They do this by anchoring negative expectations within the psyche. When we consider our unconscious thoughts manifest our expectations into our waking reality, it is essential for us to deconstruct these stories in order to take back our full creative power as sovereign beings. For just like the dinosaurs, if we don't evolve our thinking we will wipe ourselves out through unconscious action!

Time to Unplug from the Matrix

Many of us are tired of enacting the same unenlightened stories which have kept us bound to struggle in reruns of our own Olympiad soap opera. But there are many still sleepwalking amongst the distractions of politics, sport, entertainment & gossip, unconsciously worshipping the latest celebrities as screen Gods & Goddesses who are playing the roles of our modern day demigods, enacting their universal stories as larger than life characters on screen & off. So if you are ready for a fresh script, a 'choose your own adventure' life of free will, the first step is to unplug from the matrix of 3D (lower self) programming that is continuously anchoring these unconscious perversions of our archetypes, offering us disempowered patriarchal prototypes. Fortunately as more folk wake up the stories being made for our consumption are also changing. For example, an increasing number of fairy tales are being remade as feature films with strong & smart female protagonists who can save themselves - a welcome return from the mythic inversions written by Hans Christian Anderson & the Brothers Grimm, (aptly named) who distorted the seeds of feminine wisdom, providing patriarchal retellings that disempowered the feminine as either weak & naive or cruel & manipulative. Similarly, the teaching parables used by Christ & his disciples were edited & distorted when recorded for future generations in the Bible. In 'Harlot, Forbidden Tales of the Bible' by Jonathan Kirsch he provides documentation of the five storytellers hired to write the Bible who altered the us myths to serve the patriarchal agenda. For example, instead of the Egyptian Goddess, Isis parting the sea they inserted a male protagonist, Moses. The Dead Sea Scrolls discovered between 1946 & 1956 on the northwest shore of the Dead Sea also revealed the many books written by the disciples of Jesus that were omitted from the Bible because they gave instruction on how to become self-realized beings, a fact those in power wanted hidden from the people.

Just as Pandora was provided as a role model to disempower the feminine in ancient Greece, the Bible introduced Eve as the equivalent female scapegoat for all of human suffering. Her male counterpart, Adam, the patriarchal prototype of an unconscious male rejected his first wife, Lilith because she refused to be dominated by him & then he blamed his second wife, Eve for everything that was wrong with his life. (A story many may identify with if they are truly honest with themselves when reflecting upon their own lives.) Since the feminine is the aspect that awakens the masculine to ascend the Tree of Life this deception of the truth can only suggest a deliberate act to avert the evolution of our species. As we question the distorted mythologies of the Greek & Roman societies upon which our modern day culture is based, we will transform our civilization from one which values duty to an empire which enslaves its people by valuing the accumulation of wealth & territory...to one that honors the natural evolution of our species based on the higher principles of love & service to the greater good.

The Descent of Orpheus

Rescuing the Inner Feminine

In this chapter we're going to specifically look at the reclamation of our feminine archetypes that make up the feminine psyche. This is one half of us, regardless of whether we are physically male or female. The main lesson of our feminine self is to learn how to love, by truly seeing the inner beauty, perfection & Divine wisdom in every aspect of creation, starting with ourselves! To that end, it is usually the experience of unrequited love that shifts us from the outer world to the inner world, initiating our inner descent to see & fall in love with our own inner feminine.

In the myth of Orpheus, he loses his beloved, Eurydice & sets out on a perilous journey to the Underworld to find her. He is cautioned to not look back, for if he looks back, he will lose her forever. This indicates he must focus on his own journey, confronting all his fears & wounds rather than look to her to heal his pain. If he trusts the Divine plan & is earnest in his quest for self fulfillment he will be rewarded with an external love reflecting his commitment to love himself. In the patriarchal version of this tale, he looks back & loses her forever, anchoring a subconscious expectation that true love is unrequited. So if you would like to change this old story, I invite you to see Orpheus triumphantly returning to his everyday world where he is reunited with Eurydice, (who is also wiser for her journey to the Underworld) so is ready for a mature & conscious sacred union.

The moral of the story is that every man is destined to meet a woman with whom he falls in love, as she is a mirror of his own inner feminine which he is yet to consciously see & embrace in himself. It is therefore necessary for him to lose her so he may begin the process of finding those traits within himself & become whole. If, however a man does not accept the loss of his external feminine, (i.e. focusing on possessing or grieving his lost love instead of developing his own inner feminine) then he will lose her forever as he can only keep the love of a woman if he has developed those traits within himself.

Similarly, the journey of descent undertaken by women has been recounted as the myth of Ishtar, the Queen of Heaven who descended into the Underworld to help her twin sister, Ereshkigal give birth. This signifies that a woman must go to Hell & back to relinquish all the preconceived ideas she had about herself as a way of truly knowing herself so she can love her true self & allow her true self to be seen by others. Both men & women must take this journey of descent to rescue all the aspects of their inner feminine. This awakens the power of their Divine feminine essence, known in Tantra as 'Shakti,' which is the feminine meridian of energy that runs from the base of the spine to the crown. When Shakti is awakened, (known in Sanskrit as kundalini) it enhances one's vitality, creativity & sexual charisma.

The Map of Female Archetypes Which Govern the Seven Major Chakras

Below is a map of the feminine archetypes. Each of the seven inner Goddesses govern a chakra (energy center) & so when we afford each archetype expression in our lives, we emit the color rays of the full spectrum of light, symbolized by Ishtar, the Rainbow Goddess. (pictured below.) When we consciously unveil all of these aspects we access each of their strengths, wisdom & gifts empowering our feminine sense of self. (Please Note: I have provided a lengthier explanation of the masculine archetypes in this book as I have already written an entire book on the feminine archetypes. So if this whets your appetite for a more extensive understanding of these aspects, including processes to empower each feminine archetype I suggest reading my first book, 'The Inner Goddess Makeover').

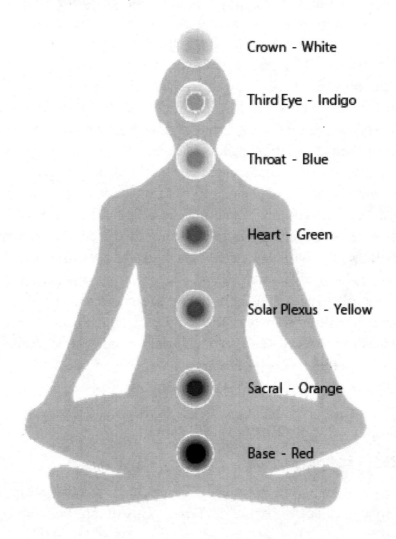

Crown - White

Third Eye - Indigo

Throat - Blue

Heart - Green

Solar Plexus - Yellow

Sacral - Orange

Base - Red

CHAKRA	INNER GODDESS
Base: (Red)	Lilith, the Wild Woman
Sacral: (Orange)	Aphrodite, the Beautiful Muse
Solar Plexus: (Yellow)	Athena, the Golden Heroine
Heart: (Green)	Demeter, the Earth Empress
Throat: (Blue)	Artemis, the Medicine Woman
Third Eye: (Indigo)	Hecate, the Wise Woman
Crown: (White / Magenta)	Ishtar, the High Priestess

So, let's go on a tour through the spectrum of feminine aspects, which collectively make up the feminine part of our psyche. And take note, if there is an archetype you have an aversion to...beware! The aspects which repel us are those which are disempowered & undeveloped so if we persist in disassociating from them, we attract folk into our lives who embody those archetypal shadow aspects so intensely it pushes all our buttons. So rather than scapegoating others to avoid looking at your own reactions, I recommend valuing these teachers on the path, as they are confronting you with your own fears & disowned aspects. Like the old adage, 'Where there's fear, there's power.' So keep asking why you are having such a strong reaction to your work colleague, neighbor, daughter's teacher, mother-in-law etc as they will be someone you simply can't avoid until you've learnt your lesson - such is your shared sacred contract! Equally, the archetypes which are empowered within you will attract others into your life who exude their strengths.

Empowering Lilith, the Wild Woman

Base Chakra: (Red)

The first archetype we meet is Lilith. She is the first feminine aspect we express in the first seven years of our life. That is, if our inner 'wild child' isn't suppressed by parents who are confronted by their child's 'socially inappropriate' behavior. This is the part of us that will explore our bodies, express our rage with tantrums, eat dirt, make noise, wear our food & run around naked! This is not an aspect which has been encouraged in most traditional households for fear of raising a child who would flaunt their body & scream like a banshee. In fact it has been so widespread for little girls in particular to be rejected for expressing their anger but embraced instead if they cry, that the majority of modern women will automatically burst into tears when they feel angry & have no idea why.

Lilith is the part of us who explores 'that which is hidden or taboo' in order to understand why it is being suppressed. In other words, she is the truth teller who will not hold her tongue to uphold falsehood. When empowered as an inner aspect, she will choose her inner circle by discerning those who are empowered enough to speak their truth from those who aren't. She does this as a matter of survival as she knows that what is suppressed will corrode from within & destroy the whole.

(Our cultural suppression of the truth in order to appear socially acceptable is why we have manifested Cancer as a corrosive epidemic.) Survival is a key issue since she governs the base chakra. If she is disempowered or suppressed she will keep a lid on the truth in an effort to survive. For example, she may keep her real opinions or frustrations to herself rather than risk being ostracized. This suppression of truth will ultimately lead to passive aggressive behavior, feelings of powerlessness & a lack of energy, drive & passion.

Power of the Pussy...Meow!

Because she governs the feminine side of our base chakra, Lilith's mouth is the yoni (female genitals), the gate of death & birth. (The death aspect being menstruation & the ego death of orgasm which means, 'the little death'.) So in order to reclaim & free one's feminine primal power one must first acknowledge any negative feelings they have towards the female genitalia. For women, any feelings of shame, sexual rejection & trauma are stored within the cellular memory of their Gspot (urethral sponge) which is located along the inside wall of one's yoni (vulva). By reverently massaging the Gspot either alone or with a partner you can release any unexpressed pain being held in this area. Once this is released you will feel more in touch with your yoni & free to really feel & enjoy your sensations so you can vocalize your pleasure, liberating you sexually. This reconnection with your authentic sexual response, (rather than trying to be a hot sexual performer emulating what you think is sexy) will empower you to always be true to yourself in every other aspect of your life. N.B. It is important when massaging the Gspot that one's full presence is engaged whether doing this for yourself or a lover. For when a woman feels truly held in this way, both emotionally & energetically she can surrender to feeling & expressing the waves of unexpressed emotion this unlocks.

For men, whether they are heterosexual or not, it is similarly an act of power to acknowledge any feelings of revulsion or fear they have towards vaginas. That is, natural, hairy vulvas which culturally have been shamed as unsightly & unacceptable in recent years with the increase in Brazilian waxing & patriarchal pornographic images of hairless female genitals. This is quite simply the powerful image of Lilith, the primal erotic feminine being reduced to an image of prepubescent Eve / Pandora which is persistently sold to men as the iconography they should associate with sexual arousal. This cultural conditioning is anchoring pedophilia as the ultimate male fantasy via a suggested auto-response being planted in the collective subconscious with the intent of overriding one's authentic sexual urges & self expression. This is because our sexuality is powerful, so when we reclaim our erotic selves, our wild selves will no longer be enslaved by falsehood & illusion.

When you point the finger, three are pointing back at you...

Ultimately, any misogyny expressed outwardly as thought, word or action is also directed unconsciously towards one's inner feminine which inhibits one half of your self expression. So the degree to which one unconsciously minimizes, negates or criticizes women indicates how much they are suppressing & denying their own inner feminine, revealing their unconscious need to be mothered! Regardless of your gender preference, if you can't appreciate the beauty & power of a natural woman you have fallen prey to the patriarchal propaganda machine & you've got some healing to do on your inner feminine. So if you're a woman who is sporting a Brazilian wax or who still refers to your genitals as 'down there' it's time you faced your fear of rejection should you embody your natural woman. Or if you are a guy who is repulsed by vaginas, spiders, cats or snakes (Lilith's totems) it's time you confronted your fear of being castrated by feminine power.

Ways to Befriend Lilith

For the ladies, I recommend you contemplate the raw power & beauty of this erotic orchid between your legs by sitting naked in front of a mirror to view it at close range. This will enable you to face any fears you may have that it is ugly or misshapen & when you get over the shock of this physical intimacy with yourself you may start to discover it's unique beauty. Because if YOU can't be that intimate with your yoni you're sure not gonna feel comfortable with anyone else trying to! And that would mean missing one of the greatest delights available in the Garden of Eden. :) To those of you who are heterosexual men with partners, consider asking your partner if you can take the time to really get to know her yoni by admiring it without the pressure of sexual performance. You may each then draw artistic representations of your / her yoni as a beautiful flower or screaming mouth as you develop an appreciation for the power & luscious beauty of this innermost feminine bud. This may then lead those of you with your own yoni to take pride in trimming or waxing your topiary bush out of a sense of deep honoring rather than banishment. (However, I would urge you to keep some of your fertile fur to acknowledge your power as a wild cat). You may also want to buy some wildcat underwear that houses your precious bud with respect & self love. For homoerotic men, consider checking out the work of Betty Dobson who was the first to create a photographic exhibition of yonis that have inspired many others since. For, whilst it is wonderful to worship the phallus with artistic imagery, it is balanced to appreciate the beauty of both genders.

Regardless of our gender, when we are uncomfortable with the aspect of Lilith we usually are unconsciously rejecting & suppressing our authentic self as we fear letting our wild self out of the bag, lest we be rejected. Of course, if we reject our true self, so too will those around us as mirrors of how we see ourselves. So to reclaim this aspect, let your hair down, express your discontent & if people around you try to shame or ridicule you for it, be true to yourself & create the changes necessary to reflect your truth. By owning your right to express your frustration & anger, your inner Lilith can confidently assert her truth & not defer her power, enabling her to take action whenever needed. For example, mothers not comfortable with their inner Lilith may say, 'Wait till your Father gets home,' to their misbehaving children instead of daring to let their own wrath out. They do this because they fear their own power coming out in such an uncontrolled way that it will destroy those around them. As a result, mothers who suppress this archetype inadvertently give their power to their children, fearing their children will reject them if they get angry. This becomes increasingly difficult to witness as children whose parents won't express their anger often throw the worst temper tantrums as they are expressing their parents unexpressed rage to challenge their passive parents to stand in their personal power. This dynamic creates a cycle of powerlessness with children ruling their parents as little tyrants or being scapegoated as out of control & often medicated to suppress the anger which the parent finds too confronting.

The other HUGE lesson Lilith offers us is the opportunity to face & own our shadow. These are the traits we don't see in ourselves so judge, reject or ridicule in others. Understandably, when we start acknowledging our own flaws, agendas & poor choices we start resolving conflict more easily & having less to feel angry about. So to empower your inner Lilith, always ask yourself, 'What is this person mirroring for me? Where do I do that to myself or to others?' instead of reacting by judging, blaming or attacking others.

Speak Up or Your Vulva Will!

When working with women who are unable to orgasm or open sexually I often introduce a yoni puppet. (The one I made curiously bears a resemblance to 'Animal' from 'The Muppets'!) This is done to literally give their vulva a voice so we can get to the heart of their resistance. Ailments such as cystitis, thrush, eczema & STD's are often the yoni's only way of saying, 'I'm mad as hell & I'm not going to take it.' So by using a puppet it enables a woman to let her yoni say what it would say if it could talk so it doesn't need to manifest as physical symptoms. Similarly, those who don't express their rage are prone to feel irritated & itchy & scratch their skin incessantly or experience skin conditions such as eczema & rashes, indicating that their inner Lilith needs to speak up & make some changes!

Men, whilst you may not have a vulva - same thing applies if you start getting itchy feet, genitals or a general urge to scratch & shed your old skin...your inner Lilith - the serpent who sheds her skin, is asking you to acknowledge how frustrated you are with the status quo, at home or at work so you can take your power back by doing something about it.

Lilith: Myth vs Truth

The story that has been anchored in our psyche is that Lilith was the first wife of Adam, who left him because he expected her to lie beneath him rather than be true to her own erotic nature. Ultimately, we need to transcend the concept of either gender being 'on top' & agree to dance together, spiraling around the central pillar of light that ignites when we open energetically to each other without thought of domination or submission. In the patriarchal version of this story, Lilith was unmet by any man for two thousand years because of her refusal to compromise her true self - a story many strong, outspoken women have acted out for lifetimes, creating a deep & painful belief that they will never be truly met by a man. It is therefore of great importance that women who have subsequently rejected men for their role in this unconscious drama review whether holding on to this story really serves them & the greater good. Thankfully, this story was recently rewritten by the film, 'Avatar' where the male protagonist as the archetypal, Adam leaves the patriarchal war regime which seeks to dominate & destroy the true feminine & instead decides to defect from his patriarchal culture so he can come home to his own primal self. This homecoming is initiated by his meeting with the archetypal wild woman, Lilith who teaches him the ways of nature so he may live in accordance with the sacred tradition of the Tree of Life. Fortunately more & more men are waking up to follow their authentic primal desire for the wild feminine, regardless of the patriarchal conditioning they have received which taught them to dismiss the sacredness of nature & reject & fear the natural woman as repulsive & unacceptable when compared to the compliant & hairless Eve fashioned by the Patriarchy as a projection of the perfect girl. When we acknowledge we have the subconscious expectation that we will be rejected for our natural self & primal urges should we stop removing our body hair, disguising our natural scent or wearing the acceptable cultural code of clothing - just realizing the degree to which our authentic self has been suppressed will render us less able to be manipulated into rejecting our own true selves in order to be considered acceptable.

Empowering Aphrodite, the Beautiful Muse

Sacral Chakra: (Orange)

Aphrodite is the maiden part of us that when disempowered yearns to be rescued from her unhappiness by the perfect partner, whether we are male or female. Between the ages of seven to fourteen the lessons of the sacral chakra are highlighted, making this a time when we most need to be seen

& adored by our parents to anchor the perception that we are truly lovable & worthy of love. This impacts on our choices later in life, as Aphrodite's lesson is to learn how to love herself by making choices that honor her values.

In our adult life, the partner our inner Aphrodite falls for indicates how much we truly love & honor ourselves, as they externally reflect back to us our early conditioning about ourselves. So too, as we mature, heal & become more self honoring with our choices, we outgrow partners who have the same level of emotional maturity we witnessed in our parents, which signals the level of emotional support we once thought possible.

Our inner Aphrodite's challenge is to enable us to truly see ourself. This is done most easily by expressing our inner self creatively, as art is the language of the soul. So whether we doodle, bake, sing, dance or write poetry the key is that we lose our rational judging mind by surrendering to being in the moment of creation, allowing it to take us where it will without any concern for how it will be received. As our inner Aphrodite expresses herself in the outside world through acts of beauty she comes to appreciate more deeply the beauty of her inner self & falls in love with her own soul. This frees her from trying to appear beautiful to others by constructing a persona she thinks is attractive. This then enables us to relax & let our inner beauty shine through. Of course, the more we appreciate who we are, the more inclined we then are to groom ourselves in a way that celebrates our natural features, making it possible for us to gracefully accept compliments.

When this aspect is unconscious we often try to seduce potential partners using our appearance which leads to doubt & inevitable disappointment as we eventually realize that our partners haven't seen our true self so they don't love us for who we are inside. When we are chasing external love & affection we don't trust that we are lovable enough for someone to see us & choose us for who we are. Then when our emotions swing between trying to possess the object of our desire & self-pity as we crave sensual pleasure as a substitute for love, such as sweet foods or alcohol to comfort our inner child the way warm milk used to. If this becomes habitual our sacral chakra becomes blocked with unprocessed emotion creating a distended abdomen.

Ways to Befriend Aphrodite

Aphrodite is the girl / maiden part of us so tend to your inner girl's need for regular creative expression, fun, sensual pleasure & self loving acts such as bathing & pampering & you'll keep your emotional cup full so you don't seek someone else to fill it for you! This is especially important for those over thirty (past the chronological maiden phase) to keep you young at heart. Usually this archetype is the first aspect to be thrown off the bus when one becomes a parent as we often perceive these Venusian pursuits as frivolous & self-centered but if we don't continue to have a regular time & place to express this part of ourselves we become depressed & resentful with a sense of being burdened by responsibility.

Practical tips to gift your inner Aphrodite some TLC include buying yourself flowers, going to a drawing class, going out dancing, singing karaoke, having a pampering night or indulging in bathing rituals. The more you see your inner beauty, the more you will surround yourself with people who truly appreciate you for who you are inside.

Aphrodite: Myth vs Truth

Aphrodite was seen as having dramas due to marrying the 'wrong men', those who were incapable of truly seeing or honoring her, until she settled for a considerably older man. This inability to select a healthy choice of partner can be attributed to her early conditioning, modeled by her parents who anchored the expectation. In the patriarchal version of her myth, Aphrodite is borne out of her parent's conflict rather than an act of honoring love. The story focuses on the violent act of her Earth Mother, Rhea who cuts off the phallus of her Sky Father, Ourannus, so that his seed is sprayed all over the fertile waters of the ocean, out of which Aphrodite rises up fully formed. This castration is the result of her mother's rage that the male God only wants to use her for his transient pleasure without embracing the subsequent responsibilities of fatherhood needed to perpetuate the circle of life. So what Aphrodite grows up witnessing in the patriarchal mindset is the dissatisfaction of her mother who criticizes Aphrodite's immature father, which further exacerbates his reluctance to embrace his daughter. This creates a subconscious pattern within young women to seek out emotionally unavailable men (like their Dads) & idolize them as Gods, denying feelings of personal dissatisfaction lest their spoken criticism leads to them being rejected again by the masculine. In the patriarchal retelling, the locals marry her off to the blacksmith God, Hephaistos who is crippled (symbolizing the wounded masculine) who she then cheats on by having an affair with the Warrior God, Ares...a relationship which is passionate & combative. Only when she unites with the God, Hermes who is wise does she find enduring love.

So to unveil the inner workings of this myth, if we don't first address the need to heal our own inner masculine we will unconsciously agree to a marriage with a wounded partner & inevitably feel unsatisfied & look elsewhere. Secondly, we must seek to understand & balance the archetypes of Aphrodite & Ares who govern the marriage of our sacral chakra (emotional center) so we can overcome being driven by strong emotional desires that lead us to create endless cycles of karmic love & war. And finally, we must meet & develop our inner Hermes, the wise man to attract one into our waking world whom we recognize & revere as a basis for conscious partnership. Hermes governs the sixth chakra, ajna (the third eye) which is the place where internally our feminine & masculine meridians bow to each other so we may see out of the one eye, which is the perspective of our Soul. When we achieve this internally, we will then attract & consciously choose a partner who is a reflection of this inner wholeness & maturity.

For both men & women, this will transform the unconscious story & expectation that true love is characterized by emotional torment such as swings between love & hate or tortured scenarios of unrequited love. This theme of hopeless love is repeatedly anchored by fictional lovers such as Shakespeare's, 'Romeo & Juliet' & 'Tristan & Isolt' by Beroul. By acknowledging the evidence of this age old drama as simply a stage of emotional immaturity in our own lives, we free ourselves to create more mature unions. This is based on our ability to choose aloneness as a path to create Sacred Union within before realizing the fruits of this path with a lover. This is simply the lesson of delayed gratification. Relinquishing that which is offered in the short term for that which offers greater fulfillment in the long-term.

Empowering Athena, the Golden Heroine

Solar Plexus Chakra (Yellow)

The Solar Plexus chakra is stimulated during the ages of fourteen to twenty-one when we turn our attentions to how we can make a difference in the world. This is because Athena is the part of us that awakens to how we can use our talents to serve the greater good. She does this as she is inspired to restore justice & offer what she can in a spirit of co-operation. To achieve this aim she first generates an awareness of our hidden talents. For example, if our parents are unable to see & affirm our gifts, our inner Athena may encourage them to seek out a mentor to further develop our skills, ideas & confidence so we can assert ourself & our talent in society.

Athena is the most rational of all the feminine archetypes as she governs the solar plexus, which is the energy center associated with our lower mental body, which rules our thought patterns & beliefs. So as we mature, our inner Athena's challenge is to assist us in individuating from our father's view of us, so we may assert our own thoughts & gifts without needing to either rebel or seek approval from others as we share our identity with the world.

When our inner Athena is disempowered we trust outside sources for 'reliable information' rather than giving credence to our own internal guidance system via our intuitive, sensual, emotional & energetic receptors. This can lead us to being cynical (mentally closed) rather than skeptical (receptive yet discerning). Until our inner Athena learns to open to these other pathways of gnosis, she will aspire to attain the recognition of those in authority. This can underpin a relentless drive within us to achieve victories & credentials whilst accruing status & wealth to prove our underdeveloped sense of self worth. To break this pattern of chasing ambition she must learn to value the getting of experiential wisdom, rather than merely accumulating knowledge. This requires a psychological descent within to realize her fears, humility & confront her low self worth.

Ways To Embrace Athena

It is inevitable that we will each experience an unexpected blow to our ego's plans such as job loss, illness, divorce or the death of a loved one to initiate us into this inner descent so we may find a sense of self worth that is not based on what we do but who we are. So it is crucial when life doesn't go according to our best laid plans that we 'make lemons from lemonade' by looking at what our current situation is gifting us. For example, we could perceive job loss as being gifted much needed time to face ourselves. Especially those aspects & activities which we haven't prioritized. When we sit in the void of the unknowable future & connect with our own sense of nothingness, however uncomfortable it feels, we then eventually find comfort in doing that which comes naturally rather than that which is imposed by outer sources as a path to happiness & success. The key to empowering your inner Athena is to spend time doing what you love, even if you think you're no good at it as this is the fastest path to discovering your true soul gifts that you've honed in other lifetimes. Often this will develop into the creation of your dream job in a way that seems inconceivable initially to your rational mind's limited perspective. In my experience, those who struggle with this aspect, (such as doubting they're talented at anything) are usually very gifted with their subtle senses which are hard to validate. This makes putting themselves 'out there' a challenge without the encouragement of a wise mentor who can perceive & validate their inner gifts. Whether your talents are rational, physical, intuitive or sensory the key is to adopt a step-by-step approach, sharing your skills, gifts & talents with those who are dream holders (those who nurture & support your goals & vision) before exposing them to dream stealers (those who unconsciously criticize your efforts or take credit for your work.)

Athena: Myth vs Truth

Athena was the most revered Goddess in the Greek pantheon as she was the most masculine (rational) of all the ancient

Goddesses. As the patroness of crafts, her gifts were used to build cities that could boast great cultural skill & her prowess for planning & strategizing proved invaluable as a tool for amassing political power & wealth for the city, Athens after which she was named. This has subsequently sent a clear message to women ever since. That being; aspire to be more like your father than your mother if you wish to earn respect & kudos in the world of men! In addition, her mother, Sophia, the Goddess of wisdom was then appropriated as a namesake applied to man-made traditions, such as the science of philo'sophy' replacing her true patronage as one who governed the experiential & intuitive understanding that is the source of women's wisdom.

Athena's birth tells of her father, Zeus swallowing both her & her mother as he didn't want to be usurped by his offspring. (This dynamic one sees portrayed as the father's needs eclipsing the needs of everyone else in the family unit. i.e. we'll eat red meat six times a week as that's what your father wants.) Frustrated by this imposed limitation she pounded away on the inside of his head until the inventor God, Hephaistos heard her pounding & assisted her individuation from her father. The midwifery role of Hephaistos symbolizes the importance of a mentor upon our path who validates our right to express ourself & encourages us to share our inner gifts with the world, despite any lack of encouragement from our paternal father. It is after all our belief that we are worth investing time, energy & effort in that inspires us to take up our purpose. So, regardless of how talented we are, if we don't have an advocate affirm this self belief we will lack the necessary courage to birth our own ideas in the world. Those who leave home but seek to prove their worth in the great city are still metaphorically pounding away on the inside of their father's head, trying to get recognized by society - the external masculine. It is only when we forgo the allure of the bright lights of fame, wealth & status & instead attune to that which is within us which asks to be birthed regardless of its popularity, that we free ourselves from our father's view of us. This is fundamental to expressing our authentic view of ourselves & the world. The key is that rather than contribute her gifts in order to win acclaim our inner Athena must be true to herself & connect with her inner self before seeking to share herself with the greater community. Perhaps even more importantly, by taking the time to go within before embarking on a career she can find inspiration to make a difference that far outweighs her childish need for recognition. This is why venturing beyond our father's domain before committing to a career path or tertiary study assists our inner Athena to individuate from her father's values & beliefs so we can find our true purpose, free from his influence. This may take the form of travel, volunteering or moving out of home.

For both men & women, changing this story around success involves questioning where in our own lives we can see evidence of the unconscious story that we will be recognized in our own right if we are more the product of our fathers than our mothers by building a life from our heads rather than our hearts.

Empowering Demeter, the Earth Empress

Heart Chakra (Green)

It is interesting that twenty-one used to be the legal age of adulthood as it is when many feel the urge to consciously explore the legacy of their relationships with their parents which activates the archetypes of the inner parents who govern the heart. This is because the kundalini is activated in the heart from ages twenty-one to twenty-eight. This is when we draw upon the memories of our Earth Mother as a role model for our developing inner mother, known as Demeter in Greek mythology. For whilst we are being the natural, soul-centered child during the first seven years of our life, we study our Earth Mother whose positive & negative traits become the blueprint for this aspect. The mother is the first spiritual teacher we encounter who teaches us through ritual (repetitive routines) how to take care of ourselves. Tasks such as cleaning our teeth, dressing warm to cover our kidneys (lower back) in cooler weather & eating balanced meals.

She also teaches us how to live within the natural cycles for optimal well being & how to recognize endings & beginnings & cope with change. She assists us to celebrate our milestones & learn our life lessons so we grow into well adjusted individuals who can grow to contribute to society & foster the next generation. Despite all the foundation she provides, it is inevitable that when we hit puberty we will reject our mother & all of her teachings by doing the exact opposite of what she has taught in order to assert our own identity & discover first hand what works for us. Not surprisingly, this is a testing time for both parent & child. In our thirtieth year when Saturn completes its twenty-ninth year orbit & ends up in the same place as it was when we were born, we encounter a catalyst in our lives, urging us to grow up & take responsibility for ourselves. This is when we demonstrate how well we have integrated the strengths of the inner mother by taking better care of ourselves such as eating well, getting enough sleep, detoxifying & choosing partners who are not destructive to our well being.

How Healthy Is My Inner Mother?

When this inner Mother aspect is empowered we honor our need for equal rest & activity & find a balance between giving

& receiving so we can sustain our ability to nurture others & give birth to children, new conditions & creative children such as work projects. When it is disempowered we put everyone else's needs before our own & go into 'dark mother' running on empty, giving from resentment & getting ill to unconsciously take a break.

The patriarchal consciousness upheld the 'all giving mother' as the ideal to which women should aspire, which was neither balanced or sustainable, hence the epidemic of breast cancer as women's nurturing organs sounded the alarm as to how toxic this patterning was. What has compounded the burn out rate of women in the mother phase was that their husbands weren't culturally expected to grow up emotionally & take responsibility for also learning how to nurture themselves & others so not only were women mothering their children but also their partners.

Ways to Embrace Demeter

To empower your inner mother spend time at home. Like the saying goes, 'home is where the heart is' & since she governs the heart chakra, just allowing yourself the time to truly 'be' rather than 'do' by resting at home is a great way of coming home to your true self so you can identify your needs & then take proactive steps to get them met. A great daily practice for strengthening your inner Demeter archetype is to place your hand over your heart once a day & ask, 'How am I feeling?' As before something becomes a full blown emotion it starts off as a subtle feeling & if we attune to our feelings we can take appropriate action to respond accordingly so our needs get met, rather than unconsciously hoping someone else will sense & attend to our needs for us, which is unconsciously expecting others to mother us. Similarly, if we experience discomfort in our body we can close our eyes & attune to that part of the body & ask what unexpressed feeling it is holding for us. By acknowledging it, we free it to surface & be felt which then allows it to move & be expressed.

Assessing our dietary nutrition is also another fundamental part of self mothering. For example, if we eat low GI foods that offer a sustained energy release, we don't crash after a sugar high & then feel low emotionally & need others to prop us up. Eating ample raw foods in Summer gives us the energy boost of active enzymes, especially if grown bio-dynamically or organically. Whereas eating warm, cooked whole foods in Winter saves our bodies having to work so hard to heat & process our food. Similarly, eating seasonal produce which is sustainable for the Earth is also better for us since we are essentially the one organism, at one with the Earth herself. The ancient Indian science of Ayervedic eating offers a great template for this.

Spending time creating & nurturing the cyclic growth of a food garden is another great way to empower your inner Demeter, as it acts as a metaphor for your own life changes. It also improves health & immunity by grounding your energy & connecting you with the circle of life so you feel supported by the Great Mother, Earth. Just as reconnecting with nature centers us, so too does having regular body therapies. This is because touch is the most primal form of love that we receive from the Mother, which anchors that we exist & we matter. (Mater meaning mother) To that end, having a regular massage & asking for regular hugs & cuddles anchors the knowing that we are supported, held & able to have our needs met.

To further empower your inner Demeter, practice acceptance, gratitude & patience as much as possible, both with yourself & others but above all, learn to identify your needs & take responsibility for being resourceful with what you have. For example, working with your immediate community to exchange resources, time & services so symbiotically everyone's needs get met.

Demeter: Myth vs Truth

In the patriarchal story of Demeter, the mother archetype she raises her child on her own. This sets up an unconscious expectation that the feminine should shoulder the burden of parenting singlehandedly without the active support of the conscious masculine. This pattern we see evident in the number of single mothers & the cultural phenomenon known as 'married singles'. (This term describes mothers whose husbands are 'married to the job' leaving them doing the majority of child rearing in isolation.) To add insult to injury, the only intervention the mythical Demeter receives from the masculine is in the form of the child's paternal uncle, Hades who kidnaps the daughter, Persephone when she encounters puberty, exposing her to the shadow of human nature by taking her to the Underworld. This suggests that it is an expected part of life that the flower of the budding feminine will be taken by an older man rather than the maiden giving this gift freely on her own terms in her own time. As if that wasn't enough, when Demeter seeks the support of her child's father, Zeus to bring his brother to justice she discovers that Zeus had consented to his brother's plan to abduct the girl as he believed it was time she grew up. This sends the message that in a patriarchal culture it is an unavoidable rite of passage for a young girl to be abandoned or betrayed by the father who in a conscious culture would assume the role of provider / protector. It also suggests that it is inevitable that young girls can expect to be dishonored sexually by the unconscious masculine, a fact which is accepted as the status quo amongst the fraternity of the unconscious & immature masculine. It is only when Persephone's father, Zeus realizes that Demeter's grief will impact upon his own food supply that he speaks to his brother & brokers a deal so Persephone will thereafter spend six months with Hades in the Underworld & six months with her mother each year. This signals that unless the unconscious masculine is directly inconvenienced or threatened he won't rise to defend the honor of the sacred feminine. It also suggests the best a girl can expect from her father is a compromise, signaling the lack of support her mother received will then be continued in the next generation. It is no wonder women resist becoming mothers until later in life or manifest infertility or morning sickness given the subconscious expectations of what they witnessed in their own mother's journey & what they have to look forward to, should they cross that threshold into motherhood!

So given how bleak this imprint is for those living out the story of the mother, it is imperative that we now choose to consciously change this story if we are to create sustainable motherhood that is both supported & joyful rather than filled with subsequent betrayals & despair. How to do that? Well, keep affirming that the old story is changing by seeking out the friendship of conscious brothers who anchor the heart centered Green Man archetype. This affirms that this aspect exists for you & your children. Access the support of your soul community to help parent your child as the natural order recognizes it takes a village to raise a child. Protect the sacredness of subsequent generations by empowering them to intuitively recognize those who are unconscious in their intent. Ultimately, it is through the reclamation of rite of passage ceremonies, that youths will be encouraged to consciously individuate from their parents with the support of elders in the community so they don't have to unconsciously rebel in order to assert their own individuality which places them at risk of being exposed to adults who don't have their best interests at heart.

For both men & women, changing this story around the mother involves questioning where in our own lives we can see evidence of the unconscious story & expectation that a good mum does everything without expecting any help from the masculine.

Empowering Artemis, the Medicine Woman

Throat Chakra (Blue)

Journeying with Artemis is akin to a second maidenhood as Artemis is the inner feminine aspect which asks us to face our aloneness to find our inner strength. The emergence of this aspect as the kundalini moves into the throat chakra between ages twenty-eight to thirty-five can create inner conflict for those feeling confined by the patriarchal confines of marriage & motherhood. This may trigger a need to assert their strength again by getting fit & carving out more independence so they may live more aligned with their inner truth. Many women physically embody Artemis, (the Amazon) after they leave the perceived security of home or a marriage, which was ultimately wounding for them. Artemis guides us to seek refuge in nature, with our girlfriends or with our trusted pets for companionship while we learn to trust our independence & hone our survival skills. This is a necessary phase, proving to ourselves that we can fend for ourselves, without needing anyone else to protect or provide for us so we may grow beyond dysfunctional co-dependency in the future. If we don't take the time to build this sense of self reliance, we seek out the perceived security of someone else & repeat the pattern of wounding all over again.

When our inner Artemis is unconscious we often 'armor up' energetically, not allowing others to get close to us as a way of protecting our unresolved wounds & vulnerability. For those who have experienced significant abuse or trauma this aspect becomes dominant until they can find a suitable sanctuary where they feel truly safe to heal, just as an animal secludes itself to 'lick it's wounds'. Our journey with Artemis teaches us that our perceived weakness also holds the key to finding our greatest strengths. This enables us to develop our own inner healer, trusting our intuition to guide us to that which can free us from our burdens. Whether we are male or female, we all have the ability to heal ourselves & assist others in their healing process, as those who resonate with what we have found helpful, will synchronistically appear in our lives when the time is right. You don't need to become a professional healer to embody this aspect, you just need to have explored & recognized what has personally worked for you in processing & releasing your past pain.

What is important is that we trust the innate way in which we work rather than adopting some 'off the shelf' healing modality as our brand of healing. Whilst it can be helpful to learn other techniques & anatomical information, it is our Higher Self that knows what to do if we attune to this part of our being & dare to follow it. Ultimately, healing is a journey rather than a one off cure so it will take the right combination of ingredients to free you of your hurt rather than seeking a miracle worker.

Ways To Embrace Artemis

Our inner Artemis also heals through sisterhood. For men it is just as important to have trusted girlfriends in whom they can confide & access emotional support. Often those who have dared to confront their wounds via private sessions with a counsellor, healer or intuitive clairvoyant will then greatly benefit from group sessions, such as participating in a facilitated circle. This is because initially when we commence our healing journey our wounds are too overwhelming for us to expose to a group, but when we have learnt the value of opening up to a trusted spiritual midwife we are then ready to risk opening our inner self up to a safe group of like-minded people. Artemis is the aspect that asks us to reclaim our selfhood by healing all of our wounded fragments into one whole & healed identity. Sitting in circle accelerates this process as we see aspects of our self mirrored back to us. This includes our strengths, vulnerabilities & human stories, allowing us to see how universal our wounds are & how empowering & beautiful shared emotional intimacy can be in an honoring space. The sense of selfhood we reclaim through this shared experience of healing enables us to speak our truth so we may set boundaries that honor our vulnerability to avoid being re-wounded out in the world. From this sense of true selfhood we can then aim our arrows of intent, knowing that they will make their mark.

To consciously strengthen your inner Artemis consider spending time with animals, going on retreat alone in nature, strengthening yourself physically with weights so you feel strong & take proactive steps to heal & assist others to heal. Since she governs the throat chakra, chanting is a wonderful way to clear this energy center so the inner self may express itself more confidently through the outer persona.

Ultimately, our inner Artemis has to learn that her truth is her greatest means of protection. By sharing your vulnerability & speaking your truth to set boundaries you will gain confidence in expressing your inner self rather than covering it up by becoming impenetrable & emotionally shut down. According to Mayan elder, Barbara Hand Clow, a mid-life crisis is often brought about by the transit of the planet Uranus which forms a square (opposition) to where it was when you were born. I have observed many women dealing with their Artemis issues during this transit between ages thirty-six to forty-four with forty being the zenith of this transit. In other words, whatever you haven't healed & empowered within yourself during ages twenty-eight to thirty-five will come back to bite you on the bum during this Uranus opposition, kind of like a finals exam with Artemis!

Artemis: Myth vs Truth

In the myth of Artemis, she resided in the forest in Arcadia after announcing to her father, Zeus that when she grew up she never wanted to marry, preferring instead to run free with her hounds. Whilst she took lovers in the forest she spent her time residing with her sisters & offering refuge to young girls & animals who had been wounded by male hunters who had sought them as prey. The only tale of love for her was with the hunter, Orion whom she inadvertently killed when her twin brother, Apollo dared her to hit a mark out at sea with her bow & arrow, which she did, not realizing it was Orion. So deconstructing this story, we reveal the underlying assumption that if a woman chooses to follow her own path & focuses on making her mark, she will lose her only chance at love as her arrow of truth will destroy her lover. The key to breaking this enchantment is to realize this can only occur if we get caught up in a spirit of competition with our brother. So if we heal our relationship with our brother, (those unresolved conflicts with our male siblings &/or male friends) we won't unconsciously enact this unfinished drama with our lover as it creates an underlying sense of competition with our opposite, thus destroying the harmony of our union. This story also suggests that by focusing on the damage done to the feminine by the unconscious masculine rather than on healing the gender rift, the cycle of polarization of the feminine & masculine living separate lives will continue. This is symbolized by the fact that her twin brother, Apollo lived on a isle where he allowed no women & Artemis lived in the forest surrounded by mainly women, viewing men as a threat to her sanctuary. Fortunately recent films like, 'Mirror Mirror' & 'Brave' are changing the distortion of these archetypal stories in our modern day ritual amphitheaters by highlighting the conscious lesson of this archetype so we can heal the conflict we carry inside us, rather than enact it outside of ourselves continually.

For both men & women, changing this story around the cost of freedom involves questioning where in our own lives we can see evidence of the unconscious story, as a fear or expectation that if we take up the call to follow our truth we will be destined to live a life of aloneness & suffering.

Empowering Hecate, the Wise Woman

Third Eye Chakra (Indigo)

Hecate governs the third eye, the doorway to the inner realms. Chronologically during the ages thirty-five to forty-two the kundalini moves into the third eye, creating more of an awareness of our subtle senses. However, in my experience it is between the ages of forty-four to fifty-five (after the completion of the Uranus opposition & in conjunction with our 'Chiron return' that Hecate puts us through our paces to see if we have integrated her lessons. (N.B. 'Chiron return' is when the planetoid, Chiron which has a forty-nine year orbit ends up in the same place it was when we were born.) This brings up for us the greatest wound we have come to heal this lifetime as an initiation around our fiftieth birthday. This initiation confronts us with the crossroad of death & birth. If we embrace our vulnerability & retreat to consciously heal our wounded inner child, we reclaim the innocence of our inner magical child. This is the precursor to claiming our power as an elder, by taking the high road of growth instead of the road of denial. If we do this in the lead up to turning fifty, we find this a very empowering transition. If however, we put off this call to retire, downsize our home, let go of our children or release the past the same lesson will return at age fifty-five in the form of stronger catalysts such as illness to make us stop & let go of who we were so a new self may emerge.

This starts with confronting the fears of our inner child. For if we don't take responsibility for healing our wounded inner child, we unconsciously then become more like a frightened child, giving our personal power away to external authority figures such as doctors & the fear based reality presented by the media so we become the frail little old lady or man on the downward road of decline. So this crossroads is essentially asking us to choose life (conscious growth) or death (unconscious atrophy).

Of course we encounter our inner Hecate long before this gate. Every time we encounter unexpected life changes she is there inwardly asking us to release that which doesn't serve us so we may move on. The more we can surrender our future to Highest Will by trusting the Divine plan the more graceful we will transition into our elder years, which asks us to release all that the ego thought defined us. Death of a loved one also initiates us into the mysteries of Hecate as this event acts as a catalyst for us contemplating our own death, as well as life beyond the veil of material existence. This is because once we have a loved one on the other side it helps us to open up to assistance from the spirit realm so we may serve as a bridge between the two worlds.

Hecate is an aspect that has been feared & ignored by the patriarchal consciousness, which has portrayed her as a hag or a silly old lady. Hecate is the archetype that arises in the psyche of women every time they menstruate as this is the death phase of the lunar cycle, when the spiraling blood in our wombs calls us deep within to the void of the unknowable, putting us in a light trance state. Our monthly 'Moon time' is in fact a practice for when we are said to attain our power at 'Moon pause' (menopause) & enter into a trance state walking between the worlds as the chronological wise woman. Regardless of whether we are male or female, the lunar phase of dark moon (two weeks after full moon) is when we are most likely to experience this aspect within our psyche & coincidentally this is when most women bleed. When we feel Hecate's presence within us we often feel tired, inward, depressed & are more likely to wear black, purple or navy. Migraines are another Hecate symptom if we haven't heeded the call inward to meditate or sit motionless in the bottom of the well to access our inner knowing & wisdom.

Ways to Embrace Hecate

To empower your inner Hecate by attuning to your inner wisdom, attend a psychic development class, Red Tent (women's circle) or Brotherhood Lodge (men's circle), study herb lore, have ritual baths, meditate & study esoteric texts or oracles for greater insight. Above all, take the time to reflect as Hecate assists us to make sense of our past so we can allow what needs to be let go of gracefully & sit in the void, trusting that in this place of receptivity & humility we will then be shown the next step. If you are rejecting or suppressing this aspect you will be afraid of change, aging & death.

Hecate: Myth vs Truth

In the ancient Greek version of her story, Hecate as a girl was said to have stolen a pot of rouge (indicating her desire to grow up) but fearing the wrath of her mother on Mt Olympus, she runs away & hides in the bed of a birthing mortal woman! As a result, the fire spirits (said to be the sons of the blacksmith God, Hephaistos) came & placed her in the waters to 'wash her clean' & she was swept away on the current to reside in the Underworld where she stayed & learnt the divinatory arts for which her wisdom was sought.

So this tale suggests because of her own 'dark mother' Hecate is exposed to maturity beyond her years, as many girls are who are raised by women who unconsciously project their dark emotions onto those around them, without acknowledging & taking responsibility for the effects of their own dark side. It is therefore symbolic that Hecate doesn't share her desire to become a woman with her mother, as she doesn't want to become a woman like her mother but instead wants to share that transition with a birthing mother - the Holy Cow Goddess, Europa who is full of the milk of human kindness embodying the other side of the dark mother which is Demeter, the 'all giving' mother. It is also significant that Hecate suffers because of her silence, indicating how important it is for girls to be listened to & held emotionally by other women - which is one of the main functions of the Moon Lodge or Red Tent.

Since Hecate governs rites of passage I find it interesting to note that she never receives her birth rite of menarche by being welcomed to the Red Tent to sit in counsel with the menstruating women when she becomes a woman. In fact, both tales of female puberty in the patriarchal myths are of maidens who don't have the support of their mothers at this gate. Persephone is abducted by Hades as she is deemed ready to be taken to the Underworld as his sexual consort & Hecate is also taken by males to be 'washed clean'. This suggests the power we have to change these dysfunctional stories just by reinstating our Red Tents & rites of passage to heal ourselves so we can properly support our daughters to become women who see & honor themselves as sacred & sovereign. This omission sadly has been the case for countless women who never received a sacred welcome to their womanhood by their mothers so were left to their own devices to explore their own private transition into womanhood. As a result the first initiation they received into their womanhood was through childbirth which was a shock without first being prepared in the teachings of the blood mysteries. The omission of Hecate's other female mentors such as aunts & grandmothers who would've welcomed her to the Red Tent in matriarchal times signal how, without this circle of support, young girls would be destined to enter the Underworld during childbirth & repeat the cycle of the unsupported 'dark mother' with their own children. That the patriarchal writers describe the sacred act of birth as 'impure', signals the power they sought to denigrate by the blatant misogyny inherent in this re-telling. Hence midwives, herbalists, oracles & wise women were portrayed as ugly hags or evil sorceresses who couldn't be trusted because of their 'black magic'. The irony is that the Olympiad demigods sought her for her wisdom, indicating that they used her for their own ends but discouraged mortals from seeking answers to become wise. Hence the masses were taught to fear women's wisdom by depicting the maiden as being repeatedly manipulated by the figure of an evil elderwoman. This occurs in every fateful tale told to girls such as 'Snow White', 'Hansel & Gretel', 'Cinderella'

& 'Sleeping Beauty' where the only good elderwoman is a dead one, aka the fairy Godmother in 'Cinderella'. The message here is that if we are to balance the sides of dark mother / all giving mother we cannot omit our need for feminine support in the form of rites of passage & ongoing wisdom circles that assist us to embrace the cycle of death & rebirth. For the cultural cost of denial is facing them alone. This chaos & confusion understandably takes us down into the Underworld of rage, grief, depression, fear, isolation & despair. The evidence of this we can see in our own lives, emphasizing the importance of having wise male & female elders whose insight can assist us through each milestone. By ensuring we give ourselves this support we stop the cycle of abuse that occurs when the parent is raising a child while lost in their own dark psyche. Similarly, when we acknowledge this we can ensure our children have regular access to wise elders who can support their internal growth as their earth parents are often so busy just meeting the immediate physical needs of their children.

WHO ??

Reclaiming The Validity of Intuitive Truth: Cassandra

Given the lack of stories surrounding Hecate, leads one to postulate that these were perhaps more plentiful during matriarchal times when this aspect was highly revered, given the number of crone amulets dug up such as the 'Venus of Willendorf'. For this reason, I would also like to include here the deconstruction of the Cassandra myth, as it plays a pivotal part in reclaiming the archetype of the feminine mystic.

Cassandra is symbolic as a daughter of the Hecate archetype. Legend describes Cassandra as the most beautiful daughter of King Priam & Queen Hecuba who presided over the ancient Greek city of Troy. One version of her myth says when she & her twin sister were children, serpents were found writhing over them as they slept. Serpents, were renowned for their trance inducing venom used by ancient priestesses to access insights so this was taken as a sign that Cassandra was bestowed with the gift of prophecy, having such a personal affinity with this sacred feminine totem. The patriarchal version attributes the male God, Apollo as gifting Cassandra the gift of prophecy just as he assumed authority over the oracle & serpents at Delphi. The story goes that he promised Cassandra the gift of prophecy on the condition that she lie with him but once the gift was granted she refused him so he spat in her mouth cursing that her words would never be believed. Regardless, of how she became prophetic, the story anchored is that no one believed her insights, despite history later proving her predictions were correct. So instead of her being listened to, heard, understood & acknowledged for her service her father locked her away in a pyramid to avoid her words creating public embarrassment for him. (Although it is interesting to note that he asked the guards that he be informed of all her predictions. Kind of like someone who mocks astrology but secretly reads their personal horoscope!) Unlike the ancient wise kings who sought the services of priests & priestesses to interpret their dreams, advise strategy in alignment with celestial transits & read omens as part of their decision making, the Greek King Priam never acted upon any of Cassandra's channellings which was the ultimate cause of his demise. Had he actually acted upon her intuitions he would never have opened his gates to allow the Trojan horse to enter - one of her most well known prophecies.

So too, this story has embedded the subconscious belief in our collective consciousness that should we attune to our subtle senses we will be ridiculed as mad & locked away. This has led to a cultural stigma of the supernatural, so that the archetype of the mystic was silenced & suppressed by fear & superstition. A fear perpetuated by the media as the propaganda machine of the elite who feared a populace waking up & thinking for themselves. For when one shuts down the third eye in an effort to appear normal they lose their ability to discern truth. Without access to our built in 'bullshit-meter' we become gullible to the hypnotic programming of our minds through billboards, print, radio, television & online marketing. This can only continue when our inner Apollo, who governs the rational mind is unconscious. When he is disempowered, he will unconsciously & constantly seek approval from outside himself causing him to suppress all of our intuitive urges & observances, dismissing them as unreal. Equally, all we have to do to re-empower the inner mystic is to notice, share & act upon our insights to reclaim our inner truth & wisdom to discern. Like any muscle, the more you use it the stronger it gets.

Empowering Ishtar, the High Priestess

Crown Chakra (White / Magenta)

Ishtar is the essence of the Magdalene, the awakened Divine Feminine in human form. Her lesson is to embody the Divine through sacred practices that align the body, mind & soul. Practices such as Yoga (meaning 'union'), Qi gong, Tai chi, Tantra & Feng Shui. When empowered, our inner Ishtar honors her body as a temple that houses the Divine. In practical terms this means she generates her own light through devotion inspired creativity, including sacred sexuality with her inner lover so she doesn't need to defile her temple with anyone offering to light her wick! (Like 'The Doors' song, 'Come on Baby, Light my Fire'!) When our inner Ishtar is consciously expressed we become discerning about who we allow into our inner sanctum, be it our home, heart or body. This means we retain our high frequency rather than burn out accommodating those who haven't shown themselves to be truly honoring of our sacred time, space & inner eternal flame. As one learns to embody this aspect, it becomes an increasingly important lesson as your increased light will magnetize more people towards you. This is because Ishtar (meaning 'Star') is the energetic aspect, the lightbody or stellar feminine. So when we honor our energy levels we honor our Divine spark. Similarly, this means limiting contact with those who drain us as they haven't yet found their own inner light.

Ishtar was said to be, 'the maker of kings', meaning she would insist on a man being able to answer her riddles to prove his wisdom, demonstrating his genuine deep reverence for the feminine mysteries as a condition of entering into union. Knowing this, ensures one's temple is not desecrated by an unconscious lover, regardless of our gender. Similarly, whether we are male or female, Ishtar is the part of us who ensures a prospective partner has made a deep commitment to serve the light through conscious service & right action as a condition of our involvement. If we compromise on this condition, we prostitute our own sacred space as it is guaranteed that the liaison will drain us if our partner hasn't found their own connection & commitment to Source.

Ishtar is the one who sees & embodies all the aspects of the inner feminine, knowing they each have their place as equally sacred & necessary to the whole. Having descended to the depths of herself to reclaim these inner aspects she asks that others do the same in order to share her sacred space, be they lovers or close friends. When all of her aspects are consciously on board, she uses the sum of all her parts to serve the All by anchoring Heaven on Earth. Her shadow lesson is to remember to sustain her inner light so she doesn't burn out in service to others.

Ways to Embrace Ishtar

Ishtar, (the Magdalene or High Priestess) governs Sacred Union so when embracing this aspect it is particularly helpful for us to read up on what sacred partnerships look like so we have a blueprint to anchor them in our own lives. If we are in partnership it is wise to commence a sacred practice with our beloved, such as those outlined in Volume Two. If single, we can fill our own cup sensually & sexually by self pleasuring & dedicating our raised energy as a gift to all of humanity as the sacred prostitute who is wedded to Spirit. N.B. During the patriarchy the aspect of the sacred prostitute was reduced to a nun, a woman who dedicated herself to sacred service but did not allow herself to experience direct communion with the Divine through ecstatic sexual & sensual pleasure. This suppression of Ishtar was sold to us as the penultimate 'good woman' whereas a sexually vital woman was denigrated as a profane whore. This split the archetype into a dualistic notion of Hell.

So marrying our spiritual connection with our creative expression in the form of sensuality & lovemaking reawakens this aspect. We do this by focusing on Divine appreciation & devotional worship of ourselves & our Beloved, opening us up beyond the goals & self consciousness of the rational mind to experience multi-sensory bliss & ecstasy. This frees the true self to dance with the light in one's beloved & the All. The more one expresses their naked soul in this way the less they can make choices which are out of alignment with their highest truth so their life becomes an expression of love. If single, invoking a deity to dance with energetically when self pleasuring is another way of experiencing this ecstatic union of masculine / feminine energies.

Ultimately, connecting with Ishtar is about marrying the celestial with the physical which is done simply through intent. For example, if we practice Yoga but are more focused on achieving a pose than on truly being unified we are imposing the will of the lower mind upon the body. If however, we set sacred space & intent before we begin we transform our practice into one of pure alchemy, the transformation of ourselves into our Divine truth & potential. We can transform any sacred practice from meditation to self pleasuring by doing any or all of the following first:

Cleansing: Showering, washing ourselves with a facecloth, smudging with the sacred smoke of herbs or leaves such as sage or eucalyptus or spraying our energy field with an auric spray, aura soma or salt water. Alternatively, we can cleanse using energy by visualizing violet flames spiraling up through our field or by rubbing our hands together to create energy then using our hands to swipe along our field, removing any dross.

Setting Sacred Space: Ensure the room or outdoor area is clean, uncluttered & uplifting to the senses. We can do this by creating a simple altar consisting of fresh flowers, candles, an essential oil infuser or incense, a crystal grid & pictures or statues of the deities we feel aligned with in our heart. Personally, we can do this by anointing our chakras with essential oils before we begin & sitting in silence, calling our energies back into our heart.

Setting Sacred Intent: When we dedicate our practice to a higher purpose such as to strengthening the light of the World Soul, we elevate our practice by imbuing every moment with greater meaning than just our own personal gain. Invoking our Higher Self to anchor within us & opening our stargates so we may be a vessel for Divine Will is another powerful daily intention, whether we choose to do yoga or not. You will notice when you enter a high frequency space like a healing center, temple, ashram, church or mosque that the room feels charged so we become more self aware within that space of our thoughts, words & actions. This is because when high intentions are set, they amplify all that is not in accordance with that intention so we just feel wrong if we dishonor the space in any way. So too, we can raise the frequency of our homes & workplaces just by dedicating a room to a higher purpose such as a designated meditation room or alternatively by creating altars - places of beauty to elevate the spirit at the entrance, in the garden & in every room. By simply attuning to a space we can intuitively feel the best place to position furniture to optimize the flow of chi (energy) & by regularly opening the curtains & windows to allow sunlight, fresh air & the scents & sounds of nature we invite the negative ions of nature in to cleanse our space of electro magnetic pollution, dust mites & negative thought forms. Needless to say, if we are surrounded by sound pollution, sight pollution or air pollution this is more of a challenge but can be done through sound, aromatherapy, color therapy, sacred symbols, energetic visualization, good design & use of space, natural materials such as river stones, seagrass matting & bamboo & artwork that invokes serenity.

When we create sacred space we raise the vibration of all who enter to match the intended frequency. We then experience a sense of being held by the space. Like the saying, 'God is in the details' when we take the time & care to create a loving environment through our choices we bring out the best in all who enter. This means we don't have to work so hard personally to assist people to see & know their highest light which can drain us. Whereas setting sacred space is a meditative activity which soothes & uplifts our own soul.

Ishtar: Myth vs Truth

Ishtar, the ancient Babylonian Goddess previously revered as the Queen of Heaven was reduced to the 'Whore of Babylon' in the Bible & those that kept amulets of her were accursed as worshippers of false idols. In the ancient Babylonian myth, Ishtar descended down through the seven spheres (the planets) to enter the Underworld where her sister Ereshkigal was birthing. (As in the Hecate myth, birth is again associated with a descent to the Underworld.) In this instance it is associated with a loss of one's power via a descent where she is stripped bare, suggesting the shift from maiden to mother entails a fall from grace. The evidence of our belief in this subconscious story can be seen in the pedestal status afforded a maiden in our patriarchal culture where she is valued for her youthful looks, sexual availability & innocence. As such, she is celebrated as the ideal woman as she poses no threat to the status quo of the ruling unconscious masculine. This is another contributing factor to the epidemic of post natal depression as independent young women endure the shock of medicalized childbirth & then realize that in their new role as mothers they are culturally isolated whilst being overworked & undervalued. Understandably this leads to resentment which gets targeted at her partner, as a representative of the unconscious masculine. This is when her other aspect as the warrioress is evoked & she turns her evil eye on her husband, determined to kill off his immature ways like the Queen of Hearts, 'Off with his head!'. In fact, if one was to read the Wikipedia facts about Ishtar which sympathizes with the masculine one would think her a cruel & vengeful deity who killed her lovers. Whereas Joseph Campbell (the mentor of George Lucas, creator of Star Wars) draws a comparison between Isis who mothered Horus & Ishtar who mothered Tammuz, illustrating an understanding of women who were cast in the role of mother to their immature consorts which becomes unsustainable after the descent into motherhood & birth of a child.

This is symbolized in the myth by the fact that Ishtar's husband, Dumuzi does nothing to assist her return from the Underworld but instead sits on his throne smoking a reed pipe. In other words, he has not developed the capacity to face his own fears so avoids empathizing with his wife by distracting himself with substances to dull his conscience which would impulse him to respond. It is instead Ishtar's handmaiden, Ninshubur who petitions the other Gods & Goddesses for help & only one, the God, Ea responds by sending two beings who empathize with Ereshkigal during her labour. So thankful is she that she grants them what they ask, that being the safe return of Ishtar. This part of the myth highlights the one quality both men & women must develop if we are to ascend & that is the ability to empathize. This requires us to open our heart so completely that we become one with another & so feel what they are feeling. This is emotional intelligence, perceiving through the neurons of the heart. It is the innate quality all true midwives possess. For when we are truly suffering, this is the greatest gift anyone can give us, complete understanding. (More about this in Volume Three when I speak about the shift into heart consciousness known as the fourth dimension)

Unfortunately this story sets up the expectation that one cannot rely on one's husband to be emotionally mature enough to be fully present during childbirth. So this plays out & sets up a divide I see in many couples where the wife never recovers from the sense of disappointment she feels toward her husband for not staying present & connected on all levels of his being as she made the descent to the crossroads of death & birth. Fortunately, a growing number of men are awakening the sacred masculine (Shiva) so are now taking this conscious journey of descent with their beloved. This involves surrounding & holding their partner energetically as she surrenders to the chaos of the feminine act of birth. Without his unwavering support she feels out of control, anxious & terrified. If a man has not found his connection to the light of Source within, he can not maintain this focus which sustains his partner. So too, a great lover instinctually surrounds & holds his partner energetically so she can continually open to deeper & deeper states of surrender, enabling her to ride the rhythmic waves of her multi-orgasmic state. This is why the act of birth can also be orgasmic when a woman is held energetically in fierce love & passionate reverence for the chaos of the sacred feminine. When we reclaim these aspects of the holy couple, birth can once again be as joyous & transcendent as the conception.

To view examples of conscious couples journeying orgasmic birth together visit: Orgasmic Childbirth Video: http://www.youtube.com/watch?v=0lfdnL_SdEs

Ishtar presides over Sacred Union as the feminine aspect of the holy couple so it's worth also noting the ancient Greek archetype of 'wife' that's been embedded in our subconscious. This was the Goddess, Hera who was the Greek version of the Queen of Heaven. Rather than being revered as a Queen though, Hera was mocked as an angry, sour woman for not being able to keep her philandering husband Zeus faithful to her, (hardly the blueprint for conscious Sacred Union!) This lack of recognition for her regal stature & power is anchored also with another Ishtar archetype, Mari Magdalene who was dismissed as a lowly whore whereas her consort, Jesus was worshipped as the saviour. I find it ironic that the group mind has lamented the persecution of Jesus whilst continuing to persecute his Queen. So whilst he was afforded kudos & devotion for his wisdom, compassion & service these traits were not equally revered in her, his Divine complement who was vilified & scorned.

To further ridicule the aspect of Queen, the ancient Greeks said Hera plotted the demise of Hercules because he was an illegitimate child of Zeus. This portrayal is a complete inversion of one who is a deified (conscious) wife & mother. As with most of these Greek (demi) Gods & Goddesses, Hera was worshipped long before the patriarchal rewriting of her story. Originally her husband's affairs were said to have derived from the earlier matriarchal story where the reigning God / King would be killed as a sacrifice as part of a rite that was said to ensure the fertility of the land. (Illustrating how unhinged the matriarchs were in their views about men!) So, little wonder that men tired of conforming to that story. This also explains the deep seated fear of commitment & marriage within the male psyche when you consider a man would die if he consented! The only truth in that concept is that psychologically both the unconscious & immature aspects of both men & women must die in their transition from single life to the next phase of partnership & parenthood. If they don't, the relationship will die, along with the family unit. If this isn't understood they will unconsciously compete with each other to avoid being the 'loser' or the one who dies, creating a fight to the bitter end. This is a sad fulfillment of the subconscious belief, 'til death do us part!' Whilst the start of a new life chapter signals the end of the old & along with it the death of those immature aspects - we can learn to surrender gracefully with support from one stage to the next rather than betray our partner when the descent into the shadowlands begins. (More about surrendering rather than falling with your beloved in Volume Two.)

⚕ The Journey of Isis

Re'membering' the Inner Masculine

In this chapter we're going to specifically look at the reclamation of our masculine archetypes that make up the masculine psyche. This is one half of us, regardless of whether we are physically male or female. The main lesson of our masculine self is to find our purpose so we may take up our rightful place & serve the greater good. To do that we must unveil all of our inner masculine selves who together will enact our highest potential out in the world. When these aspects are disempowered we become disoriented, unaware of our special gifts & abilities with no personal discipline or focus. The following mythology holds a key in reclaiming the multi-faceted God within.

In ancient Egyptian mythology, the God, Osiris was murdered by his brother, Set who usurped the throne. The Goddess, Isis then set about gathering the pieces of Osiris' body to restore him to wholeness. When he was whole, she managed to become impregnated by him resulting in the birth of Horus who after many conflicts with Set, triumphed & restored justice to the land. Those familiar with the film, 'The Lion King' will recognize the retelling of this journey of the Holy Son, who must reclaim his kingdom from tyrannical rule. So too, we must each awaken the Holy Son of the Divine Father by awakening our inner feminine who then seeks out & assembles the facets of our authentic masculine.

The parable of 'The Lion King' is a timely metaphor for each of us as we collectively question the scruples of patriarchal power brokers who have ruled the masses for their own greed & power, resulting in the depletion of the land & the suffering of the people. This myth symbolizes how the inner feminine within us all needs to seek out & heal the disparate parts of our wounded masculine so we are once again whole, powerful & fertile. For then we are able to seed & manifest our true heart's authentic life externally. To do this we need to have a map of our male archetypes so we can take proactive steps to empower them out in the world. The murder of the good King, Osiris indicates how we each have killed off the sacred masculine & replaced it with the ego as ruler. Only when we have awakened the sacred inner feminine by swearing our allegiance to a higher power, can we transcend our ego desires to take this inner journey to awaken the sacred masculine. Then, just like Luke Skywalker (from the film 'Star Wars'), when we have learnt to respect & use 'the Force' by attuning to our intuition, our phallus can then be used as a magic wand of creative light rather than a wand of destruction. (A symbol recurrent in our patriarchal culture with it's focus on guns, swords, knives, clubs, batons & drills.)

A Changing of the Guard

I have deliberately omitted the patriarchal Gods, Zeus, Hades & Poseidon as they have only served to embed the negative traits of the masculine in our collective psyche as the three ruling male icons in ancient Greco / Roman mythology. I base this decision upon the fact that these shadow masculine role models exhibited only unconscious & immature behavior, akin to criminals who considered themselves above the law. A legacy which can now be seen in the CEO's of unethical corporations who have sat above the general populace in their ivory towers behaving in a way that is unconscionable in their bid to increase profits whilst remaining unaccountable for their actions. For it was six thousand years ago that the matriarchy ended & the patriarchy began with the imposing of a new mythology. This involved Zeus, Hades & Poseidon gifting themselves each a third of Mother Earth to dominate & plunder by drawing lots from a helmut. (Kind of like the deals done on golf courses!) As a result, we internalized our fear of these three 'Godfather's', keeping us in the Underworld until we remembered our ability to exercise our free will. Now through conscious choice we can take our power back mentally from Zeus (the Sky Father), emotionally from Posiedon (the Sea God) & physically from Hades (the Underworld God). For when we are not ruled internally by these unconscious aspects we will no longer externally give our power to those who are.

For us to transcend our destructive masculine patterns as a species we need to first refute the idea that a God is one so immature & unconscious that he would dishonor & destroy the feminine. This patriarchal agenda of male dominion over the feminine is illustrated in the endless tales of these unevolved male aspects attempting to kill all of their children, abducting young girls & taking women sexually through either rape & deception. Personally, I see these aspects as defunct 'dinosaur prototypes' - misleading male icons whose poor examples of standard male behavior has obstructed the emergence of the conscious masculine within the psyche. All of these false Gods have therefore been subconscious role models for the unconscious masculine as they portrayed unbalanced men through their refusal to honor their feminine traits within themselves, which then manifested outwardly as misogynistic behaviors.

Take for example, Zeus, the now obsolete pin up of male authority who was the classic stern & distant father figure who ruled from above, (his head) by instilling fear in those within his dominion, acting more like a dictator than a Dad. I have instead replaced him with the re-emergence of a more ancient father figure, the Green Man. As highlighted as a footnote in Jean Shinoda Bolen's book, 'Gods in Everyman' this new aspect is awakening in post modern men who want to be heart centered in their role as fathers rather than rule from a distance. For patriarchal fatherhood only modeled one who was distant from his spouse & children as he was disconnected from himself. This changing of the guard in male authority figures is also thankfully changing the face of many corporations which now have both an ecological & social conscience.

The Map of Male Archetypes Which Govern the Seven Major Chakras

Just as there are seven feminine archetypes at the seven gates within our energy system, there are also seven aspects of the sacred masculine which govern the seven major chakras (energy centers). When all are consciously expressed, they activate the Pingala (solar) nadi, the masculine current of energy that runs from the base of our spine to the crown in our heads. Each chakra acts as a key, both in the sense that they emit a frequency like a musical note & open a vortex which collectively creates a full spectrum of light & color. This opens our lightbody to become a rainbow bridge so we may outwardly become a rainbow warrior & take right action to restore Eden.

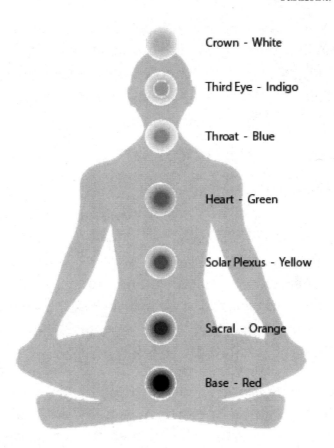

Crown - White

Third Eye - Indigo

Throat - Blue

Heart - Green

Solar Plexus - Yellow

Sacral - Orange

Base - Red

CHAKRAS	INNER GODS
Base: (Red)	Pan, the Wild Man
Sacral: (Orange)	Ares, the Warrior
Solar Plexus: (Yellow)	Apollo, the Statesman
Heart: (Green)	The Green Man
Throat: (Blue)	Chiron, the Wounded Healer
Third Eye: (Indigo)	Hermes, the Magician
Crown: (White)	Dionysus, the God of Ecstacy

Below is a tour through our inner male Gods which make up our collective masculine psyche, whether our physical gender is male or female. Since we live in a holographic universe, the aspects which are disempowered or unexplored will attract into our lives mirrors who show us the shadow of these aspects externally & the archetypes which are empowered within us will equally attract others into our lives who exude their positive qualities.

Empowering Pan, the Wild Man

Base Chakra (Red)

Pan is activated during the first seven years of our life as connecting with the natural world helps us to really anchor on the earth plane. In these formative years, the more we are encouraged to run around 'nudey rudey', study bugs & catch tadpoles the more we will be able to express our primal masculine later in life, despite counter cultural conditioning. In our unconscious masculine dominated culture that has worshipped money & celebrity as false Gods many have unconsciously tried to attain these goals, which suppresses the natural self in order to appear civilized & successful. This then creates ego addictions & manic / depressive emotional swings. To get off this destructive see-saw of striving for success & coping with failure we simply need to 'come back down to earth' & reconnect with the masculine archetype of Pan by asking ourselves, 'What do I really need to survive?'

If we're honest with ourselves, we'll acknowledge that we do not need the latest model car or luxury home. For our desires simply create more stress as we have to work harder & longer to keep up with all the repayments. So getting back to basics by coming home to our natural selves enables us to simplify our life so we need less to survive. For the creature comforts we surround ourselves with just create a sense of security, to mask our survival fears. If we don't stop to examine our base fears, our compulsive behavior & stress accumulates as manic overdoing. Because the archetype of Pan governs the base chakra, he asks us internally to face what we fear so we don't inadvertently destroy ourselves & our life by trying to avoid them.

Coming, Ready or Not!

An initiation with Pan often looks like our worst nightmare as Pan (from which we derive the word, panic) asks us to face our survival fears. However given that our rational mind, (in the name of progress) has sought to protect us from the elements so we live our lives in the comfort of air conditioning, central heating, artificial lighting & double glazed windows, we have over time become so disconnected from the elements that we fear them out of ignorance. This is why we've collectively had such a fascination with pop culture icons who don't fear nature, such as 'Tarzan', Steve Irwin ('The Crocodile Hunter') & TV shows like 'Survivor' & 'Man Versus Wild'.

As Gaia (Mother Earth's) rebirth continues, her Earth changes are reminding us that we must maintain a healthy respect for the natural elements & cycles of creation & destruction. As a result, many are experiencing initiations of one sort or another where they have to make an effort to understand their natural habitat in order to survive. For myself, my initiation with Pan included a year of homelessness - including being evacuated from bush fires. Like many I was ignorant but fortunate. Despite living in a land that renews itself through fire, the majority of us living in rural Victoria (Australia) didn't understand the element of fire, such as how it moves & how to survive in the face of this raw element. (This fact was sadly illustrated by 70% of all bodies recovered from the 'Black Saturday' fires being found in bathrooms, where many had sought refuge as they didn't understand that water is a conduit that would not offer cool refuge but would instead literally boil them as our bodies are 70% water.) In our region, fire education programs have since been implemented so locals have learnt when faced with a bushfire, it is practical to seek out the opposite element, Earth for protection. i.e. standing behind a brick wall or behind a car under a thick woollen blanket. Unfortunately it took such a devastating event for our communities to understand the element of fire, rather than simply fear it.

Ways to Embrace Pan

Ultimately we are made up of the five elements, as is everything in the physical realm (3D). When we align with our inner Pan we come to respect & recognize the elements both within & without as the outer macrocosm reflects any imbalances in the microcosm. To do this we must consider the natural elements that we are made up of & balance these elements so we don't end up with such an elemental imbalance that we create our own natural disaster that threatens our very survival.

Below is a description of elemental imbalances. Consider how the elements are being reflected back to you in your life, letting you know where you are personally out of balance. For example, if you negate or suppress an element such as fire (anger) you will attract others who have an excess of this element which may trigger your survival fears. Through understanding the behaviors of the raw elements (internally & externally) we can harness their raw energies creatively rather than be destroyed by them.

Excess Elemental Imbalance

Fire out of balance destroys rather than creates through rage in the form of abuse & violence. (Alcohol known as 'fire water' fuels latent rage so it is expressed uncontrollably.)

Water out of balance drowns in constant dramas of their own making rather than soothing with love. (This is when it becomes all about them, their high's & low's so they are not centered enough to truly give to others.)

Air out of balance over analyses & criticizes all our efforts rather than assisting us to simply use logic to problem solve. (Those prone to smoking their drugs tend to paralyze themselves with over-analysis, spending their time daydreaming & talking rather than doing.)

Earth out of balance results in us becoming so bogged down by responsibility that we build limiting structures & routines that are so fixed we are not flexible enough to try a different way.

Balancing Fire: When we experience heat wave days it is easy to see how quickly this excessive solar energy gets us physically & emotionally prickly & 'hot under the collar'. This is often illustrated by 'hot headed' young males revving their engines along the sunset strip, looking to blow off some steam. On 'Black Saturday' when the soaring temps & dry winds created bush fires that took hundreds of lives, I returned home to find my male housemate had exploded in a fit of unexpressed rage by tearing down all my sacred feminine furnishings - illustrating how the out of balance fiery, yang energy had catalyzed his out of balance yang energy to blow it's stack destructively also. Both men & women who have Mars or the Sun in a fire sign such as Leo, Sagittarius or Ares are most in need of learning to channel their inner fire creatively rather than destructively, as well as how to literally 'cool down' by immersing themselves in the element of water, (the feminine) by having a swim or cool bath on days of extreme heat. And when Gaia (Mother Earth) heats our core with extreme temperatures it is an invitation to access our passion, what we feel most strongly about, observing feelings of anger as an indicator of what action needs to be taken creatively rather than exploding uncontrollably in a fit of rage!

Balancing Water: When we experience grief it is as if our emotions have drowned out our inner fire so just looking into the raw element of fire will help us to revive & uplift our spirits. Likewise, during monsoonal rains or endless foggy drizzle, to avoid feeling sad & apathetic, get your fire going with a creative project you can work on indoors. Those who have water signs heavily aspected in their natal charts such as Cancer, Scorpio or Pisces often need a bit of help lightening up with some fun creative play as a way of balancing their tendency to become insular due to their emotional & psychic sensitivity. Similarly, when Gaia floods she is acting as a catalyst for us to express any sadness we have not acknowledged. This occurred in the very masculine 'sunshine state' of Queensland here in Australia which flooded, creating a public outpouring of emotion rarely seen by Queenslanders who are renowned for speaking with a stiff upper lip. (The sun rules the masculine, hence my assertion about those in the sunny state.)

Balancing Air: In hurricanes, cyclones & strong winds our thoughts can become easily scattered as air rules the rational mind. Those who live in high altitude areas benefit from learning to still the mind through meditation to avoid insomnia due to the mental stimulus mountainous terrain offers. This heightened state of mental clarity & insight is why mountains have been climbed throughout time as a way of seeking perspective. It has long been understood by Gypsies that the 'winds of change' disseminate new thoughts & possibilities around the planet which is why all indigenous tribes listened to the voice of the wind for inspired thoughts. If you find yourself with your head in the clouds or confused by over-analytical thinking, you simply need to unwind your mind by reconnecting with the elements of earth & water. To do this, take your shoes off, get out in the garden or go bush & eat some grounding foods such as beetroot, kidney beans or nuts. Then take a warm bath & drink some chamomile tea with boney & you'll sleep more soundly & be less prone to anxiety.

Balancing Earth: Those who become too sedentary, stuck in their ways & attached to the material realm often need an earthquake to wake them up & shake them out of their complacency! (Not that I'd wish a wake-up call that big on anyone.) Given how dense & slow our vibration has become as a species, with so much emphasis on the economy over our evolutionary growth it is no wonder that we've had so many earthquakes in recent years to awaken us from our unconscious slumber. Often if we are out of balance in our Earth element we use food as a 'cure all', eating to comfort ourselves & to avoid looking at our issues so we literally become slow & heavy like our consciousness. This is why the more someone heals their old issues, the pounds literally fall away but if they just try diet after diet without resolving the core issues they will never break the habit of over-eating. Reading books that activate the higher mind such as channelled books create the inner shifts needed before outer ones can take place.

Pan: Myth vs Truth

If a man communes with Mother Nature he will develop a healthy respect for the feminine, so he doesn't unconsciously use & abuse nature & women. Hence men in traditional cultures did survival missions such as vision quests alone in nature as rites of passage to mark their transition from boyhood to manhood.

Without building this self reliance a man, regardless of his age will remain an eternal boy like Peter Pan, running away to Never Never Land to distract himself with the other lost boys rather than grow into a truly empowered wild man by accepting & taking responsibility for his inner beast! When a man can accept & learn to love his wild self he can then more readily own & accept all aspects of his lower nature. This includes his lust, temper & fear based behaviors. By accepting & taking responsibility for his animal urges rather than hiding or suppressing them out of shame he can then express them in a balanced way. This also includes accepting his physical self since Pan governs the base chakra, which corresponds to the physical body. The more he rejects his own body hair, nudity & bodily functions the less he will be able to accept them in others. (On that note - love your phallus guys just the way it is rather than comparing its size or shape to others. To the women, consider way in which you could worship the power of the key to the temple, the wand of light - whether hetero or lesbian.)

The archetype of Pan was once a pre-Olympian nature God who was a worshipper & protector of nature (the feminine). He was then denigrated to a lowly predator of women. So what has been subsequently portrayed to us is an unconscious & disempowered Pan archetype. A male who is dominated by his lust, causing him to sexually harass & pursue women, even if the attraction isn't mutual, inciting panic. One can see plentiful depictions of this unconscious Pan in our pop culture, such as the TV show, 'Law & Order SVU' which reenacts criminal cases of sexual deviants, further anchoring a dark association with primal male sexuality as that of a dangerous predator. There are however a few positive portrayals of wild men who honor women sexually like the gardener in the novel, 'Lady Chatterley's Lover'.

I feel a key to reclaiming the true essence of Pan lies in the remembrance that Pan is half goat, an animal totem associated with spiritual ascension because it thinks for itself unlike a sheep. What's more, it scales difficult mountains, considered places of spiritual insight, just as Pan was said to reside in the mountainous forests of Arcadia. In opposition to this, the patriarchs portrayed Pan as dangerous. When unconscious, yes, he does pose a threat to the sacred feminine which is why porn, which propagates the expression of unconscious Pan energy is an industry which threatens the sanctity of the natural feminine. However, when Pan is consciously embodied, he is a symbol of male empowerment who poses a threat to those who don't want us to think for ourselves. For he is the one who possesses an innate wonderment & understanding of natural law, which fuels his own fertility & sexual potency. (The loss of this being evident in the low sperm count of men who are completely disconnected from nature.) Pan is the one who learns to harness the life force known as kundalini (serpentine energy) up through the chakras which is why Pan was said to have fashioned a panpipe from seven reeds out of a woman whose sisters had turned her into a reed. (Her sisters represented her inner feminine archetypes, which when conscious opened her seven gates of consciousness.) So too, each reed represents the seven keys or chakras in our energy system, which when open, allow the breath of Spirit to move through us so we become like a reed pipe, an instrument for the Divine whose song uplifts all who hear it. For if we honor the power of this force of nature within us, we can transcend our lower animalistic tendencies to become the 'King of the Beasts' - one who can't be trapped or consumed.

Beastly But Not A Brute! Pan As A Lover...

So you could say Pan is the part of us that knows how to 'blow like a flute', a talent he develops through unashamed self pleasuring which grants him a healthy love of sex & an ability to perceive the subtle rungs on his inner 'Stairway to Heaven' so he doesn't blow his seed on the welcome mat with a partner. What's more, when a man is empowered in this archetype his breath alone can produce an orgasmic quiver when received by his lover. He is the aspect that instinctually knows how to make a woman sing by playing upon her flute (chakras) with the reverence of a worshipper of nature! And that's the key - worship! The more one earnestly worships, the more energy is generated sending his mate into orbit! However, if he seeks to dominate the feminine rather than revere her, she will close down energetically & neither will climb the 'Stairway to Heaven', despite her well rehearsed fake orgasms. This, sadly is the pallid diet of sexual interaction being sold as pornography to a global audience of men, which disempowers them with an instruction on how to be a lousy lover!

Another version of the inverted Pan archetype is the Christian concept of the Devil, causing people to fear their natural self & disown their shadow for fear of being scapegoated as unacceptable or evil by the unconscious mob. So if you have a son be sure to provide him with positive depictions of Pan such as 'Tarzan' & 'The Jungle Book' to counteract this & never shame his body or sexuality.

Empowering Ares, the Warrior

Sacral Chakra (Orange)

Ares is activated between the ages seven to fourteen, when boys seek out more rough play in the form of wrestling & take more

interest in competitive sports. As an archetype, Are'
reduced from a sacred warrior trained & skilled in the ..
to hunt & defend his kin to a mere pawn in tactical manoeuvres.
A warrior has a strong sense of self whereas a soldier is a man
whose Spirit is deliberately broken so he will follow orders
without question. If this was not done there is no way their
humanity would enable them to carry out the orders handed
down by militant leaders who head corrupt war machines that
dominate other cultures. So instead of fighting to uphold truth
& justice they are simply viewed as the expendable 'manpower'
needed to pillage the spoils of other nations so the elite may
amass more territory, wealth & dominion over others for their
empirical rule. In the U.S. the indoctrination of their 'Aryan
youth' into a blind allegiance to the military starts with the daily
pledge of allegiance & is further anchored by a school culture
that worships the boys who play grid iron (armoured) football.
The arts of dance & music are also militarized with the girls &
less brawny boys steered into cheer squads & marching bands
that glorify organized, precision based group moves wearing
military style uniforms.

Alternatively one can use creative & peaceful resistance as the
rainbow warrior to gather the power of the people. One can
look to the example of Ghandi or Martin Luther King who
inspired so many to join them in making a stand for what was
true & just. This ability to gather 'people power' has become
more accessible than ever with the advent of social media
causes which raise public awareness & apply global pressure
to efficiently & effectively petition the need for change. In just a
short space of time I have witnessed many injustices
overturned due to this process of peaceful activism.

The usurping of the warrior by the introduction of the militant
soldier has caused many Ares dominant men to feel ashamed

of this aspect, leading them to suppress it for fear of becoming a brute with no conscience. However if this aspect is not expressed in a healthy way, for instance with martial arts to channel this masculine aggression it becomes bottled up & expressed uncontrollably like 'The Incredible Hulk.' Sadly this is usually unleashed on those nearest & dearest when frustration cannot find expression through words. This dynamic occurs more for men who have not developed the next archetype, Apollo who governs the rational mind so they can assert their frustrations strategically through the law of the land.

When Ares is out of control he literally kills his alter ego: Adonis, the Lover. This creates a pattern of destructive /abusive behavior towards his partner followed by shame & regret which anchors a deep sense of powerlessness linked to his inability to control his rage. Men who have a dominant Ares (emotional center) can easily become overwhelmed by their lower emotions so their remorse is equally overwhelming & painfully genuine, leading to a destructive cycle of forgiveness & repeated emotional abuse. To break this cycle they need to do more than seek forgiveness, they need to take responsibility for their own emotional growth by joining a men's group to examine & learn from their emotional responses. This is best done with a band of trusted brothers who are rainbow warriors, dedicated to healing the war within so they don't need to act it out on those around them which destroys everything they hold dear as they inflict their wounds on to their families.

Ares governs the sacral chakra so men who have a strong Ares aspect make generous, sensual lovers who express their big emotions with unashamed romance. This can make it very challenging for shadow Aphrodite women to leave abusive relationships with unconscious Ares men because they feel more passionately loved than ever before, even though the love can quickly turn to abuse should he become frustrated & lash out, verbally or physically.

To express Ares energy positively; sports & activities such as paintball, laser gun & go carting as part of a regular boy's night are great to let off Ares' steam, especially for men who are over thirty. For men who are parents or step-parents, making set times to give their 'inner Ares' a chance to play, test their limits or vent their frustrations will avoid potential eruptions on the home front, such as drinking to excess to suppress emotions or being unconsciously competitive with children which destroys their children's trust in them.

Many Ares men feel like black sheep in terms of their perceived inability to meet with their father's expectation of them. This is because they find it hard to stick at that which doesn't excite them, so they can often run away from their responsibilities if they haven't found a way to turn their joy into their livelihood. This is why sports stars are worshipped by the collective unconscious masculine as the shadow Ares aspect vicariously living through those who have managed to turn their fun into glory & an enviable income to spend on fast cars & adventures. Instead of worshipping athletes, to empower our 'inner Ares' we all need to exercise our own inner athlete & dare to risk being bad at physical pursuits until, through practice we can find our inner superhero & shine in our own life.

For women dealing with Ares men who are out of balance it is best to get out of the way until they have let off their steam. Women married to alcoholics know which nights to avoid their partners if it's a regular booze up night because whilst 'fire water' temporarily helps an upset Ares to forget his troubles it unfortunately lowers their vibration & puts fuel on the fire (especially spirits) so that he acts without thinking, often in an aggressive manner. (This is equally true of women with a strong Ares aspect!)

Why Beer Guts & Bloated Bellies = Disempowered Ares

If alcohol becomes a dependency for a disempowered Ares aspect to cope with their big emotions their bellies will become distended signaling the number of unprocessed emotional wounds they are yet to heal. This is because they are being stuffed down with alcohol or other substances such as marijuana or food. This is because Ares governs the sacral chakra which is situated in the belly, the emotional center where our inner child resides. In other words, if you want to spot a disempowered Ares a mile off, just look for a guy with a big gut. This symbolizes he is unconsciously being led around by his inner child! Men in this cycle of emotional disassociation & drug addiction often unconsciously seek out maternal women to process their emotional states for them but are so unhealed & immature emotionally that they are unable to offer any real emotional support in return. Men in this state are unable to effectively father as their own unhealed inner child is so reactive they often compete with children behaving childishly by being emotionally reactive rather than being heart centered & paternal.

The Classic Bar Room Brawl

If there are two Ares men who are about to express their pent up emotion on each other in the form of a brawl, no woman can break it up as she will get clobbered in her attempt. This is because some young guns go looking for a fight just to express some of their pent up rage, which is ultimately at their fathers

& themselves - even if they think it's about the world, their girlfriend or some guy that pissed them off. When there's that much heat, it takes the cool rational logic of an Apollo dominant man to talk the men down so they can once again see reason. Ultimately, this is the aspect they must develop to raise their energy up to the next gate to avoid spiraling down into a re-enactment of their inner child's tantrum.

Ways to Embrace Ares

Any physical activity will immediately help to balance our inner Ares as it provides an outlet for any pent up frustration. So whether you prefer to sweat it out solo by training in a gym, punching a boxing bag, running, team sports or rallying with a friend in a squash court after work...it doesn't matter what it is, but getting off the couch watching others play sport is the first step to empowering this archetype. This could also take the form of regular & informal games with friends & family in a local park such as 'Lions & Gazelles' where each team has to outsmart & outrun the enemy to retrieve the prized possession of the other team.

When this aspect is really empowered he is akin to a superhero that uses his brute force to serve & protect. So you may even consider joining your local CFA (country fire authority) to fight fires as a volunteer or sign up for a fun run to raise resources for a community in a less affluent country.

Being honest with the state of your inner boy is also key. In other words, do you wear oversized kid's clothes such as long shorts, caps & novelty underwear & spend most of your free time watching sports, drinking beer & playing violent video games? If yes, then I recommend going to see a male psychotherapist to explore some of your inner child's unresolved issues as your emotional immaturity will threaten the quality & longevity of your core relationships. This is a great preparation for attending rite of passage initiations into manhood such as conscious men's groups & retreats.

If, on the other hand, you view anything macho as lowly or base, you have disowned this aspect completely & need to discover the joys of being a boy, such as building & racing a go cart or the rush of an adrenalin sport like white water rafting. Unfortunately, due to our lack of community many of the men I see in my couples coaching have very few male friends as their partners are left to organize all social activities. This lack of 'bro-mance' leaves many men isolated & cut off from falling in love with their own masculinity. Joining clubs or taking up a hobby you can share with other guys is a great way of accessing more male friendships. 'The Men's Shed' movement for those in Australia is also a great way for men to connect with older male mentors in hobbies such as woodwork, which may help to heal the inner Ares wound of not being seen & understood by his Dad. For more info visit: www.mensshed.org/find-a-shed/.aspx

Since Ares is also the sacred warrior who would dance both before battle & to recount his efforts to his tribe, sacred dance is a very therapeutic way of expressing one's inner conflict & frustrations. Whether you seek out a native American Sun Dance ceremony (where you dance from sun down to sun up without food or water to access other states of consciousness in a sacred space held by a experienced shaman) or whether you seek out a regular fix of dance meditation such as '5 Rhythms', sacred dance frees the spirit & is a great way to express our inner fire creatively rather than destructively.

Ares: Myth vs Truth

In ancient Greek mythology, Ares, the archetypal warrior / dancer / lover was the least revered God. This is because he possessed the physical strength to overthrow those who ruled the corrupt empire. So to circumvent this possibility Ares was scorned & mocked as 'an angry hothead' or 'dumb beefcake' rendering him powerless as an archetype. The legacy being that young men would be so consumed with their own inner conflict that they would self-destruct rather than retaliate against the regime that had enslaved them. This is why the film, 'Gladiator' had such an effect upon young men who felt ashamed of their inability to find the courage to rise up in spite of their perceived limitations.

Ares was the least liked son of Zeus, (the archetypal dark father) as he was the one least likely to follow in his father's footsteps & take up a strategic role to ensure the continuing power of the empire. The emotional abuse by Zeus toward his son is summed up by the following quote of his, 'To me, you are most hateful of all Gods who hold Olympos.' Probably the most damaging illusion cast upon our psyche was that war was the first & true love of Ares. Like the childhood character, 'Ferdinand, the Bull', Ares preferred to be a lover rather than a fighter but it was for his heroic efforts on the battlefield that he was praised rather than rebuked by his father, which motivated him to fight in a bid to unconsciously win his father's love. This was mistakenly perceived as bloodlust, a personality trait which is fostered in our growing boys by patriarchal toys & games which predominantly focus upon beating or killing the enemy as a way of earning value as a man.

Similarly, he was portrayed as a handsome heartbreaker who instead of seeking to resolve his inner conflict, (which would've enabled him to win the hand of Aphrodite), he indulged in destructive & promiscuous behavior which resulted in many other unloved children being born, perpetuating his own unresolved wound as a karmic legacy. In Greek myth, he was often accompanied by Eris, the Goddess of chaos, denoting how his inner conflict created trouble for him wherever he went. Personally I read the cause of his personal torment as not just his unresolved rejection by his father but his inability to create a marriage with Aphrodite, who is his corresponding counterpart archetype in the sacral chakra. By being repeatedly exposed to a misleading story that Ares was never able to marry Aphrodite, we have re-created this subconscious drama in our own lives by falling for those who are unattainable as they reject us or threaten to destroy us with their own unresolved inner conflict. More importantly, by believing it impossible to create inner harmony emotionally at this gate by finding a truce between the forces of love & war we have been unable to transcend our old emotional dramas to continue our upward journey on the mystical inner tree of self-awareness.

So Ares was embedded in the male psyche as cruel, vindictive & vain. As, again it was only the negative traits of Ares that have been highlighted by patriarchal mythology, so he was portrayed as fighting only for personal glory or to settle a personal grievance rather than to serve the greater good. Fortunately, films such as 'Spartacus', 'Rambo' & 'Gladiator' portray those who are used & spat out as pawns in the war machine but who discover the inner strength to awaken the hero within & win their freedom through the completion of many challenges. (For more about this journey read the chapter on 'The Twelve Trials of Hercules' in Volume Three.)

Another myth which is key to freeing Ares from his dark story is his imprisonment by the twin giants who threatened to destroy his home. As a result of him being defeated he was imprisoned in an urn for thirteen months. The thirteen months denotes the thirteen lunar cycles in a year, suggesting Ares had to go within & ponder the thirteen faces of his feminine nature before he could successfully embark on his outward twelve trials to empower his outer masculine. I see these two giants as parental or authority figures who often seek to confine or control Ares rage by medicating or incarcerating rather than assisting the emotional healing & rehabilitation that will calm his inner storm. Interestingly, it is the God Hermes, the archetypal wise sage who assists Ares to escape. In other words, if a man doesn't develop his inner wisdom by consciously seeking to understand himself & his journeys in the Underworld (which are the experiences created by our unconscious choices & behavior) he will remain forever trapped by his unresolved rage at his authority figures. This rage stems from the fact that Ares feels he is not truly loved unconditionally by his parents. This leads him to rebel, which only further accentuates his sense that he is expendable, the one who would be sacrificed in order to create peace. Unfortunately many parents respond, not by reviewing how their own actions & family dynamics could be fueling such a rebellion, but by undermining their young Ares emotionally & psychologically so his brute force is continually used against him, creating a cycle of destruction & punishment. This means he is only given positive reinforcement when he allows himself to be used as a sacrificial pawn either on the battlefield or sports field, risking injury to provide violent entertainment for those unable to directly access their inner Ares so they can feel the primal high of beating an opponent.

Men who fear their large emotions just as one might fear their own reactions turn themselves unwittingly into 'The Incredible Hulk' causing them to live a double life like 'Dr Jeckyl & Mr Hyde' but if they find the inner courage to face the ogre within by confronting their pent up emotions with the help of a psychotherapist they will come to see their emotions as a source of strength rather than weakness. (Core Energetics is another great Ares therapy where the therapist dons padding & lets you beat the crap out of them & unleash all your big emotions!) When they experience this sense of inner strength by awakening the wounded healer aspect, Chiron they no longer feel the unconscious need to prove their masculine strength outwardly as brute force. Similarly, therapy gifts them an experience of being listened to by someone in authority so they feel empowered enough to never allow themselves to be used as a life size 'action figure' (at their own expense) as a modern day gladiator or soldier. In addition, if we also empower our inner Ares by learning the sacred arts of war, we will honor the teachings by only using them in that arena, thereby retaining our personal dignity & power like a Samurai warrior. As it is the concept of violence as entertainment repeatedly being fed to the masses which keeps their vibration low as it evokes their core fear of survival. This encourages the general populace to make limited life choices based on ensuring their security. When Ares refuses to be part of this destructive game like in the sci-fi film, 'The Running Man' the game must end.

Empowering Apollo, the Golden Hero

Solar Plexus Chakra (Yellow)

Apollo governs the solar plexus, (the inner sun) which is activated between the ages fourteen to twenty-one when pressure to achieve is felt more than ever before. Apollo's mission is to not settle for being the 'golden haired boy' who fulfills his father's wishes. His greatest challenge is to risk societal disapproval to find his true purpose. A man without a purpose is lost without a cause greater than himself to devote his energy to so he feels worthless, despite what he earns. However, before he can find his purpose he must first find himself.

Those who have a strong Apollo aspect find this difficult as they are so multi-talented that giving up all that praise & approval to risk looking like a fool is a big ask, especially in a society that rewards those who tow the line & don't rock the boat with corporate carrots in the form of bigger offices, parking spaces & the illusion of financial security. I have observed this to be a far greater challenge for those born into wealthy families as there is a distinct pressure to 'make something of themselves' as quickly as possibly after graduating in lieu of the expensive private school tuition that has been invested in them.

An Apollo man is ruled by his intellect, making the search for his soul an even greater task. This is further impeded in his early life as he is more likely to surround himself with male friends who are goal oriented rather than female friends who question his inner life & motives. In his myth, Apollo was polarized from his twin sister, Artemis to the point where he didn't even allow women on his island! This is because out of all the masculine archetypes he is the most rational so is most inclined to polarize in the masculine polarity & dismiss the feminine altogether as insignificant. On the surface he'll seem like a great catch; bright, talented, wealthy & well respected but scratch the surface & you'll see a boy who doesn't know himself, resulting in a lack of depth & passion.

Music is his great love & particularly helpful on his quest as it connects him to his feelings & his soul. Taking up an instrument is a great form of meditation as it gives his soul self expression rather than just being content to live through the expression of others. Apollo dominant men will often have a huge music collection which is a great starting point but the real shift happens when they dare to create their own music. Expressing their soul through music enables them to see & fall in love with their own soul, enabling him to find their true self.

On the positive, he is a great team player but his greatest challenge is to learn to take charge & assert himself as a leader. By following his own heart he will inspire others to be part of his quest to achieve something greater than any of them could do on their own which will serve the greater good.

Often men with a strong Apollo archetype have a dominant father who only grants loving favor when they perform in a way that is suitable. Given that the masculine part of us, our ego looks to the father for validation as we're growing up it often takes a complete individuation from the father for an Apollo dominant man to take the reigns in his own life & develop a sense of self worth that isn't defined by his father's measure.

Ways to Embrace Apollo

We can empower our inner Apollo by playing strategy games such as Chinese checkers, chess & backgammon. These assist us to think things through using discrimination & risk assessment. These are skills we can then apply to any endeavor which assist us to rise above the reactions of our primal & emotional selves which are governed by the base & sacral chakras. This enables us to literally 'cool down' by applying logic & reason to a situation so we can respond in a way that is ultimately more beneficial. It is imperative, however that we do not become so 'stuck in our heads' that we use our intellect to make all our decisions or our lives will appear successful outwardly but lack any real personal fulfillment. Without being balanced by the wisdom of the heart our masculine self can become cold & callous. A trait summed up by the saying, 'It's not personal, it's business.'

As already stated, music holds a key in awakening a man's connection to his soul so it is necessary for a man to find his voice by connecting with the sounds that most reflect his moods. This is a necessary step in expressing his own true voice in the world. This true voice is one's ability to find meaning in something greater than the achievement of personal success. This inspires one to devote their time & energy to serving a higher purpose which resonates with their soul's authentic values. This might be working pro bono as a human rights lawyer rather than in corporate litigation, or using one's skills as an ad exec to create & promote an innovative project for charity.

It is therefore helpful for our youth to be encouraged to find themselves through travel & life experiences which expose them to different points of view before they embark on a path of long-term study. For the more they complete of tertiary study or the higher they climb in their chosen profession before really stopping to consider their inner calling, the more they fear they have to lose by following their heart's urge to try a different path.

As money is the outward measure of one's self worth in a patriarchal culture, more pressure has traditionally been applied to young males to pursue financial success ahead of personal fulfillment. This preoccupation with outer value over inner truth only serves to disconnect them further from their true selves, making intimacy virtually impossible as they have uncovered no true self to share with another. So the status quo has been for a large proportion of men to invest the majority of their time accumulating wealth, assets & external status, thinking this will then attract a mate. The obvious problem with this scenario is that whilst they may attract a mate based on this patriarchal mating dance they will understandably suspect that unless they continue to acquire more perks they will be rejected, making it even scarier to follow their own conscience. It is therefore the loss of their wealth, assets & status that ultimately act as a much needed catalyst for growth for men who have focused on the external world & neglected their inner world. Such an event is an opportunity for a man (or woman) to examine how they have denied the importance of the feminine, both internally & externally so they can create a more balanced life where they are not married to their work. This 'dark night of the soul' connects them with their own suffering as they have the time & space to just feel without being distracted by their work. This ability to truly feel their own pain then develops within them the ability to empathize with the suffering of others. It is the development of this emotional intelligence that curbs their tendency to be rigid in exacting excessive punishment on those who don't follow the rules. This is because they have taken the time to question where following the rules has got them, realizing that blindly following the rules has lead to their own loss of self. As a result they become less inclined to judge others who live outside the status quo, creating a humbling of their ego. This occurs when they can admit they don't have life figured out so then real personal growth can occur. The evidence of this can be seen when they no longer try to buy their way through life but start relating to others as fellow souls on a journey rather than as mere opponents or objects of desire to be either destroyed or won over. This ability to question themselves, enables them to question the ideals & values of their father & the society that raised them so they can develop their own path based on their own realizations. Ultimately this will lead to using their strategic mind, skills & talents to create new solutions & structures that enable not just themselves to shine, but others in a spirit of co-operation rather than competition.

Developing the archetype of Dionysus is often very helpful in freeing Apollo from his fixed thinking & view of the world through the direct experience of altered states which expand his vision beyond the rational or 10% part of his mind. Similarly, practices which still & clear the mind such as meditation & sound healing also help to connect him directly with his heart.

Apollo: Myth vs Truth

According to the patriarchal legend, Apollo's first act was to request a bow & arrow so he could destroy a serpent. (It is interesting to note that the serpent had been cast as an evil instrument of the Goddess when previously it had been sacred to the Goddess & revered as the awakener of truth.) So this serpent had supposedly been sent by Hera to torture Apollo's mother while she was giving birth. (As already discussed, Hera the archetypal wife & queen was portrayed as a spiteful, jealous & vindictive woman throughout Greek mythology rather than the noble, benevolent & wise 'Queen of Heaven' that was known to the people during the pre-Olympiad era.) When we consider that Apollo was the most celebrated son of Zeus, we see how symbolic it is that the golden haired child of the patriarchy was the one who attacked the serpent. In other words, by casting unconscious Apollo as the successful icon of manhood most worthy of emulating, men would subconsciously view serpents & the archetype of the Queen of Heaven / High Priestess, (who governs the crown chakra) as the enemy. This would mean subconsciously they would refute the feminine so they would not awaken their subtle senses. This would keep them mentally stuck in the prison of the limited rational mind, following orders & conditioning without question, thereby upholding the patriarchal status quo. It is interesting to note that Apollo was said to have created the Pythian Games, held every four years to celebrate his victory over the serpent symbolizing the oppression of the feminine. These games became the Olympics - a ritual held on a cyclic basis (four years being symbolic of the four directions to anchor the patriarchal intent within the Earth plane). Similarly, Apollo assumed control of Delphi where oracular prophetesses accessed trance states by inhaling sulphur from the cracks in the Earth & infecting themselves with the venom of their pythons so they could channel insight for the people. Despite the priestesses continuing to utilize their traditional means of divination, it was the demiGod, Apollo who was credited with having the gift of prophecy.

As the reinvented holy (son) Sun God, Apollo was said to have drawn the sun across the sky in a chariot everyday so he was also revered as the bringer of light. This was the hallmark of the timeless saviour God who brought the consciousness of Heaven to Earth to enlighten the minds of the people. A role enacted by Buddha, Muhammad, Christ & Ra. Apollo, on the other hand as an inversion of the sun God cast a dark shadow by using his gift for mental strategy to settle personal scores & inflict pain upon the people such as using his bow & arrow to disseminate plagues. (Research findings by Dr. Leonard Horowitz, a public health authority, and author of the bestselling book "Emerging Viruses: AIDS & Ebola, Nature, Accident or Intentional' suggest Apollo's shadow has been re-enacted by the U.S. government, through the creation of biowarfare viruses such as Ebola & AIDS to cull the populace in resource rich third world communities.)

'"I've reprinted the U.S. Government contracts under which numerous AIDS-like and Ebola-like viruses were bioengineered by the Army's sixth top biological weapons contractor. At the time," the late 1960s to mid-1970s, "such viruses were hybridized from other germs using crude laboratory methods compared to today's sophisticated biotechnology," the doctor said.'

http://eugenicsanddepopulation.blogspot.com.au/2009/01/aidsebola-reports-outbreaks-man-made.html

Apollo was said to preside over the colonization of people & as such was used as an instrument to amass more power for his father based on the disempowerment of others. Hence the Apollonian icon of the golden haired Aryan youth was idolized as the helpmate of the New World Order. So too, those who have been most successful during the patriarchy were those who served the dark empire at a great cost to the people. Take for example, IBM (International Business Machines) the most successful company in U.S. history until Apple usurped them. It's ingenuity provided the means to record via punch cards the data necessary to colonize the Jews, gypsies, free thinkers & homosexuals who were used then exterminated to further cull the population in the Nazi work camps of World War Two.

'But Jews could not hide from millions of punch cards thudding through Hollerith machines, comparing names across generations, address changes across regions, families trees and personal data across unending registries. It did not matter that the required forms or questionnaires were filled in by leaking pens or barely sharpened pencils, only that they were later tabulated and sorted by IBM's precision technology.' Black, IBM and the Holocaust, Second paperback edition, pg. 107.

Out of all of Zeus's sons, Apollo was shown as the greatest helpmate to his all powerful father but was not empowered enough to follow his own destiny. He was unsuccessful in love, despite his handsome appearance because of his sole reliance on his rational mind he was disconnected from his heart. This was symbolized externally by his estrangement from his sister, Artemis suggesting he had a deep mistrust of women & the feminine. This also prevented him from going within to find his own inner feminine so he never found his true passion & purpose.

Given Apollo's misogyny & destruction of the feminine, it makes sense that he fell in love with men - Cyparissus & Hyacinthus, both of whom he lost due to an excessive compulsion to compete. On the other hand it is suggested he only became infatuated with his greatest female love, Daphne because of an act of retribution by Eros who shot him with an arrow & then shot Daphne, casting an enchantment that she would be unable to love him. Once again, we see the reiteration of the concept of hopeless & unrequited love between the sexes. This inability to create a sustained & loving partnership did not however prevent Apollo from fathering twelve children, a legacy we see with unconscious men not bearing the responsibility for actively fathering their offspring. More revealing, however is that again in the myths of Apollo, we find his two greatest loves, Daphne & Cyparissus were turned into trees! For me this symbolizes how they transformed themselves into microcosms of the Tree of Life, transcending the dramas of the karmic interplay of archetypal energies. In other words, by disengaging from love & war they instead focused their intent to open the seven doors of consciousness, (the chakras) to awaken the twin serpents of kundalini up the inner Tree of Life to awaken them as sovereign & enlightened holy hermaphrodites.

Apollo was also a gifted musician but presented in his unconscious expression to us, he was competitive to the point of maiming those who preferred the talents of others. (Now that would make for an interesting reality show!) Yes! He reputedly transformed the ears of King Midas into that of a donkey after he voiced his greater appreciation of Pan's musical ability. In another instance he won a musical competition against the satyr, Marsyas by challenging him to play his instrument upside down, a feat which is possible with a lyre but not with a flute. Then not content with winning by unfair means he skinned his opponent & nailed him to a tree. Similar to the Roman authorities who nailed Christ to a tree to avoid being outshone by his superior intelligence & leadership. (It is so symbolic that one who had ascended his inner Tree of Life & Knowledge was made an example of by being tortured with a tree, just as the patriarchy chops down trees in the name of 'progress'.)

Empowering the Green Man, Earth Father

Heart Chakra (Green)

Between the ages of twenty-one to twenty-eight the kundalini is activated in the heart. This brings up all of our issues with our parents from our own childhood to prepare us for our own expression of the Green Man post Saturn return. (This is an astrological transit that asks us to grow up & take responsibility for ourselves in our twenty-ninth year when the stern paternal energy of Saturn returns to check on our progress!)

The Green Man is an aspect of the masculine that is being reclaimed after countless generations of children grew up with the distant Sky Father known as Zeus (who later became the image of the old guy in a white robe & sandals that many of us were told was 'God' growing up.) This image, along with the industrial age saw men treating themselves more like machines than men, working long hours in all male environments & ruling the roost from a distance so that they were often feared more than loved by their children as they never got to know their father's true self, his soul.

You've only got to look at the number of men in prime time TV shows now cooking & gardening to see that the post modern male is finding his roots, working from home, helping with the child rearing & developing new technologies that work in collaboration with Gaia & her creative elements rather than working against them.

The Green Man is an Earth Father, a man who is centered in his heart so he is connected to himself, to his partner, to his children & to the natural cycles. Because he honors the natural cycle of death & rebirth he is able to grow his legacy in a way that is sustainable both for himself & those around him - no longer working long hours away from his family & dying of a stroke at age sixty. A prognosis that makes a lifetime's effort invested in return for a gold watch at retirement a poor investment & an even poorer joke when you consider all it essentially does is remind you of the quality time you will never get back!

Ultimately the fastest way to activate the Green man is to spend time growing a garden as this reconnects us with the circle of life which like the fable of 'The Lion King', puts a man in his heart, renewing his respect for life so he finds his courage to take heart-centered action as needed.

Women can midwife the birth of this aspect in their partners by actively supporting them to leave the perceived security of a job that is slowly killing them & actively encouraging them to take the leap of faith on their true heart's desire. N.B. When an unconscious woman just wants to be fathered by her husband by having him kill himself to provide for her, she often doesn't respect the value of money & makes unnecessary purchases like a child. When this is the case, she needs to activate her own inner masculine by identifying & sharing her gifts with the world to help contribute so he is not bearing the weight of financial responsibility on his own.

Because the majority of men didn't grow up being mentored by a father who had anchored this aspect, role models were birthed in our pop culture by those who did. Enter 'Kermit the Frog' created by Jim Henson & 'Shrek' created by Mike Myers who have together helped us to birth this new archetype of the Green Man, a leader who overcomes his fears by following his heart to manifest his dream.

L Plate Green Men: Get Thee To A Brotherhood Lodge!

Finding other conscious men you can share your heart with on a regular basis is a key ingredient for developing the Green Man archetype, especially for men. Through the practice of 'Brotherhood Lodges' boys & men from 15 years of age can offer mutual mentoring & support through the high's & low's of life. This can be created by gathering in circle once a month when the sun shifts into a new sign to discuss the lessons that lie ahead of them in the coming month through an awareness of the strengths & weaknesses of that zodiac sign. (I provide this info in the chapter, 'The Twelve Trials of Hercules' in Volume Three.) In addition, by confronting your heart's truth with witnesses each month, you can't not act upon your conscience so each month you grow incrementally into the best man you can be.

Who's Your Daddy!

Having a men's circle is particularly important for men once they become fathers as often all the attention is on the new mother & little support is offered to the father who has the added pressure of providing for three instead of one (or more), in addition to his own fears of repeating his father's mistakes or feeling like a walking wallet as the sole provider. Receiving understanding & insight from men who have made this transition into conscious fatherhood, strengthens a man's ability to stand tall in his new role, even when he makes mistakes. I recently spoke with a brother who had been attending men's groups for the past six years since he became a father. He told me he had grown incredibly as a result which I could see in how he fathered his two girls & partnered his wife whilst honoring his own needs.

A New Breed of Fathers

Many men are now more present & active in their children's lives. This affords them the opportunity to attune to their children's feelings & witness the consequences of their own actions upon their children. This helps them to change the pattern & understand the wounding of their own inner child. For a positive father has the confidence to instill structure & discipline within a child, which is as necessary as love & nurturing in equal measure, if you want a happy, confident & well balanced child who can grow up to apply self discipline & structure in their own lives.

Fortunately there is a 'Green Man' approach being applied in schools to ensure children adhere to the rules. The emphasis being to create a healthy mutual respect between teacher & child rather than the 'old school' approach of authority figures demanding rather than earning respect which results in kids resenting & rebelling against authority to avoid their spirit being broken. It is simply the concept of 'certainty not severity'. In other words, follow through with consequences that fit the crime incrementally rather than letting them get away with stuff to avoid being the bad guy & then losing it & hurting your kids when they take it too far, either verbally or physically.

Another fundamental difference between the archaic role model Zeus, the distant Sky Father & the earthy Green Man is that the Green Man will never undermine his partner, the Earth Empress as he knows united they stand, divided they fall & that their kids need a strong foundation rather than one where the kids are watching the cracks widen, wondering when the 'D' word is gonna surface! The unconscious father by contrast swings between attempting to rule the entire family unit, including his wife by over-riding her decisions & putting her down in front of the kids or alternatively acting as if he is one of the kids by rebelling against her rules, alienating her as the only responsible adult.

This re-emergence of The Green Man is why men who are initiated into into the heart through becoming parents are now more likely to reassess their work / life balance. Ideally this is best done before the added responsibility of children comes along. N.B. Developing the counterpart energy of Demeter, the inner Mother will assist men in opening their hearts which in turn empowers their outward expression of their inner Green Man. She does this by encouraging us to 'come home' to nature, where the heart is - out of the madness of the mind & the city!

Ways to Embrace The Green Man

Create a garden! Whether it's a balcony garden of veggies in pots or doing a weekend workshop in permaculture, getting your hands in the Earth & directly working with Mother Nature to create life will be quietly empowering, centering & grounding for your inner Green Man. Another great way is by restructuring your work if possible so you can work from home rather than feeling like a cog in the wheel of the metropolis. Working from home or near home enables us to feel more connected to our home, our loved ones, our land & our inner circle of friends which provide the joy to sustain our outward service. By contrast, the old paradigm prioritized work seeing money as that life blood which sustained life. This inversion of priorities affirms poverty consciousness as it causes us to put money before doing what we love & in the place that makes our heart sing with our nearest & dearest. The irony is that when we make this shift, we become happier which frees up our creative mind to be resourceful to generate abundance in ways we couldn't have dreamed of while stuck in a mindset of financial dependence.

Structuring your work to reflect the natural cycles also is a great practice for embodying the Green Man. In other words, just as the native Americans did most of their physical labour in Spring & Autumn when the weather wasn't extreme you may plan to expend more energy at these times of the seasonal wheel so you can retreat & reflect in Winter & relax & play in Summer. The bestseller, 'The Four Hour Work Week' by Tim Ferris may also be helpful in changing your view of how to schedule your work around your life instead of the other way around.

Be Part Of The Solution (not part of the problem!)

Learning about the unethical & unsustainable farming practices used by large agribusiness will also inspire you to actively participate in the return of Eden by buying, bartering or raising your own free range organic produce. If our choice is now whether to live in love (expansion & growth) or fear (contraction & atrophy) it makes sense that our food source carries the vibration of love rather than fear. When we consider that fear is the emotion coursing through an animal's veins at the time it is killed in our modern day meat processing plants, if we then ingest that animal we are adding to our own density by anchoring more fear within our energy system. Like the old saying, 'You are what you eat.'

Green Man: Myth vs Truth

Well, if we rummage around in the subconscious to discover what stories are embedded about the archetypal father we find numerous examples of Zeus, the Greek Sky Father abandoning his responsibilities as a parent to pursue other fertile women. So instead of sticking around to provide for & protect his children, he saw his role as father as merely the act of procreation. This implies that fathering is only physical, rather than it also being emotional, mental & energetic. Subsequently many modern men have perceived their duty as fathers as providing for their family physically, with no concept of mentoring their young or being an emotional support to them on an ongoing basis. So, while many modern fathers may feel resentful of working themselves into the grave for their offspring they may fail to see where they didn't seed a closer & more meaningful bond with their children by getting to know each other emotionally, intellectually & creatively in the form of play. In fact, in our 3D uni-verse (offering replays of the one story) there are only negative imprints of fatherhood offered through our Western mythology, a fact we see reflected in our society. Instead what we have had repeatedly ingrained is that fathers compete with & undermine the efforts of their children, illustrated by all the myths which show Zeus swallowing his children for fear of being usurped. We are also given the expectation that our fathers won't be there for us when we need them, as illustrated in the myth of Persephone, the archetypal daughter. In this myth, she is abducted by her uncle. (A man who consumes & possesses the sacred feminine externally rather than developing it in himself.) When her mother, Demeter seeks out Persephone's father, Zeus for help he refuses to assist her until his own food supply is threatened. Repeatedly we are also shown that the distant Sky Father punishes his young from afar rather than consistently, guiding & correcting their errors in judgement, signifying that he ruled from the head to instill fear rather than showing strength from the heart.

When we consider that the archetypal husband & father are the same archetype that governs the heart we can see why heart disease & heart attacks are so prevalent in Western men who have been so disconnected from the positive qualities of the Green Man. These destructive mythic patterns within our subconscious also explain why men have struggled to wholeheartedly embrace fatherhood. Unconscious men also fear commitment, causing them to sabotage relationships that could offer them the experience of raising a family. This is evident in the Greek myth that depicts the birth of Venus. In this story, Zeus, the Sky Father won't commit to Rhea, the Earth Mother to raise children which would sustain life on the planet. Enraged, she castrates him by cutting off his penis & out of the foam it scatters on her fertile seas, rises Aphrodite. So too, life has imitated art as women, fed up with bearing the load of parenting have further emasculated their immature husbands by verbally pointing out their shortcomings as husbands & fathers. This loss of male power on the domestic front lay in the basis of all 1950's 'take my wife' jokes as unconscious men tried to reclaim their sense of manhood by putting down their opposite. This fear of being henpecked by a woman who perceived his masculine weakness was the unconscious reason Zeus (& now those in his likeness who follow his example) have an insatiable desire to seduce younger women. In other words, in an effort to assert their male power they seek to sexually dominate as many women as possible to prove their masculinity to themselves. Unfortunately for them, this type of sexual behavior gratifies only the ego, making the soul more hungry for true union. Such a soulful union however is not possible until they stop to question why they flee from women who would stimulate them mentally, energetically & emotionally. This means allowing themselves to open to an experience beyond their control - which is the secret to really living & feeling alive, rather than trying to capture a new lease on life by dating someone half their age. (Pedophilia is the extreme of this dynamic illustrated by Hades abduction of fifteen year old Persephone.) This means, like Zeus they become a caricature of the 'Dirty Old Man' as they age, pursuing young girls who are mirrors of their emotional immaturity. The more they shape shift or use their status, wealth & assets to seduce, the more they affirm how unlovable their true self is, creating an obsessive tendency to prove themselves lovable by securing the affections of physically attractive young women. Ultimately, a man will always fear intimacy with a mature woman if he hasn't sought out his own rite of passage initiations to mature himself. This is why the cracks often appear in a marriage after the birth of the first child. Since his partner has been put through menstruation & childbirth as rites of passage to prepare her for parenting, he must equally undergo conscious transitions to mark his shift from boy to man & knight to king if he is going to feel inwardly equipped to match his partner in their new roles as parents.

The Dark Father's Legacy: Fear of Marriage & Fatherhood

While growing up if boys perceive their father doesn't wholeheartedly embrace the role of fathering they will assume it is a burden rather than a joy & seek to avoid it in their adult life. This rejection of the role of father can be conveyed through never prioritizing one's home life over work, body language, facial expressions & looks that signal imposition when asked to contribute to family life & of course, derogatory remarks. Similarly, daughters growing up with such a Dad will settle for a man as a partner who hasn't developed his inner Green Man as they will accept his closed hearted & immature attitude as normal.

So if a man does not grow into his heart by examining the behavior of his immature self he will not respect himself & this lack of self respect will be mirrored back to him by his partner. (This lack of respect is the main reason women stop feeling sexually attracted to a man.) So instead of scapegoating her criticisms as the problem or blaming his children for being needy, the conscious man will recognize his need for emotional, mental & energetic fathering & take proactive steps to access it in the form of men's circles, retreats & rite of passage ceremonies with other conscious men of different generations. And yes, it is very sad that the majority of men (& women) did not receive the necessary influence of a conscious father whilst growing up. However, it cannot be embodied for the future generations without men taking responsibility in the present by accessing the support of self aware men to make up for this cultural epidemic of 'the absent father'. Fortunately, this can be healed in circle, as every man present plays the role of 'the good father' enabling them each to explore their hurts, wounds, insecurities, strengths & dreams. As they explore their inner world in the company of heart centered men they feel validated by the archetypal father, healing the invalidation that has led to their subsequent disempowerment. In other words, the buck stops with us! Then regardless of whether a man consciously chooses to have children of his own or foster, adopt or assume a parenting role with step-children or whether he fulfills his Green Man by mentoring others, he will then be able to fully open his heart to his partner & enjoy a true relationship of equals without fear of not measuring up. For true peace of mind comes with opening the heart!

Embodying Chiron, the Wounded Healer

Throat Chakra (Blue)

From the age of twenty-eight to thirty-five our throat chakra is activated by our kundalini rising into our fifth gate as we enter our fifth cycle of seven years. This presents us with whatever hurts from our past we haven't yet resolved within our psyche. If we embrace our vulnerabilities as they arise by expressing our tears we clear our channel of blocked energy so we can receive insight into how our wound has served us. When we identify the lesson, we feel enlightened with conscious understanding rather than weighed down by unexpressed pain & fear. This enables us to appreciate why as a soul we chose to be wounded in this way, turning our shame into gratitude & empowerment. For ultimately every wound we receive in this life brings to the surface the wounds we have repeatedly manifested & carried for lifetimes. So when we understand our part in attracting these karmic lessons we no longer need to repeat them.

If we don't address our need for personal healing during this time we will have what's known as a mid-life crisis during our next cycle (from age thirty-six to forty-four.) If we still avoid dealing with our past pain by applying more distractions in the form of substances, work, travel or sex our unresolved issues will hit us like a freight train prior to turning fifty. This is because during our forty-ninth year the planetoid, Chiron completes it's forty-nine year orbit so it ends up exactly where it was in our solar system when we were born. (A planetoid is a celestial body which is half way in size between an asteroid & a planet.) The return of Chiron, the Wounded Healer brings up for us the biggest wound we've come here to heal this lifetime as a catalyst for personal rebirth.

The ultimate lesson for our inner Chiron, is to see our biggest wound as our greatest teacher. So our journey to heal & understand ourselves serves as our apprenticeship to awaken the spiritual teacher within us. For when this aspect is empowered we teach all that we have learnt from journeying with our wound. By openly sharing our human frailty with such honesty that it speaks directly to the wounded aspect of others we assist them in healing their sense of shame & separation.

This aspect of the spiritual teacher is within all of us. For the greatest teachings of truth are simple but it is the degree to which we connect with the universal soul in others as to whether our words will hit their mark & catalyze a personal shift in others. This end result is dependent on our ability to completely unmask our ego as the universal, 'Everyman'. Chiron is therefore the aspect of the inner masculine that must risk the ultimate test of courage. That being, to publicly acknowledge his 'achilles heel' which will both humble & initiate him into his service as a teacher.

Through this humility he comes to a place of gratitude for his wound, for all that it has gifted him. This is compounded by the knowledge that he chose to be wounded in this way so he could heal what he has carried for lifetimes. For only then can he fulfill his potential as a spiritual teacher & assist others to face their wounds with the same dignity.

At first when we accept that we need help in order to heal, our wound is so overwhelming or confronting that we can only cope with one trusted other, poking around in our area of acute vulnerability such as a reader, healer or counsellor. Through this process we become more accepting of our vulnerability which readies us for the next stage of healing. This is being truly seen beyond our social mask in a group. It is for this reason that facilitated sharing circles offer a safe forum for us to publicly acknowledge the wounds & scars of our journey, along with any insecurities that have created patterns of self sabotage or overcompensation. By speaking our personal truth & insights in an environment that is emotionally safe & supportive we gain the confidence to share our experiences with others, enabling us to be less guarded & more open on a daily basis. By participating regularly in a sharing circle, our self understanding & wisdom accelerates because we gain a deeper understanding of human behavior. This enriches all of our relationships so we feel more optimistic about our ability to form enduring partnerships.

Chiron teaches us the gift of true brotherhood, which goes far beyond the realm of 'mateship' or friendship as his ability to communicate his inner self offers a soul connection with other men beyond the superficial discussion of the mundane. This willingness to share truth attracts true soul brothers into our waking world who will honor our bravery when we dare to share our deepest pain. For only one who has embraced their own pain is capable of holding a respectful emotional space to witness others release theirs. However if we deny our hurts by suppressing our sadness with substances we unconsciously recreate our wounds.

Men deserve the same depth, trust & support many women share as soul sisters. Without this gift, the majority of men are isolated & prone to addiction as they feel powerless to awaken their true inner power. For whilst many mainstream men run from the idea of attending a men's circle, until they find the inner strength to revisit their greatest wound they will be ineffectual as men.

Equally, women need close soul brothers. Men who will not feel threatened by emotional intimacy, nor view them as a potential sexual partner but simply offer an honest perspective from a male point of view. For women working with their inner Chiron, this first involves developing compassion for men by understanding the wounds of the masculine. This is ultimately healing for all of our relationships with the men in our lives. It also enables us to attract & cultivate beautiful brother / sister relationships with men if we are not sizing them up as potential partners but content to enjoy candid soul sharing. This experience gently heals our relationship wounds with the masculine & restores our trust in intimacy with our opposite.

Proof Is In The Pudding!

After working for so long on my inner feminine aspects, after I began consciously working with my own inner masculine archetypes & doing masculine archetypal chart readings for men I was moved to run a Brotherhood Lodge as a one-off test case to see if I could adapt the monthly Red Tent women's circles format to create a wisdom circle template to assist men for their emotional needs. (Working with couples had also highlighted how much men now needed their own support circles. A need which was being accelerated as the Earth's kundalini continued to rise, as this meant everyone's wounds were being triggered so relentlessly in relationship that no relationship stood a chance without both men & women having a regular forum for truth & healing).

Shortly after running this circle I returned to where I was born & for the first time, had an enjoyable visit where I was able to see the beauty rather than the pain of my childhood home. This indicated I had achieved a certain level of healing as my Father's inability to relate to me no longer triggered hurt but met with gentle acceptance of him & everything we had journeyed. I figured this was in part because of my efforts to understand the masculine so I could heal that part of myself & assist my brothers to heal. This had in turn engendered compassion for all men, including my father who now pleasantly surprises me with his openness to my alternate viewpoint!

Ways to Embrace Chiron

Any kind of soul therapy session is the best place to start. This could take the form of ongoing sessions with a psychotherapist, art therapist, hypnotherapist, shamanic healer, soul centered counsellor, clairvoyant or spiritual healer. The key is working one on one with an experienced spiritual midwife who focuses on the empowerment & emergence of the inner self rather than analyzing or encouraging you to talk endlessly about your past which can further anchor the victim archetype rather than empower the true self to emerge victorious with greater understanding & appreciation for how your past has served you.

In addition, to committing to ongoing sessions with a therapist it is also essential that you take full responsibility for your own healing journey, rather than use your therapist as a sounding board for one hour a week like a surrogate parent. This may include spending time journalling, drawing, analyzing dreams, pulling oracle cards, going to meditation or attending psychic development classes which all deepen personal awareness & allow for greater communication with the inner self. Since Chiron rules the throat chakra, expressing your inner self is the key to freeing & opening this energy center. Daring to 'open up' to male friends & spending less time with those who you can't be your true self with is also characteristic of a strengthening Chiron aspect.

As stated earlier & in every alternate paragraph in this book, illustrating my emphatic desire for their return - men's circles! If you don't have one in your neighborhood, consider starting one. ('The Twelve Trials of Hercules' chapter in Volume Three offers a structure to work through in conjunction with the free 'Create Your Own Red Tent Circle' PDF on my website.) Just being repeatedly witnessed in your vulnerability is the only practice that will help you to feel increasingly accepting of yourself & comfortable with your human frailty.

Reading self help books & books that empower the masculine through the insights of spiritual teachers will also accelerate your inner Chiron's development.

Here's a few titles I recommend:

'The Myth of Male Power' by Warren Farrell
'Manhood: An Action Plan for Changing Men's Lives' by Steve Biddulph
'Raising Boys' by Steve Biddulph
'Iron John' by Robert Bly
'Gods in Everyman' by Jean Shinoda Bolen
'Way of the Spiritual Warrior' by Dan Millman

N.B. To further empower your inner Chiron one must embody the strengths of his counterpart, Artemis, the Medicine Woman who learns to defend herself by speaking her truth to uphold boundaries that honor her vulnerability.

Chiron: Myth vs Truth

Chiron was said to be the child of two serpentine parents indicating they were fully conscious beings who had awakened their kundalini. True to form, Greek mythology infers his parentage was unnatural as they claimed Chiron was born a mutant who was rejected by his mother at birth, which meant he was left to raise himself. What it does suggest, is that he was instead raised by the Great Mother, Gaia (Mother Earth) as he spent a lot of time in a cave, which is akin to a womb within the Earth Mother's body. As a result he became wise. However the story we have been told is that despite his getting of wisdom, he could never heal his childhood wounds. (This suggests one would be forever trapped by their karma on the wheel of suffering & not be able to transcend into an awakened & whole state.) Due to Chiron seeking out the mentoring of the solar plexus governing entities, Apollo & Athena in music, war & medicine he was valued as a teacher in Greek legend & had many students, including Asklepios (the father of modern medicine). This infers that what Chiron accessed intuitively within his cave was not worth any credence unless validated by the rational mind in the form of external study that could be formally recognized. (Fortunately there were a few subsequent fathers of modern medicine who acknowledged the role intuitive wisdom had played in the development of the healing arts. Parcelsus, considered one of the greatest physicians of his time, burnt his official pharmacopeia to protest the burning of female healers stating, **'he had learned from the sorceresses all**

that he knew.' Source: 'The Wise Wound' by Penelope Shuttle & Peter Redgrove.

The fact that Asklepios was renowned for carrying a staff entwined with a serpent suggests he also acknowledged the feminine mysteries as necessary for one seeking to understand the healing arts.

Some versions of Chiron's myth say that it was the God, Apollo who reared Chiron but this feels like a red herring as Chiron represents the masculine who embodies the wisdom of the inner self or feminine side of his nature. It does makes sense, however that due to his Tantric parentage he was perhaps placed in a cave for a year at the age of nine, which was customary when a child suffered multiple illnesses in their ninth year. Since the ninth year marked the end of their first numerological cycle if a child underwent a marked initiation at this time in the form of illness, (known traditionally as a Shaman's death) it alerted the rest of the tribe to their abilities as a healer. For unlike western medicine, a shaman was one who was initiated through their own illness or depression into the archetype of the 'Wounded Healer'. Only through their first hand experience of illness could they understand the nature of it & find a cure. When they had overcome their own disease, they would then assist others with what they had learnt. This ensures that healers have compassion for those they assist because they know what it is to experience their symptoms, unlike modern Western medicine which can view patients with cold indifference like a research subject rather than a fellow soul. Likewise when one views illness as an initiation rather than as a failure or weakness, one feels empowered to take an active role in their own healing rather than just giving their personal power over to the condition or their treating physician. Adopting a defeatist, aggressive or passive approach merely anchors 'victim consciousness'. For it is through illness, that one stops 'doing' in the physical world & goes within to contemplate themselves & existence. This is what the cave signifies in Chiron's myth. He is not shunned & hidden away but rather recognized as one who can walk between the worlds to gain insight for himself & others. It is for this reason that shamans are often depicted as being an even blend of both genders as they are a bridge between the inner world of the feminine & the outer world of the masculine so they can disseminate what they have learnt. This makes sense when one considers that when a man has found his inner Father / King by opening his heart, the energy can then rise up into his throat enabling him to really get in touch with his vulnerability. In other words, when he has been validated by an older male, anchoring a solid sense of his own masculinity he can then allow his inner feminine to be expressed.

Chiron's greatest wound was said to have come from Hercules. While out hunting together, Hercules accidentally shot him in the leg with an arrow dipped in the blood of Medusa, (the snake haired Gorgon Goddess representing the dark feminine or primal aspect of Lilith who governs menstruation.) The patriarchs have subsequently lamented there was no cure for this & Chiron was destined to suffer after being 'contaminated' with the most potent substance of the feminine. This injection of the feminine death phase was akin to Chiron's menarche (menstrual) initiation into the feminine mysteries. However instead of it being revered as a great honor, it was viewed as an incurable wound - I dare say this is where the playground concept of being contaminated with 'girl's germs' came from!) What this tells us is that he had to deal with his own inner feminine. For he would not feel healed or whole until he attended to that wound. The fact it was done by a male companion inadvertently suggests that young men, in an effort to assert their manhood often stifle, reject or ridicule the feminine in each other as they find it threatening in themselves & therefore in each other.

Because of Chiron's developed feminine sense of compassion he was the one that offered to take the place of Prometheus. Prometheus was the mortal who was punished by Zeus for his efforts to bring spiritual enlightenment to his people. So, despite being rescued by Hercules - Zeus still demanded someone take his place & Chiron offered, losing his immortality in return. On the positive side, this suggests the degree to which the archetypal Chiron is selfless. I also read it as signaling the following caution: another can rescue you (such as Hercules or a medical doctor) but unless you take responsibility for healing yourself you will end up in the same place if your mental outlook remains unchanged. (This is represented by Zeus's remaining stuck in a mindset of seeking someone to blame & punish.) For we develop illness when we lower our frequency through fear based thinking which perpetuates lower emotions like anger, resentment & shame. If we hold on to our hurts seeking continual retribution we inhibit our bodies natural ability to heal. Similarly, if we become so over-identified with a created ailment to the point of forgetting our true self we will be destined to suffer. Like the old saying, 'misery loves company' so we then unconsciously lower the vibration of those around us by telling them all about our suffering as a way of seeking validation. This is a far cry from acknowledging our wound & what we're personally doing to resolve it. These are the people who just want someone to listen to them complain rather than taking proactive steps to help themselves. So for healers, this is a warning, only help those who demonstrate they are willing to help themselves otherwise you will be drained to the point of suffering also. Hence the burn out rate of those working in the health professions & human services as culturally we have struggled to transcend our sense of victimhood.

Empowering Hermes, the Magician

Brow Chakra (Indigo)

The third eye chakra is activated during the seven year cycle from age thirty-five to forty-two, if the lessons with Chiron have been learnt in the previous cycle. For we can't perceive the subtleties of 'The Force' if we have not first embraced our own personal sensitivity. Hermes is the wise sage (like Yoda or Mr Miyagi in 'The Karate Kid') who offers a wise perspective to the young hero because he has been to the dark side & returned to tell the tale. So understandably, many young men with a strong inner Hermes are attracted to the Underworld of crime, vampires, goths, depressive music & virtual realities as this is a necessary chapter in their getting of wisdom. In fact, the rise of IT along with Harry Potter indicates how many computer wizards can create worlds out of thin air just with intention of thought, computer code & late nights spent in cyberspace.

A tell tale sign of a shadow Hermes man is a silvery tongue that he uses to wangle his way out of any sticky situation. That is, until one day his luck runs out (often around the age of thirty) when he is caught in the act. This usually results in his freedom being curtailed in some way so he has no choice but to examine his own behavior. It is through this imposed sabbatical that he learns to use his quick mind to grasp insights that free his inner child from his inner jail of depressive & critical fear based thoughts that took root in his teens when his elders failed to provide him with much needed existential answers.

His charm, combined with narcissism makes him a deadly bedfellow for those who succumb to his sparkling wit & quick mind. For like the planet, Mercury he is slippery & hard to pin down should you ask anything in return for your time, commitment or affection. That is, until he faces the death of his old ways at the crossroads where he must wake up to himself if he is going to live another day. Given how effective he is at dodging close scrapes it often takes a spectacular fall from grace to bring about a life review or psychological death.

Just as Chiron begins to empower himself & heal when he accepts that his illness or wound was a necessary initiation for his growth, so too Hermes begins to mature when he can make his peace with his shady past by first owning his own unethical behavior as this leads him to appreciate his unsavory past was an essential part of his journey. Hermes, (as the governing male aspect of the third eye) has the ability to manipulate, influence, deceive, charm & outwit others. (I have seen this in grande scale NLP practitioners who use their knowledge of hypnosis to take audiences into regressed states of receptivity then implant the urge to buy their products. Resisting their intent in such a strong energy field generated by the group mind places great strain on one's own third eye!)

When Hermes is still immature he does this purely for his own gain & so long as his focus is upon getting his own way he will not confront the effects of his actions or his own conscience. Simply because things come easily to him he often lacks respect for those who work hard & play by the rules. For rebelling against the fear of being 'straight' or the gullible 'good boy' can lead him to self destruct by getting lost in an 'after dark' smokescreen of Underworld glamour, such as indulging in a cocktail of booze, drugs, prostitution, illegal activities or violence (be it actual or virtual) which distract him from confronting himself clearly in the light of day.

Ways to Embrace Hermes

For men who do not see themselves as possessing cunning, ingenuity or wisdom, a good way of developing one's inner Hermes is to start by applying wit & strategy to increase your ability to earn or restructuring your approach, enabling you to work smarter not harder. Those who have completely disowned this aspect may feel phobic about computers & technology so starting with a patient IT mentor is also good start. Similarly, those who dismiss the esoteric sciences are also denying their inner Merlin so reading how exoteric science such as Quantum Physics is now proving esoteric science true is helpful to open the fixed thinking of the rational mind to the more expansive occult concepts. For example, what every Star Wars fan knows as 'The Force' science calls 'The Field' based on Lynne McTaggarts' research. Those who have suffered acute depression, felt like loners & avoided real life responsibilities also benefit greatly by seeking out a truly wise mentor (not a shrink who will nod his head or prescribe you happy pills) but one whose truly insightful advice you can humbly follow to become a better man (or inner man) who you can feel proud of.

Reading books such as 'Psychic Self Defense' by Dion Fortune or attending a psychic development circle is another practical way to strengthen this archetype so you can better attune to & utilize your extra sensory gifts rather than dismiss them out of ignorance. The secret order known as 'The Knight's Templar' provide another example of Hermes role models as Jedi warriors who used their knowledge of occult lore & alchemy to protect the Essene teachings which proved a threat to the plans of the Priory (Illuminati). As such, they were said to be adept at maintaining a psychically clear & protected space for the continued work of the Magdalene, the aspect of the High Priestess which is the awakened feminine. This is therefore a particularly relevant skill set for men to develop as they prepare to support their partners during childbirth. For during childbirth a woman must journey inwardly between the worlds to the void of death & birth to retrieve the soul whom she is birthing. If her partner has awakened & empowered his inner Hermes he won't end up feeling like a third wheel because he will use his energetic focus to create a force field of protection around his loved ones as they take this perilous journey of death through the seven veils. By affording her this protection energetically she can surrender more easily, so the labour is not prolonged & she will not be open to attracting lower entities on the astral who can attach when she is in such an acute state of fear, which is an unacknowledged contributing factor to post natal depression. This application of an awakened Hermes, one who guides souls at the crossroads of death & birth is the energetic warrior being called forth by pop culture icons like Harry Potter who acknowledge all of life, not just what the 'Muggles' (uninitiated) can perceive through their five lower senses.

The fastest way to open the third eye chakra is through a sense of fantasy play. In other words, one must reconnect with the innocence of the magical child before one can truly journey between the worlds. For most, this aspect is suppressed when they become teenagers leading to depression & mental rigidity. So it is the role of Hermes to rescue the magical child from the inner dungeon of doom & gloom so one can once again access their subtle senses through the portal of the imagination. (or 'I of the Magi nation' as I used to explain to my knee high faeries at children's parties.) It is for this reason that quest dramas &

games are initially healing & empowering for men whose inner children are trapped in the labyrinth of their rational minds. So initially, indulging in flights of fancy such as sci fi, animation & gaming conventions, comic book & action figure collections & role playing games like 'Dungeons & Dragons' stimulate the imagination of the inner magical child. This assists the joyful opening of one's third eye so innovative new solutions & insights can be perceived which offer the improvement of one's quality of life. That said, if one becomes lost in a virtual quest & never learns to apply the lessons they have learnt there in their daily reality they will become parodies of their altar egos. (aka 'Comic Book Man' in 'The Simpsons'.)

One can bridge the gap back to this reality by reading magazines such as 'Nexus' (which explores paranormal phenomena) & doing online research into sacred geometry, crop circles, ancient & galactic civilizations which can expand one's view of this reality to make it worth showing up for rather than escaping. So too, watching interviews with those who bridge the worlds of shaman & scientist are highly recommended. (Nassim Haramein & Drunvalo Melchizedek are two who come to mind.) A word of caution however for those who seek to astral travel, bend spoons & manifest their desires...before attempting to change your physical reality you must first learn the art of internal alchemy. To do this one must seek to embody the strengths of his counterpart, Hecate, the wise mystic who creates sacred ceremonies to assist us through change so we can continue to transform ourselves & respect with humility the process of death & rebirth.

Hermes: Myth vs Truth

The story goes that when Hermes was born, he distinguished himself by escaping from his crib & stealing his brother, Apollo's cattle. To confound his brother he literally 'covered his tracks' by removing the herd's hooves & reattaching them so they were facing backwards. This created the illusion that they were heading in the opposite direction to lead his trackers off his scent. Once back in his crib he was discovered but charmed his way out of being punished by inventing a lyre out of a turtle shell & gifting it to his brother. (How hard would it be to parent a demigod!) This sequence of events illustrates one who pulls pranks simply to amuse himself because of his quick mercurial mind which needs constant stimulation. Without this stimulus his mind becomes destructive, devising plans that undermine or destroy the creative efforts of others. (Like the boy up the back of class who disrupts the efforts of the whole class to demonstrate his boredom to his teacher.) So sharp was Hermes' mind, he could outwit his authority figures & offer his own reprise despite their intention to punish him for his actions.

This lack of consequence creates one who has no regard for others, especially authority figures as he quickly finds he can manipulate everyone around him. This story paints a clear picture of a young Hermes who is selfish, reckless & manipulative - a trait embodied by many clever young men in the IT industry who provide their wizardry at an exorbitant cost & then don't deliver what they promise to those they see as schmucks for not being able to read & write computer code with the ease that they can.

As with the other archetypes, in Greek mythology Hermes has been portrayed more for the devious use of his gifts as an immature young man than as a wise master who learnt humility, leading him to use his quick mind, silvery tongue & subtle senses for good instead of evil.

Similarly, magicians in our culture have been portrayed as shysters who perform hoaxes such as sleight of hand trickery or on a grander scale, Las Vegas showmen who hypnotize volunteers for laughs or cast theatrical feats of illusion & glamour without getting caught. This is a far cry from the empowered embodiment of this aspect, the wise sage who has a deep reverence & understanding of universal law & the conscious directing of energy to manifest one's intent. This is because Hermes, the God of manifestation & magic was reduced to the God of trickery, thieves & business in the Greek pantheon. The evidence of how the immature expression of this archetype is anchored within our psyche is evident in the amount of trickery & deception dismissed as merely 'business'. Take for example, the ancient magical practice of creating a sigil. A sigil is a symbol which embodies the energy of one's intent. Today the majority of people only know such symbols as corporate logos which companies use repeatedly to charge their brand with recognition, power & wealth. Homer portrayed Hermes as the author of 'skilled or deceptive acts which brought good luck', the quintessential financial wizard. Not unlike those on Wall Street who produce the illusion of wealth with fabricated projections on the stock market, despite most countries being billions of dollars in debt.

In Greek mythology Hermes was employed on numerous occasions as basically a private eye for Zeus, who made use of his gift for tracking & retrieving those who were supposedly victims of enchantments or prisoners. Hermes also played the role of accomplice to Orestes by suggesting he disguise himself to carry out the murder of Clytemnestra. This does not align with one who carried the staff of the caduceus, an awakened one who would not willingly create harm or carry out the bidding of a dictator. Apart from his staff, the only indicator that Hermes indeed matured was in his role as the guide of souls to the Underworld. Again therein lies a discrepancy as one can only take this journey if one has been to the Underworld & returned with the knowledge that death imparts.

Another example of his complicit nature is in the myth when Zeus ordered Hephaestus (the inventor God) to create Pandora (the Greek version of Eve) to punish humanity for Prometheus's theft of the sacred fire which he gifted to his fellow humans. (Is it just me or does it seem like a bad running gag that Zeus just can't seem to move on from punishing the daring of Prometheus! Reminds me of the villainous Sheriff of Nottingham who continually schemes to destroy Robin Hood.) Anyway, back to the story...when each of the Olympiad Gods was asked to contribute qualities of suffering to the global feminine, Hermes put in Pandora's jar, 'lies, seductive words & a dubious character.' Again, this kind of black magic is dismissed by a complete novice who knows the law of threefold. That being, 'whatever you send out returns to you threefold' kind of a wizardry version of 'do unto others as you would have them do unto you.' Fortunately, just like a murderer is brought undone by his need to boast about his dark acts, denoting his ego's need for recognition - so too, these Olympiad false Gods wrote of their acts which would lead us to one day question them as 'Gods' & reclaim our fire. (Again, we notice another inversion where the element of fire has been sold to us as an association with Hell & punishment & yet it is the very sacred spark that will illuminate the darkness of our unconsciously created Underworld.) Another sign that Hermes was an enlightened master of energy & alchemy is that he was accredited with inventing the panpipes for his son, Pan & the flute, both of which symbolize one who has opened their chakras & learnt to harness the power of sound to change states using vibrational keys. N.B. Awakening the counterpart archetype of Hecate ensures Hermes is brought to his knees to face himself by spending time consciously in the Underworld via nightmares, anxiety attacks or depression so he may become wise & fulfill his potential as a guide, magi & alchemist.

Empowering Dionysus, the God of Ecstacy

Crown Chakra (White / Rainbow)

From the age of forty-two to forty-nine if we have opened our third eye, our kundalini rises into our crown to activate the archetypal energy of Dionysus. Dionysus is the masculine aspect who governs the crown chakra, which is the portal to our Higher Self so he is like the inner Buddha. When he is unconscious & disempowered this part of us seeks ecstatic union through substances. This leaves us dependent on those substances to feel high as they further highlight our sense of separation when their effect subsides, creating a cycle of addiction. This can lead us to become very ungrounded if we chase high's to avoid feeling the low's. For it is in the low's that we reflect upon our 'out of body' experiences, enabling us to integrate the lessons. This tendency is common in the rave culture where funsters combine both natural & synthetic high's such as drugs & trance dance to access altered states simply for the thrill without any reverence for the shamanic journey or respect for balancing their polarities. If this behavior continues for any length of time, Bi polar (manic depressive) mood swings are inevitable.

When working in the positive, our inner Dionysus honors mind altering herbs, fungi & grapes of the vine as sacred allies that assist him to see beyond the illusions of the rational mind. He does not use them merely to escape his reality & responsibilities.

Out of all the inner masculine aspects, Dionysus is the one who seeks out the wisdom of the feminine mysteries so he can explore the chaos of Shakti & experience the Shaman's death of all mental limitation. This knowledge ends his destructive cycle of wreaking havoc whilst under the influence of substances (often to the point where he has no idea of the effects of his past actions). Because of his seeking & integration of the feminine mysteries, he was the only Greek God who was said to have 'saved his mother' from the Underworld. This referred to his ability to awaken the sacred feminine within himself so he knew & understood firsthand what it was to be feminine. This enabled him to outgrow any childish projections or expectations about women that were instilled in him whilst growing up. A trait which endeared him to women & enabled him to connect with the sacred fire in every woman.

Men who haven't connected with their inner Dionysus are often afraid of losing control for fear of what they'll do. So they might strive to be straight, upstanding citizens who attend a church or adopt a devout spiritual practice rather than risk a truly intimate experience with Divinity. This is because their rational mind is afraid to let go. This is why traditionally one would see groups of women dancing around their handbags on suburban nightclub floors while the 'manly men' sat around watching them & drinking. Only the men who had awakened their Shakti (feminine essence) such as the flower power hippies & gay men would dare to let it all hang out on the dance floor. When one considers that one makes love as one dances, it is worth loosening up so one doesn't remain a plank living vicariously through others! Fortunately, drag queens in the outback, Zumba, trance dance festivals, 5 Rhythms & flash mobs are changing this scene.

Dionysus is the part of our inner masculine that enables us to be unconventional. To wear kaftans, visit exotic lands, try exotic foods & dance like no one is watching - all of which are very attractive to women as he genuinely 'digs' what they're into. This is what gives a man his 'mojo' coined by camp Aquarian loverboy, 'Austin Powers' - a quality which makes him 'irresistible to the ladies.' These same qualities however will be confronting for men who have not developed them in themselves for fear of appearing 'poofy' or 'queer'. It is for this reason that boys with a strong Dionysian character may be ridiculed or dismissed by their more conventional Dads. For should they express these camp traits in their youth their Father may react from a fear of what others will think of him for having such a flamboyant son. This fear may lead him to unconsciously criticize his boy when he finds this liberated self expression too confrontational for his own rigid code of behavior.

To the women who have neglected this inner archetype; chances are you will fall in love with that which you have disowned in yourself. I fell on this sword, after eight years of denouncing pot, cigarettes & alcohol as 'beneath me' I then fell in love with a sensual man who indulged in many sensate arousing pastimes & helped me to stop being such a prudent nun by allowing myself to experience hedonist pleasures in moderation.

Ways to Embrace Dionysus

As Dionysus is the God of ecstasy connecting with this aspect is about allowing oneself to release the dualistic mind's moralistic judgements & surrender to deeper & deeper states of pleasure. (This is why Buddha has a belly!) So if you've been a bit uptight or prudish might I recommend cultivating your sacred inner hedonist to embody a healthy expression of your inner Dionysus. :) For the more we allow ourselves to experience sensual pleasure the less it is perceived as a forbidden fruit. For it is the very concept of a taboo which leads one to consume guiltily in excess

& then regret or purge. The key is to indulge in quality rather than quantity. For example, picture if you will...savoring the transcendent pleasures of a single handcrafted Belgian truffle. First you inhale deeply becoming delirious with the intoxicating aroma which excites your other senses, causing you to sigh, murmur & salivate. You then admire the artful presentation, it's satiny touch & then close your eyes to focus intently on the taste & texture as you take it into your welcoming hot tongue & mouth. Compare that symphony of sensory pleasure with stuffing a family block of cheap, commercially manufactured milk chocolate in your gob while staring into a TV screen. For the more you personally engage & relate to your food, the more you will enjoy it & it will in turn fulfill you, so you need less of it. It is this sense of communion that we have lost. For example, once upon a time we made our cheese with milk we had fetched from our hand reared cow or alternatively, it was made with love by our neighbor, which we swapped for some hand picked berries or a loaf of our home baked sour dough bread. This sense of relationship heightened our appreciation & pleasure. So if you don't currently have shares in a cow consider how you can engage & awaken your sensory anticipation by buying your fruit & vegetables, eggs, hand made preserves, cheeses & bread from a farmer's market rather than buying them from a large supermarket chain. Or even better, make them yourself by enrolling in classes at your local community house, night school or community garden. At the very least talk to your check-out operator & thank all who played a part in your food chain before chowing down your next feed. Below are a few more examples of ways to awaken & delight in your inner hedonist. (Hugh Fearnley Whittingstall, Jamie Olivier & Nigella Lawson are also fine role models for sucking the marrow from life.)

Dionysian Pursuits 101

- Take a wine appreciation course
- Enroll in a home brew workshop & sample designer beers
- Try your hand at making apple cider or elderflower champagne
- Sample a range of different liqueurs
- Try cooking with & sampling foods from various cultures
- Experiment with a variety of coffee & tea blends, as well as different accompaniments such as cinnamon quills, mint, lemon, ginger & ground cardamom pods
- Learn the art of marrying culinary herbs & spices
- Try your hand at making cocktails, mocktails, spritzers & juices
- Experiment with euphoric herbs such as damiana
- Purchase a hookah (Turkish smoking pipe) & share various flavored molasses fibres such as apple cinnamon with friends after dinner (tar & nicotine free!)
- build a wood fired pizza oven in the back yard

Also consider how you eat & drink. You can heighten your sensory enjoyment by doing some of the following:

- dine al fresco (outdoors) as much as possible in warm weather
- eat around a low table, on cushions rather than at a table which is more formal
- eat with your hands & break bread. In Middle-Eastern cultures they eat from a central serving dish communally rather than having separate plates
- eat a box of assorted chocolates like the Swiss by taking a small bite & sharing the flavor with friend

When we bring sacred intent to our hedonistic pleasure we heighten our pleasure beyond the five earthly senses & engage our subtle senses. To do this consider the following:

- set sacred space by taking the time to light candles
- put on relaxing, rhythmic music
- lay a beautiful table with a fresh table cloth, flowers & place mats
- bless the food & those who grew & prepared the meal

Befriending The Love God

Obviously the more pleasure we obtain through regular practices such as sharing creative meals, hot tubs & body therapies, the less we are inclined to obsess about sex as our only form of physical pleasure. Similarly, if we aren't fostering a deeper connection with the love arts such as poetry, music, dance & art to express our devotional heart & 'get high' energetically we will develop a dependency on sex & substances as our lower selves only paths to pleasure. Sex addiction is currently rife in the West, highlighting the lack of reverence & sacredness associated with pleasure. For even in the Western Tantra scene, sex addiction is often justified as a decision to be polyamorous, meaning 'sexually loving the One in all'. Whilst this is a lovely existential concept, it doesn't allow for or honor the personal or small self's emotional needs, which a holistic approach to love does, by acknowledging the needs of the whole person. For example, if one has a sexual addiction they may seek out multiple partners to satisfy their sexual urges & their lower selves' need to be embraced, loved & held. So they connect physically & even energetically with another but stop short of connecting deeply in their emotional & mental bodies to avoid the risk of exposing their deep vulnerabilities or having their fears of dependency, betrayal or rejection triggered. For those who feel they need another to experience greater states of bliss through sexual union I recommend exploring the art of self pleasure from a Tantric perspective. In other words, instead of merely 'beating or rubbing one's nerve endings' to release stress, instead try really making love to yourself as a multidimensional soul. This involves honoring both the yin & yang orgasm to open to greater states of awareness. (For a greater understanding read the chapter, 'How To Make Love Like An Hermaphrodite' later in this volume.)

Accessing Altered States

As Dionysus is the part of us that seeks out altered states of consciousness, consider attending a sacred ceremony facilitated by an experienced shaman to journey with visioning herbs such as mugwort, magic mushrooms, ayawaska or peyote to further explore this aspect. I do however, emphasize doing this under the supervision of an experienced facilitator as the plant devas who govern these plants will often show you your fears & unresolved karma before opening subsequent doors to experience the multiverse. When one considers these trance inducing plants are powerful medicine that command respect by all the native traditions we must afford them this same respect or risk mental illness & anxiety disorders. Given that these plants precipitate the opening of vortexes to other dimensional states of being it is essential that someone stays present & anchored in this realm by abstaining so they can guide those back from between the worlds to avoid any scattering of personal energy between the dimensions. If one has journeyed without a guide to hold a safe container for their consciousness, a soul retrieval session may be necessary to call back energetic fragments still trapped between the worlds.

Dionysus: Myth vs Truth

In Greek mythology Dionysus was described as the God of pleasure & pain as he could be both loving & carefree as well as violent & destructive. This polarization was said to have been enacted by his followers who would drink wine & dance themselves into a frenzy with highly emotive music, then eat the raw flesh of an animal as an act of communion with the God. (Perhaps this is the origin of the saying, 'Now just settle down kids or someone's going to get hurt!) This behavior exemplifies the unconscious expression of this archetype such as a drunk or drug addict who is so intent on fulfilling his own gluttonous desires for sensate pleasure that they are oblivious to the pain caused by their behavior. This however is not the case when one sets a sacred intention & raises the energy in alignment with that intention. For example, if one attends sacred chanting at an ashram, evangelical singing at a gospel church or ecstatic trance dance at a sacred space there is no chance of participants becoming destructive as the energy raised is done so with devotional intent, evoking the Higher Self & celestial beings who can be seen in photographs as orbs of light filling the space. If, on the other hand one goes to a house party where kegs of beers are being swilled to gang rap music the chances of destructive behavior are heightened. I believe this negative representation of Dionysus has imprinted a subconscious fear in the collective that inhibits many from being able to truly surrender to deeper states of pleasure for fear of what they'll do. Again, the likelihood of doing something you'll later regret is a valid concern if you are altering your mind state in a low vibrational space. However, if we suppress this aspect for fear of losing control we become increasingly disconnected from our experiential senses so can find it hard to open to the intensifying waves of pleasure that build into a sexual climax. Similarly, hallucinogenic herbs have been criminalized which we are told by government agencies is for our safety, suggesting we can't be trusted to be self governing in such matters. Ultimately, these plants awaken the consciousness so are a threat to the regimes that seek to enslave the people to fulfill their agendas of greed & domination.

Ever since the beginning of the Aquarian Age in the 1960's the reawakening of this aspect has created more of a public demand for mind altering plants. However those who journey with these powerful medicines unconsciously risk mental illness if they don't integrate & ground the experiences they have 'between the worlds'. Because these mind expanding plants offer an opportunity to get out of one's head & experience 'being' rather than 'doing' they are particularly popular with young men as the masculine is more dominated by the rational mind than the feminine. To admonish one for drug use & expect them to 'go without' once they have opened the door to other states of reality is not possible as it does not address the soul's need for expansion beyond the rational.

So, accessing the counterpart Ishtar's natural approach to 'getting high' is a great way of balancing one's Dionysian need for hedonism & pleasure. For example, those with a dependence on 'downer' drugs such as cigarettes, pot, special k (horse tranquilizer) or acid, do well to seek out sacred practices such as yoga, silent meditation, ritual bathing, vocal harmonics, sacred art, music or creating sacred spaces to give them a healthy chill out. Whereas, those who have developed a dependence on speed, coke or ecstasy may wish to seek out active high's through sacred practices such as '5 Rhythms' dance meditation, belly dance, Capoeria, chanting, gospel singing, chakra breathing or kundalini meditation (also known as bioenergy shaking).

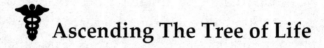 **Ascending The Tree of Life**

Activating Shakti, the Sacred Feminine

The Significance Of The Tree

The Tree of Life featured in the creationist myth in the monotheistic religious doctrines. They state God planted it in the Garden of Eden & anyone who ate of the fruit of it would gain eternal life. The Tree was said to have twelve different fruits which, if eaten would grant eternal life, health & happiness & create peace between nations. (This refers to the twelve chakras we are now unveiling as we remember our true selves, reactivating our full potential as twelve strand DNA beings. More on this in the chapter, 'Becoming a Twelve Chakra Cosmic Being' later in Volume One.)

The Tree of Life was said to be planted at the East gate in the Garden of Eden. The East is the place of the rising sun & new beginnings. It represents the element of air which ushers in new concepts of thought to awaken & inspire new growth. The Goddess, Ishtar (said to reside in the branches of the Tree of Life) was also celebrated as the ascended Venus who returns as the dawn star, rising in the East. References to the Tree of Life appear in many cultures & there is evidence of chakras in indigenous rock paintings, architecture, chants & dance around the globe.

'The Tree of Life is an important symbol in nearly every culture. In Jewish and Christian mythology, a tree sits at the

center of both the Heavenly and Earthly Edens. The Norse cosmic World Ash, Yggdrassil, has its roots in the Underworld while its branches support the abode of the Gods. The Egyptian's Holy Sycamore stood on the threshold of life and death, connecting the worlds. To the Mayas, it is Yaxche, whose branches support the Heavens.' altreligion.about.com

Can't See the Wood For The Trees?

To transcend the 3D realm of suffering we much each climb the internal trees, known as 'The Tree of Life' & 'The Tree of Knowledge'. When one overlaps these two trees as templates one sees the three pillars which comprise the internal structure of our lightbodies. The outer two pillars represent the polarities of light & shadow & the central pillar represents 'The Golden Mean' or middle path. These three pillars can be seen in the Kabbalistic Tree which incorporates elements of both.

The Chakra Goddess or Rainbow serpent was therefore the middle pillar one had to awaken within to see & know one's feminine energy as Divine. This is the bridge between Heaven & Earth (Alternatively, The Tree of Knowledge represents the awakening of one's sacred masculine by transcending the rational perception of reality as either 'right or wrong / black or white.')

This raises the obvious question, 'Why is it that in the Bible, the serpent is depicted as sitting in 'The Tree of Knowledge'? Okay, 'scuse the pun but I'm going to go out on a limb here...I think this is a red herring, (or horticultural switcheroo) deliberately done to throw the sheeple off the scent & keep the flock from escaping the pen! So before you grab your pitchfork, ring your neighbor & start boiling tar, simply humor me as one taking poetic license & make up your own mind.

Coming Home to the Goddess

The Tree of Life represents the awakening of one's Shakti (life force). The sacred feminine energy which lies coiled at the base of the spine until awakened through initiation into the feminine mysteries. This is why the ancient Hebraic feminine principle was referred to as the Shekinah, which described a heavenly apple tree reaching from Earth to Heaven. In the roots dwells Lilith, the primal & erotic serpentine Goddess who enticed seekers to taste her fruit of feminine wisdom. (This referred to a Tantric sexual initiation via the juicy fruit that lay between her legs for men with an initiated priestess. Whereas for women, this awakening occurred through their menstrual initiation if they received the sacred teachings inside the Red Tent Moon Lodge conveying the power of their yoni as a magical doorway of death & rebirth.) For once one entered the temple of the Goddess they would receive 'Shaktipat'. This meant their energy would spiral up the central pillar in their lightbody (the central nervous system along the spinal cord) to receive the ecstatic embrace of Ishtar, the celestial Queen of Heaven who resides in the branches of The Tree of Life.

This is why ancient Tantrikas would lie with men as a sacred service to open their seven channels, gifting them the blessing of the Goddess. This would awaken their yin meridian, civilizing them from Barbarians to true gentlemen. (Unfortunately for all the uninitiated sex workers out there they continue to service Barbarians as long as the archetype of the sacred whore is viewed as an oxymoron.) Similarly, if a modern man lies with a priestess woman who has opened her seven gates through being initiated into the teachings of the sacred feminine the sexual rapture may blow his circuitry releasing all that he has not dealt with within his psyche. This is why men often run away from sexually potent women for they unleash the personal demons they sought to suppress. Running however is pointless as once awakened, one cannot go back to sleep. Knowing this, many sexually charged women can forgive themselves for being promiscuous in their early adult life as they unconsciously sought to end the Patriarchy one man at a time!

Unveiling One's True Self At Each of the Seven Gates

The Rainbow Serpent awakens our knowledge of Self by dispelling the illusions of Maya (false beliefs) which have inhibited our Divine expression through each of our stargates. The awakening of this column of light up the spine, (the trunk of the Tree of Life) explains why mystics have long lived by the one idiom, 'Know Thyself.' This is also why the Biblical term 'to know' someone meant to engage in sexual union with them, literally entwining both inner serpents of light around each other's open lightbody of energy. This is because the Tree of Life is the series of electrical circuits that runs up the central nervous cord in our spine, known as chakras or energy centers. Each chakra relates to a level of personal awareness which when understood & mastered, enables us to transcend & progress to the next level of self awareness.

Lilith is in fact the rainbow serpent of kundalini (life force) who lies coiled, three & half times around the lingum (column of light) at the base of the spine until she is awakened. Then she begins her climb heavenward, seeking union with both her stellar Divine aspect, Ishtar & the Divine Masculine known as Father Sky or Shiva, the God of Consciousness. This practice is known as raising kundalini (life force). (Hence so many unconscious men are mesmerized by the sight of wild women who wrap their serpentine bodies around exotic poles!)

Just as most are familiar with our 'fall from grace' when we were said to have collectively fallen from the consciousness of

Eden, (knowing ourselves as Divine beings, at one with the 'God force') now many are reawakening the serpent of light or Divine Feminine within by climbing the inner Tree of Life which is in turn awakening the full potential of our energetic bodies, which are an internal hologram of existence.

Hmmm, You're Suggesting I Listen to a Serpent?

Many folks in the modern Western world have a phobia of snakes. This is not surprising when you consider that they have been repeatedly portrayed as evil by religious doctrines that sought to slander the iconography of pre-monotheistic faiths. Snakes were considered sacred to the pre-Christian matriarchal religions because they represented the key to our awakening so their totem medicine was honored & their venom used for visioning. Whilst women were once revered for their role as awakeners in the pre-monotheistic religions, ever since the introduction of the patriarchal religions women's wisdom was undermined & feared. Ultimately this fear of the archetypal snake woman, (or priestess) is because the truth she channels will puncture the facade of the ego, bringing about a collapse of one's everyday world before their upward ascension of consciousness can commence. For instance, in the myth of Athena we are taught that in order to build anything of lasting value we must first meet with Medusa, (the snake haired woman) who humbles us. She does this by confronting us with our disowned aspects which will otherwise sabotage our conscious efforts.

This serpent of knowledge was once revered as Lilith, the awakener (the original woman & wife of Adam) but was then scapegoated & reduced to the 'evil serpent' in later translations of the creationist myth in an effort to quell the questioning minds of the masses. Instead she came to be viewed as the one who tempted Eve, (the compliant patriarchal stand-in aka

'Stepford wife') with the apple, the fruit of wisdom. So rather than be applauded for waking Adam out of his sleep state she was blamed for unleashing evil on the world. (For a full retelling of the original myth read my book, 'The Inner Goddess Makeover').

As a result, the wild feminine aspect of Lilith was banished for 2000 years, during which time women dared not rock the boat for fear they would be ostracized by society & rejected by their husbands. Now two thousand years later, Lilith has returned to awaken our collective consciousness - in both men & women as the rising serpentine kundalini (life force) of the Earth wakes us from our sleep state to again climb the Tree of Life to become fully conscious beings, ready to enter the Aquarian Age of 'Oneness' or Eden.

The totem of snake possesses both the venom to hurt & then ultimately heal by bringing to our awareness what needs to be transmuted. In my experience taking women through their descent to see & know their shadow at each of their seven chakras, when they opened the door to each archetype they would initially come face to face with the disowned aspects of that aspect. In other words, they would see how disempowered that part of them was or become aware of the degree of its dysfunction in their life. But as the saying goes, 'Better the devil you know' so having the light of awareness shed upon this negative patterning gives us the choice to consciously change so we can integrate the strengths of each archetype & continue moving upwards to the next energy center to meet another facet of ourselves.

Working with couples, I see the same holds true. In that often they are stuck in a certain energy center when they come to see me for a session. This happens when both are polarized, with one operating unconsciously in a shadow feminine aspect &

the other operating unconsciously in a shadow masculine aspect. I simply play the role of the serpent of knowledge & hold out the apple for them to take a bite of reality by introducing them to their respective unseen traits as a mediator!

The Role of Lilith in Awakening the Rainbow Tribe

Lilith is the rainbow serpent, the dragon woman who pierces the ego with her fangs as she speaks her truth, whether we want to hear it or not. She is the messenger of Gaia, Mother Earth & her body is the major electrical current known as the dragon or ley lines that energize Gaia's form. As she moves, the earth shakes to literally wake up those who are still asleep.

As more people activate their inner Tree of Life by opening their chakras through practices such as yoga & teachings that unveil their archetypes to become aware of their multi-faceted soul we collectively strengthen the rise of the rainbow serpent within the matrix of Gaia. Each awakened being helps to awaken the collective rainbow tribe who seek to create a sustainable utopia of all colors & creeds living harmoniously under the one banner by awakening the Gaia consciousness on our planet. This is seen outwardly as the the gay pride flag celebrating diversity, earth festivals celebrating astrological & seasonal shifts & the ecological movement which is re-introducing sustainable practices such as bio-dynamic farming, recycling, reduction of carbon emissions through energy conservation, building practices & reforestation. As well as community initiatives such as veggie gardens, Red Tent Moon Lodges, seasonal celebrations & through the re-introduction of rite of passage initiations. All of these practices reconnect people with the natural cycles, themselves & each other by developing a reverence for the sacredness of life, along with wisdom & character through acts of benevolence & beauty. The more people reclaim their power through these practices the less they will be passive voyeurs, mesmerized by the acts of glory, glamour & violence enacted by celebrities in the ego driven realm of 3D or 'Hell'. Each of us who remembers ourselves to be children of the Sun & Earth are responding to an inner call to intuitively reconnect above & below. It is through this act of devotional service that we act as midwives, plugging into the ley lines of our Mother to strengthen her lightbody (the grid) with loving intent for our rebirth. Only when our chakras are open along the central pillar can we serve as a conduit to assist in the anchoring of Heaven on Earth. (More about this in Volume Three.)

Lilith Returns: The Rise of the Feminine

Nostradamus, the famous visionary foresaw that at this time in our evolution the feminine would rise up & transform society as we know it. (As I write this in Australia we have just had our first female prime minister sworn in by our first female governor General. This occurred just days after the Winter Solstice heralded in a new cycle where women would be impulsed to assume more leadership positions to address the balance of power in the West where the masculine had ruled from a very out of balance perspective.) The rising of the feminine is not about women assuming control it is about us each being governed as sovereign beings from our intuition or inner feminine, regardless of our physical gender. This is why our external leadership has become such a transparent joke to catalyze us taking back our power to become self governing. (The film, 'The Campaign' with Will Ferrell does a nice job of exposing the political system through satire...the role of the satyr, Pan (Lilith's counterpart) who mocks the civilized world.) After all, just because one is a woman does not necessarily mean they will lead from their feminine side - Maggie Thatcher being a case in point. (In retrospect, this has once again proven true as Australian PM, Julia Gillard abolished the sole parenting payment for those whose children reach the ripe old self-sufficient age of eight!)

Finally! A Happy Ending for Lilith

More than ever before, thanks to the rising kundalini within all beings, many are now willingly seeking out the wisdom & truth of Lilith! So they are finding themselves not just attracted to the erotic magnetism of Lilith awakened women but are now willing to listen to their 'inconvenient truth' in order to become more self-aware & enjoy greater intimacy. Numbered are the days of power for patriarchal females like Julia. Equally facing extinction are 'old paradigm unconscious males' who flee from honest conversation & true intimacy for fear they will be killed & devoured by the kiss of the spider woman. So...for all of you women who have been recluses, spinsters, sole parents or nuns for lifetimes rather than share your bed with the unconscious masculine THIS is the best news you may have heard for many a millenia!

'It is often the fate of a woman who is to be the consort of a king to have greater difficulty in lesser relationships'

Robert Johnson (My kind of cross-stitch!)

For men, the return of Lilith means GONE are the days of financially supporting an unconscious wife who freezes you out sexually in an effort to suppress her wild woman rage. Yes! Now you will no longer need to take a cold shower or seek out covert sexual pleasure in stick mags, brothels or affairs to fulfill the urges of your inner wild man. Now it seems both, Lilith & Pan will enjoy a happy ending (in every sense!)

Bloody Hell!

Lilith, the aspect of the wild woman (who governs the base chakra) initiates girls into their power by confronting them with their responsibility to either destroy or create life with the onset of menstruation. This rite of passage is known as menarche...It occurred to me after witnessing the oil spill in Mexico, (the largest in our history) & reading a comment by Vicki Noble, (the author of 'Shakti Woman') where she noted that crude oil is in fact the blood of Mother Earth that this spilling of her blood was our collective puberty rite! Gaia was initiating our global consciousness into the blood mysteries of the Sacred Feminine by awakening us all to the plight of the Earth & our responsibility to step up & make a difference by representing her in some capacity to anchor the new paradigm. Her fertile blood speaks to our primal understanding of our need to honor the death / rebirth cyclic nature of life which marks the end of our childish innocence & naivete. Coincidentally, just prior to this oil spill I was intuitively guided by Gaia to launch a global project called, 'Operation Red Tent' to re-awaken the teachings offered at Menarche. To view the free educational videos & find out more visit http://www.starofishtar.com/red-tent/operation-red-tent/ (Coincidentally the same week another teacher of Blood Mysteries, Deanna Lam launched her project on the other side of the world to serve the same aim!)

Addressing The Downward Spiral Taken By Teens Who Don't Receive Menarche

For 'tween (eight to twelve year olds) & teenage girls, puberty marks the rite of passage where the inner wild woman, Lilith the serpentine Goddess initiates them into the Lunar Mysteries with the cyclic shedding of their uterine lining & it's accompanying psycho/emotional shedding which occurs every month thereafter. Puberty marks a major loss of innocence for both boys & girls as they become aware of the shadow of humanity & often feel overwhelmed & powerless by the problems they see in the world which is why so many start rebelling or 'checking out' by using drugs & alcohol or indulging in reckless behavior. Many wear black to unconsciously express how they feel about themselves & the future as they focus increasingly on the dark side of human nature in an effort to make sense of it. This is why films which portray teens confronting their fears with the dark side like 'Harry Potter' & 'Twilight' strike such a popular chord.

In traditional cultures, rite of passage ceremonies at puberty assisted teens to make sense of their loss of innocence so they could embrace it as a necessary part of their journey ensuring their trust & faith in a higher power was not lost. Without this necessary mentoring which addresses the journey of the soul, many uninitiated teens become depressed & even suicidal through their ego's complete disillusionment. In the private school where I heard Steve Biddulph speak about the high rates of mental illness & sexual promiscuity amongst teenage girls, four students had ended their lives by jumping in front of commuter trains in the previous eighteen months.

http://www.abc.net.au/4corners/stories/2012/09/06/3584646.htm

For boys their puberty occurs slightly later when emotionally they mature so they are better equipped to integrate their hormonal changes. However it is often not until a sexual encounter that their kundalini is activated, awakening their base chakra energies. It is interesting to note that if a boy's female sexual partner has been initiated into Women's Mysteries & kundalini raising practises the young man will receive, 'Shaktipat' the awakening of his inner kundalini (life force) serpent through her energetic charge during orgasm.

Without this essence of 'Shaktipat', the energy generated through the sex act overcharges the base chakra creating an insatiable appetite for physical sex with no other emotional, mental or spiritual connection. This is evident in the West where anonymous sex is a cultural addiction resulting in porn, one night stands & anonymous liaisons where participants often spiral downwards into greater danger, domination or degradation in their unconscious effort to seek a sexual high which is greater than their last.

In the ancient world it was customary for boys to be initiated into their sexuality when they came of age by a trained priestess who taught them to respect women, become artful lovers & contain their ejaculation in addition to awakening their kundalini. Girls on the other hand were initiated into the Moon Lodge or Red Tent where they were instructed in the power of their bodies & taught how to honor them accordingly.

From Little Things, Big Things Grow

It makes sense that in order to grow out of the muck & mire of 'Hell' we must first reconnect with the Earth Mother by sending our roots down energetically & invoking her consciousness to activate the seed of our own self-awareness. To that end, I have recorded a simple daily practice, known as the 'Tree of Life meditation' which brings the Divine Feminine life force up into our hearts to germinate an attitude of self-acceptance, a seed which if tended bears the fruit of the inner mother who loves the small self unconditionally. (There is a link to this meditation in the Holy Hermaphrodite chapter later in Volume One.)

Just like the old saying, 'All things grow with love', so too self-acceptance is the first necessary step in our self growth. For when we have tried for so long to live up to our rational ego's expectations of perfection we end up so rigid, controlled, lifeless, anxious or depressed that we are like a scared child trying to unconsciously gain the approval of external authority figures. (Ye olde authority for those living in 'Hell' is Zeus, the distant Sky Father who presides over 'Hell' & judges everyone for not being 'good enough', a role which you may have inadvertently projected on to your boss, lecturer, father, critics, peers, neighbors or the media.) When we reconnect with the Mother we then start automatically nurturing our physical needs (base chakra), then our emotional needs (sacral chakra), then as a result we review our beliefs (solar plexus) as this current of awareness moves upward. Understandably those who are operating more out of their feminine polarity find it easier to nurture & grow through self-awareness. This explains why more women will discuss issues to bring them into the light of understanding & read self-awareness books or practice devotional traditions to raise their spirits like a plant growing toward the Sun.

Trees In Need Of a Green Thumb

Women have a natural propensity to reach skywards, toward the light of Spirit (the Sacred Masculine) as this is the counterpart energy they need to feel balanced & whole. This is why women, if not balanced with a down-to-earth connection to 'Big Mama' can allow their upward spiral to become hijacked by the mind. This plays out as an obsession with achieving perfection or attaining a spiritual ambition. i.e. if a woman attempts to climb Jack's beanstalk without first connecting with the true feminine, which is nature (rather than the distortion sold to her by advertisers) she can easily become a ball breaking corporate climber, princess bridezilla or overbearing mother superior!

Men on the other hand, who haven't found their own deep experiential connection with the Sacred Feminine seek out pastimes that spiral their energy downward in an unconscious desire to connect with the Earthy feminine. For example, they may become obsessive about their pursuit of sensual pleasure, which can easily manifest as addictions to pot & porn. This is underpinned by an unconscious urge to acquire the strengths of the feminine such as comfort, nurturance, support & acceptance. But when the cause of this dependency is unconscious these destructive tendencies create the very opposite in their lives, creating mental / emotional & psychological ill health which sabotages their attempts to form healthy relationships, further exacerbating their wound.

Snakes & Ladders For the Uninitiated!

My understanding is that before we begin consciously ascending & descending up this central pillar, fate (our subconscious or soul) initiates us into a game of 'Snakes & Ladders' with apparent external opportunities & disappointments which have us unconsciously acting out of the various archetypes at the seven gates. For example, before I began actively awakening my kundalini I first spiraled upward unconsciously seeking fame & fortune in an attempt to experience the shining charisma of the solar masculine. When fame was not forthcoming despite my ego's attempts, I then spiraled downward into a haze of substances in an effort to quiet my mind & experience a state of self-acceptance despite my perceived failures.

This acceptance can only truly be gifted by reconnecting with the feminine, via Mother Nature who never judges us. So when we feel worthless, sad & betrayed by life, like an animal we retreat to nature to lick our wounds & seek her comfort through her unconditional acceptance & natural beauty. Only from this place of true humility, like a child who has reconnected with the true power of nature are we ready to be initiated & consciously journey upward. In a more extreme case this tendency to energetically spiral up or down unconsciously is labelled, 'Bi polar'. For without sufficient grounding in the humble, natural world of the feminine our yang creative energy soars, (like the mythical protagonist, Icarus) too close to the sun as our ego feeds on the promise of shining brightly & receiving the perceived external rewards of attention, respect & validation. Gambling is another form of Bi Polar behavior, chasing the high of external success & riches to avoid feeling worthless.

This tendency to prove our worth on a grande scale is amplified if we grow up with a father who doesn't affirm our gifts by encouraging us to slowly & steadily build upon them for the greater good. As is often the case, if we are not embarking on our mission from a place of solid foundations, the tower we build with the best of intentions is destined to fall. And if we were building this tower in order to prove the worth of our very existence, the fall only serves to affirm our greatest fear, that we are insignificant, worthless & that our father was therefore right to not invest his valuable time & energy in our growth. This then results in a state of depression, a black hole into which we spiral until another idea sparks our ego's desires & we try again to build a dream upon which to gamble all our time & energy in the pursuit of success & happiness.

Awakening to Self Love

When we awaken our Shakti (light) we become aware of our shadow (unconscious) behavior. This process was misrepresented in the creationist myth as an awareness of shame when in fact it is the first step in developing a whole view of ourselves so we can see, accept & love ourselves, warts & all. If we don't look at ourselves in this balanced way we will never be able to view others & the world at large in a balanced way. Until we do, this unbalanced view creates conflict for us wherever we go. So rather than seeing this self awareness as the beginning of all suffering it actually marks the end of conflict as we see our own shadow reflected in our beloved. In other words, when the Sacred Feminine is awakened we can't stay in a state of separateness & duality. For it is by climbing the inner Tree of Life we see a bird's eye view of reality, seeing ourselves & others through the lens of our soul. This then makes it possible for us to question our mind's limited perception of dualistic thinking, reducing all experiences into good or bad / right or wrong. Similarly, when the Sacred Feminine is denied, we fall out of the tree (the central pillar) & swing between the polarities of the unconscious masculine...as explained in the next chapter.

🝆 The Tree of Knowledge

Transcending Duality, the Sacred Masculine

The Tree of Knowledge also features in the creation myths of our major global religions. It was said to be forbidden by God for Adam & Eve (the first man & his partner) to eat from this tree as it would grant them knowledge of good & evil. The story goes that the serpent in the tree tempted Eve with an apple which Eve then shared with Adam. When later questioned by God, Adam blamed Eve & Eve blamed the serpent, signifying their joint inability to assume personal responsibility - the result being that both Eve & the serpent were scapegoated for their expulsion from the Garden of Eden.

By tasting the fruits of this tree, Eve was said to have plunged humanity into a state of separation from the Divine, from oneness to duality. But if we are to truly know ourselves as Divine the first step is to know what appears to be the opposite. In other words it is only because we experience darkness that we know light or through feeling hot we can identify cold. The challenge then comes to not get caught up in the rational mind, judging either polarity as good or bad but seeing all states as different aspects of the whole, through which we learn to experience the fullness of ourselves. When we see all these aspects within ourself & accept them as part of our humanness we no longer judge them externally in others. By appreciating that all states & experiences are part of the

Divine Plan, offering us the opportunity to learn & grow we cultivate gratitude rather than bitterness. This is the return to a state of innocence, (Eden, the fifth dimensional realm of healing) which frees us from the mindset of Hell (the third dimensional realm of wounding).

To truly know ourselves experientially as every facet of creation required us to leave a state of blissful connectedness with the All to enter into a limited rational perception of reality. There we remained lifetime after lifetime, returning through reincarnation to repeat our experiences until we learned to view them through our Soul's perspective. Because we are the one collective consciousness, we remained in this cyclic wheel of karma, (learning through consequence) for many thousands of years as each soul who incarnated was taught to view the world through the rational mind. Fortunately, the ancient maps & symbols were hidden & handed down to esoteric scholars waiting for this time when we were free to openly crack their codes. And so it is through the integration & application of these two esoteric maps that we can evolve beyond our identity as homo-sapiens operating as 'monkey see, monkey do' to stellar beings who have climbed out of their trees to reside with the Gods in the stars.

How Could Knowledge Be Evil?

For over a millenia many have tried to prove their puritanical mettle by dispelling knowledge in favor of blind faith in an effort to win approval from their projected Father God. Ironic as the cosmic joke is, we actually need to question ourselves & life itself if we are to come to understand the greater meaning behind our existence. If we don't learn, we don't grow into our destined potential ascending into the consciousness of Eden & oneness again. (N.B. Heresy laws punishable by death & public fear mongering made the teaching of such spiritual teachings clandestine until recent years.)

Take a Walk on the Wild Side

So for those wanting the 'Clarke's Notes'...ultimately, the greatest lesson one must learn when ascending the Tree of Knowledge is to acknowledge one's own shadow or dark side. To willingly take this journey to truly know oneself requires leaving a state of blessed ignorance. A path which is both humbling & challenging to one's ego. The pay-off for opening your personal Pandora's box of unconscious thoughts, beliefs & behaviors is that your sexual mojo will be unleashed making you into a very charismatic Love God! This last comment refers to the activation of your kundalini (sexual / life force) which is freed when we unlock all the energy we have been suppressing for fear of being inappropriate.

Is It Just Me, Or Is Hot In Here?

Ever since the time of the Great Flood when as a species we were said to experience a fall from grace, we have predominantly operated out of our lower three chakras, which kept us in a perpetual mindset of Hell - anticipating struggles from a perception of fear & reacting accordingly. (N.B. The Christian concept of 'Hell' was named after the Norse Goddess, Hel who led souls through the Underworld, the place of unconscious souls.) So for those frightened of falling any lower, the good news is you're already here, your baggage is checked in & the only elevator in the lobby is going up!

How A Mindset Of Hell Creates Conflict Externally

If we don't take responsibility for owning our shadow by seeking to understand our unconscious thoughts, words & behaviors we project them on others - ye olde 'pointing the finger'. In the organized religious cults this was collectively projected on to a mythical being, such as the Christian notion of Satan whom everyone would blame for all their woes & then fear as an external force. So when we 'judge not lest we be judged' & make the shift to view our own small, fearful, wounded, suppressed & rejected animal self with compassion it becomes easy for us to forgive & accept ourselves warts & all, knowing that all we have done or experienced was necessary for our highest growth & understanding. The more understanding we have the easier it is for us to transcend limiting behaviors that dishonor ourselves & others.

Transcending the Illusion of Separation

The lesson we learn as we ascend the Tree of Knowledge is to transcend the illusion of separateness. We do this by seeing ourselves reflected completely in another. Only when we truly get the adage, 'I am you & you are me' are we freed from swinging between the mindset of 'us & them' which keeps us caught in a conflict of duality & opposition. The teen flick, 'Freaky Friday' offers us a modern day example of how conflict escalates between a mother & her teenage daughter when both polarize into their own world view as righteous & therefore superior to the other's. Only when they have learnt the lesson of true empathy is the curse broken & they are returned to their true selves. For only through spending a day in the other's shoes do they experientially come to appreciate what life is truly like for the other, which develops greater understanding, compassion & mutual respect. Like the native American saying, 'Never judge a man until you have walked a mile in his moccasins.'

The Key to Healing Relationships & Ending Wars

So too it is with us. Only when we can 'love thy enemy' as Yeshua (the Christ) taught as a teacher of the Sacred Masculine, can we stop perpetuating conflict. To do this we must find our shared humanity, our common ground & humbly accept that whoever is in front of us is our teacher, showing us that which we don't see in ourselves. This is the greatest lesson we must learn if we are to create loving partnerships where we don't unconsciously compete with the other to be right.

Conditional & Unconditional Love

The truth consists of paradox, being the sum of all parts & so it is that we are here to learn both conditional (personal) & unconditional (transpersonal) love. On the Tree of Knowledge we learn unconditional love by looking beyond our mind's personal agenda to see the universal Soul in our sister, brother, mother, father, son or daughter. I experienced this teaching a few years ago when I asked Spirit what I needed to do to prepare for an Equinox ceremony I was facilitating & the answer came, 'Forgive your mother & sister.' This was not what I was expecting but conceded that I needed to acknowledge with them that I had withheld my love because my small self was angry that they had not loved me in the way I wanted them to.

Josie Mirabito as a beautiful embodiment of the compassionate bodhisattva, Kwan Yin reminded us at my most recent Red

Tent that we experience grace when we learn to love others, regardless of their degree of consciousness & how they respond to us. Simply accept where they're at & what they're able to give rather than resenting them for not living up to your expectations. (This doesn't mean staying in a partnership that minimizes or dishonors us). What it does mean is accepting what is & unconditionally loving a fellow being as a soul doing their best, even if it's from a distance! Again this notion is summed up in this quote by Mother Theresa, 'People are Unreasonable. Love them anyway.'

This transpersonal love is the gift of the Sacred Masculine. The benevolent king or chieftan who loves all in his jurisdiction or the leader who loves all who work together to enact his vision of benevolence. This is transpersonal love that opens our heart to love strangers through the recognition that we are all one as the children of God.

Personal love is therefore the gift of the Sacred Feminine. As little girls we love everyone innocently as Aphrodite but we get hurt so we have to learn self love by learning to assert boundaries that honor us before we are ready to re-enter into personal intimacy as the mature Venus, known as Ishtar, the queen. Then we can strike a balance between love of self & love of other. Both personal & transpersonal love are important lessons & qualities which are necessary & complementary if we are to ascend our trees.

Christ came through to anchor a positive archetype for the Sun God but unless we also acknowledge & embody the lessons of the Magdalene, the Star Goddess we won't create the alchemy of the inner marriage to ascend our inner Trees. Just as it takes the joining of male & female to create life, we require that same union to transform & rebirth. Coincidentally in the Kabbalistic Tree, the middle path from the heart to the crown is the path of the The Magdalene (High Priestess). This is path number 13, the longest & most arduous path whose faith is tested through the chaos of the black hole, the sephirot of Da'arth.

Recognizing Polarization: The Seven Vices & Virtues

When we polarize on either side of the Tree of Good & Evil, trouble ensues so below is a quick way to identify how you tend to polarize on the Tree so you can adopt a more liberal approach. It occurred to me that the 'Seven Deadly Sins' taught by the Christian faith are another representation of the Tree of Knowledge as they polarize our perception of our behavior & our reality into sins & virtues. Personally, I see sin as our karmic lesson or the result we experience when we are out of balance. In other words if we indulge this ego tendency or desire without balancing it with the virtue there are undesirable consequences to pay. Keeping in mind, however that neither polarity is balanced, so it is wise to follow the middle mystical path of moderation, referred to as 'The Golden Mean' by the ancient Greeks which is ultimately sustainable. If we aspire to either polarity we will eventually swing to the other side, such is the universal law of the balance of opposites.

Base Chakra:
Vice: Lust
Middle Pillar: Sexual Self-Pleasure
Virtue: Chastity

Sexual arousal has been demonized out of fear that we will descend completely into animalistic behavior if we indulge it, never to again regain the civility befitting our social standing. However if we seek to suppress a force of nature it becomes more powerful as a hidden obsession. Similarly, if we indulge every sexual impulse, we abuse both ourselves & others emotionally, energetically & psychologically. The key is to become a self-fulfilling sexual being who doesn't need to suppress one's urges nor fulfill all of them, regardless of the consequences. This leads us to take full responsibility for our own sexual arousal rather than unconsciously use another in a vampiric way. One can see this in shadow Hermes & Pan men who use their charm & charisma to awaken the serpent in priestess women then siphon off their raised kundalini through transient sexual encounters that bolster their mojo. Similarly, women who prey upon men to 'get off' sexually because they carry too much shame & self loathing to climb their inner staircase themselves. When one literally 'fucks' another person (regardless of what Tantric terms they dress it up with) they are using the other person as both a host & a receptacle for their pent up stress. To avoid these mutually abusive scenarios one can find 'The Golden Mean' through self-pleasure. If done with the sincere intent of loving oneself completely, self-pleasure can be a full communion with the whole self in ecstatic rapture, rather than a subversive pastime manufactured by repression & guilt. Betty Dobson's book, 'Sex for One' challenges our cultural belief that sex is only sex if it is couple sex. If we commit to become more attentive & loving sexual partners to ourselves, abstaining from sexual partners that don't meet us on all levels of our being then we balance our base chakra.

Sacral Chakra:
Vice: Gluttony
Middle Pillar: Sensual Self Pleasure
Virtue: Temperance

We tend toward gluttony when we are attempting to self-soothe our wounded inner child's emotional state with comfort food or drink. Men tend more toward beer which is brewed by yeast & women tend more toward cakes derived from wheat. Both of which are symbolic of the grain goddess Demeter, the mother archetype. We all need to access her strengths internally or we will unconsciously attempt to fill our bottomless pit of emotional need with sensate pleasure which results in excess. If on the other hand we have swung into temperance we are attempting to temper our desires by carefully monitoring what we are allowed & what we aren't. Eventually the inner child will rebel against these imposed limits & splurge or binge undoing all of our best intentions. This is the classic 'yo yo dieting' or binge drinking we see in those who aren't dealing with that which is making them unhappy. For when we spend more time doing that which is truly joyful we need less sensate comfort like an upset child seeking a bottle of milk. For example, exercise kindness towards yourself by regularly gifting yourself with a massage. Massage is a great way to balance the swing between desire & denial as touch is the most primal form of love which soothes our inner child. Our modern culture has become so centered in the head that our bodies are starved of physical touch. That is touch that has no sexual expectation or agenda but which is given & received purely as an act of sensate pleasure. Self pampering is another great way to keep the sacral balanced & the child within, loved.

Solar Plexus:
Vice: Greed
Middle Pillar: Self Worth
Virtue: Charity

If we don't have a solid sense of our innate worth as a sacred being in our own right we tend to unconsciously aspire to attain great wealth & status to prove our worth, resulting in greed. Similarly, the same wound in our solar plexus creates the other extreme of charity - giving constantly to others but not ensuring we have what we need for ourselves. If unconscious, this can be driven by a need to prove to ourselves that we are truly 'good' & worthy of external approval, whether from a higher power, peers or authority figures such as parents. The old saying, charity begins at home applies here. If we give to ourselves so our cup is full then we can give in an authentically generous way without unconsciously expecting anything in return. The balance is learning to give & receive in equal measure, demonstrating an innate acknowledgement that energy is in constant flux & that by moving energy we attract more. If the solar plexus is unbalanced we either undercharge or overcharge for our time & efforts. If we isolate which polarity is more confronting for us then we know which one we need to learn to do to strike a balance.

Heart Chakra:
Vice: Sloth
Middle Pillar: Self Love
Virtue: Diligence

I see the lesson of this chakra as finding the balance between service & self-fulfillment or more simply put, being & doing. If we only attend to our own needs we become complacent & uninspired to assist others. If we focus on meeting only the needs of others we burn out & then swing into the other polarity of slothfulness. By accepting our own limits & needs as being equally important as those of others we find a balance in saying both yes & no from a solid foundation of self love. When we polarize at this gate we attract & resent our opposite. For example, women who do everything while their partners sit around the house or women who spend money on themselves as fast as he earns it.

Throat Chakra:
Vice: Wrath
Middle Pillar: Self Acceptance
Virtue: Patience

I think the key here is about clear communication so if we have a healthy level of self acceptance stemming from a deep sense of compassion for the Self, we are then able to assert our needs without self-doubt or guilt inhibiting our speech. By using our voice deliberately with the energetic commitment of our intention behind it we need not swing between anger or sublimation of our our needs. If we are stuck in polarized thinking at his gate we can become enraged with righteousness or allow ourselves to be used as a doormat with no voice. When we learn to be our own best friend we can speak up as needed & honor others right to speak up on their own behalf equally without taking offense.

Brow Chakra:
Vice: Envy
Middle Pillar: Self Understanding
Virtue: Kindness

When we covet the apparent assets or good fortune of another we are placing ourselves in the role of victim, denying our personal responsibility for every aspect of what we have created in our own lives with every thought, word & action. Through reflection on our own harvest we develop self understanding, opening the third eye so we can see clearly how we have attracted or created (consciously or unconsciously) everything we have experienced. This enables us to feel genuinely benevolent towards others whether they have attained more self-mastery or less than we have. At this gate we are reminded of the classic faery tale, 'The Prince & the Pauper' which reminds us the grass isn't always greener on the other side. For unless we've walked a mile in their shoes we can't be aware of the tribulations of their path. (The monologue Julia Roberts gives in the film, 'Notting Hill' about how excruciating it is to live the life of celebrity is a case in point.)

Crown Chakra:

Vice: Pride
Middle Pillar: Gratitude
Virtue: Humility

This chakra relates to whether we get caught up in pride: having an ego attachment to the gifts we receive when we open ourselves to Spirit...or whether we minimize our light with humility: denying our own Divine presence as equal & indivisible from Source as this 'playing small' anchors a sense of ego separation. The balancing quality is gratitude because only gratitude enables us to acknowledge the gift from Spirit that streams through us as sacred vessels & messengers with grace so we can share it without our own ego getting in the way. At this gate if we get caught up in comparisons of 'us & them' we can view our gifts as better or worse than another's. This inhibits us from being a clear channel dedicated to bringing through exactly what our area of unique service is. When we are truly grateful for our gifts & the opportunities afforded us to share them we can be who we truly are without fears of being too big or not enough.

Awakening The Higher Heart (World Soul)

When we see ourselves completely in the other we awaken empathy - the wisdom of the heart which lights up the central pillar so we see each other through the heart rather than the head. This is our current lesson in our shared humanity to transcend the concept of 'us & them'. When we see ourselves in every other aspect of creation it becomes unthinkable to turn a blind eye to animal cruelty, support a war on other cultures, perpetuate prejudice against other races or mock someone with a disability. Neither can we withhold our loving compassion by expressing an attitude of righteousness towards those who hurt others or break the law. The activation of the higher heart (located between the heart & the throat chakra) signals the attunement to the one global heart, known as the World Soul (the final lesson in the Tarot.)

The Kabbalistic Tree

The Kabbalistic Tree is a template which features 22 paths which we journey on our way to become enlightened (full of conscious understanding). The lesson the initiate must master on each of these paths relates to the 22 Major Arcana cards in the Tarot, which also illustrate as the life transitions we each enact in our own lives from 'The Fool' (uninitiated) to 'The World Soul' (one with the Divine). If we are actively seeking to understand ourselves & fulfill our highest potential this result is inevitable, it's just a matter of long it takes us. The Tree of Life ultimately teaches us about the polarities of duality, which were simplistically reduced to 'good & evil', a mindset which must be transcended if we are to once again experience ourselves as one with God.

Below is a diagram of the traditional Kabbalistic Tree. There are three pillars, on the left is the dark pillar of severity, on the right is the white pillar of mercy & in the center is the pillar of equilibrium. Also featured are the Sephirot, the spheres of energy which represent the major aspects which must be balanced. (N.B. The spelling on this diagram differs from that which I was taught & use below.) The top Sephirot, Kether represents the gateway to the Cosmos which I relate to the crown chakra. I then perceive the three Sephirot on each of the outer pillars as the three stages of masculine & feminine maturity. Below are the planetary correspondences & stages of feminine / masculine maturity.

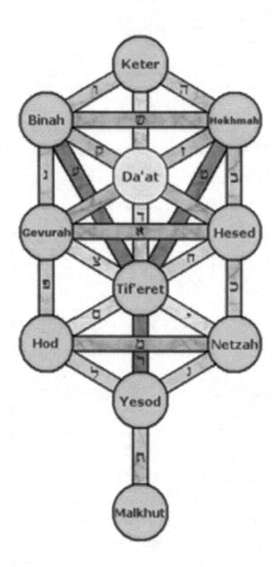

The Three Pillars

In the table below I have listed the planetary & archetypal correspondences. (N.B. The archetypal correspondences are my personal interpretation.)

Severity (Masculine)	Equilibrium (Spirit / Matter)	Mercy (Feminine)
	Kether (Sun) Ishtar / Dionysus	
Binah (Neptune) Hecate		Chochmah (Mercury) Hermes
	Da'arth (Uranus) Artemis / Chiron	
Gevurah (Saturn) Green Man		Chesed (Earth) Demeter
	Tipareth (Jupiter) Apollo / Athena	
Hod (Mars) Ares		Netsach (Venus) Aphrodite
	Yesod (Moon)	
	Malkuth (Pluto) Pan / Lilith	

(N.B. Personally I still question whether it is yet another 'red herring' to have Chochma heading the "Pillar of Mercy" and Binah heading the "Pillar of Severity." However, one possible explanation I can come up with to explain this switching of feminine / masculine poles is that Binah and Chockma represent the right and left hemispheres of the brain. So as the solar logos (Sacred Masculine) energy courses down the tree in the form of a lightning bolt from Source into matter, the masculine principle of Chochma influences the opposite side of the tree, down the Pillar of Severity & equally the feminine principle of Binah influences the Pillar of Mercy.) (Refer to the diagram below.)

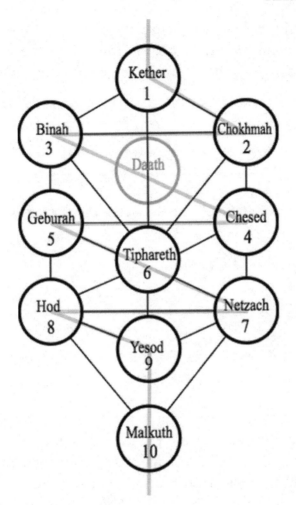

The Lightning Bolt From Father Sky

The Tree of Knowledge illustrates how our Sacred Masculine energy is activated within us: as a flash of awareness which enters down into our crown, (hence the old saying of 'a lightbulb moment'! This energy travels downwards from Source (the Sacred Masculine) into matter (the Sacred Feminine) seeking union with his Divine complement. Just as Shakti, spirals up our spinal cord seeking union with her Beloved. This interception of the polarities of Sacred Feminine

& Masculine can be seen pictorially in the six pointed star. The triangle denoting Shiva points upward to the Sun & the triangle denoting Shakti points downward to the Earth.

This activating principle of the Sky Father travels down through our personal awareness like a lightning bolt, with each Sephirah decreasing the voltage of this incoming high powered current like an electrical transmission substation so we can integrate new paradigms of thought without it blowing our circuitry! The more we seek to clear our karma at these gates by consciously understanding our lessons the more light we can absorb into our light bodies from Source. (More about this later on!) This current of energy also maps the path of manifestation, from an inspired idea to its physical creation.

The 9 Stages of Manifestation

By mapping how an inspired idea takes form in the physical we anchor the awareness of the Magi, one who can birth regardless of their gender because they have mastered the steps of alchemy. To do this one must first master personal alchemy by awakening their own awareness & mastery over their lower self. Then, like Jesus who embodied the energy of the awakened masculine operating in perfect alignment with the Divine Plan you can manifest with grace everything you need in the perfect time & the in the perfect way by acting intuitively & observing synchronicity. 'All comes to he who waits' does not mean standing around passively with no intent. It means putting out a clear intent & surrendering it to Highest Will trusting that you will always be given what you need but not always what you want. This attitude transcends scarcity consciousness or competition. When enough people are operating at this frequency 'in perfect love & perfect trust' we will see the dissolution of the monetary system.

Stage One: The Fool (Kether to Chochmah)
We trust what is needed is given. We are in complete receptivity to Divine Will.

Stage Two. The Empress (Chochmah to Binah)
We receive intuitive wisdom on how to best apply what we receive.

Stage Three. (Binah to Chesed)
We open our heart in complete gratitude.

Stage Four. Strength (Chesed to Gevurah)
We believe in our ability to manifest.

Stage Five. Justice (Gevurah to Tipareth)
We expand beyond what we thought possible.

Stage Six. Death (Tipareth to Netsach)

We release all attachment to what we desire.

Stage Seven: The Tower (Netsach to Hod)

We observe power of word by not undoing our intent with spoken doubts.

Stage Eight. The Sun. (Hod to Yesod)

We magnify our intention with the joy of receiving.

Stage Nine. The World. (Yesod to Malkuth)

We embrace our physical manifestation with love.

Making the Return Trip Home

So if we wish to evolve from dense matter to inspired awareness we simply need to reverse the process by following the path of the lightning bolt to raise our frequency at each of the gates of understanding. This makes a total of nine evolutionary steps, which is the number of steps on the Mayan calendar.

The Nine Paths to Awaken the Solar Logos

Malkuth to Yesod.

This path pulls us from operating from mind in our everyday world into the shadowy depths of our subconscious to view our fears, memories & deep emotions that we have suppressed. It is the journey from the Earth (Earth Mother) taking care of our physical needs to the Moon (Spiritual Mother) where we learn to attune to our emotional & soul needs. This path is not particularly comfortable, as our inner world surfaces to eclipse our outer world so we may experience depression, lethargy, vivid dreams & anxiety....all are a sign we have cracked our shell & we are growing! To master this path we need to acknowledge our own dark side which is surfaces to show us what we need to let go of. I see this initiation as Pandora's Box being opened & dealing with our past so we can move forward.

Yesod to Hod.

In this path we journey from the subconscious to the conscious. So this is when we make sense of what we experienced in our recent descent. this is when we take action to individuate from our conditioning. We may distill what we learnt by creating an invention, writing a book or birthing a fresh outlook. The Tarot card which relates to this path is 'The Sun' which signals the return of our optimism for living.

Hod to Netsach.

In this path we journey from the extremes of the dark pillar to the white pillar, from the rational mind to our emotions. This path is about the power of the spoken word. We learn how to express what we feel not just what we think. The Tarot card which relates to this path is 'The Tower' which means that because we have grown mentally & now emotionally, all that doesn't match our new vibration will fall away. We may need to express sadness at what has ended.

Netsach to Tiphareth.

In this path we journey from our emotions to the centeredness of our heart. It relates to the Tarot card of 'Death' which teaches us that until we surrender ourself & our life to a Higher Power we will keep creating drama for ourselves by desiring that which we don't have. We transcend love addiction by filling our heart with the light of Spirit.

Tiphareth to Gevurah.

Having truly relinquished our ego's control over our life, we then experience a new opportunity that reflects we have learnt to balance our lower thoughts & feelings so we can receive a more honoring set of circumstances. The Tarot card for this path is 'Justice' indicating that when we have the courage to leave situations where we were emotionally or mentally dominant or submissive we then attract others who have balanced these aspects.

Gevurah to Chesed.

This path teaches us to balance severity & mercy by finding our own inner strength so we can be firm but loving, the traits of our inner parents. This enables us to step into our personal power so we may serve as a leader. This path relates to the Tarot card of 'Strength' which reminds us we have the strength within to overcome what we thought was beyond us, which expands our reality.

Unchartered Path: Chesed to Binah.

This is the shift from service to stillness. It is when we go deep within, surrendering to the void of Great Mystery. I see this path as letting go of all that you thought you knew to enter the silence & await rebirth. Here we experience the aspect of Sheila Na Gig who is the death crone who births the universe. Just as the Earth Mother births us into the physical realm, the Spiritual Mother births us into the Cosmos. This is the deepest level of feminine receptivity we can surrender to so we are completely open to Divine Will. (I see this as the boarding lounge for the return trip home!)

Binah to Chochmah.

This reminds me of the light people report seeing at the end of the tunnel when crossing over. It is the blinding light & love of the Heavenly Father welcoming us home as we birth our evolved consciousness. In the Tarot this path is represented by the card, 'The Empress' signifying birth.

Chochmah to Kether.

This is the moment when we simultaneously experience ourself as the All. Every path, every pillar, every sephirot, every aspect which is symbolized by the Tarot card 'The Fool'. the Fool has returned home to a state of grace, 'innocence' seeing all things as equally Divine. Wearing a rainbow to symbolize the synthesis & integration of all his diverse facets. This is path 11 indicating both yin & yang serpents are fully awakened to activate the 11 Master being. One who has mastered their lower self by recognizing & transcending all illusion.

The Return to Innocence

Ultimately climbing the Tree of Knowledge means becoming aware of how polarization of our perception creates imbalance within & subsequent conflict externally. To transcend the viewpoint of right & wrong (black & white) we must join the dots (Sephirot) to see how all is related in the greater plan. This means that once we have been stung or bitten by someone's shadow behavior we then seek higher wisdom to make sense of it so we don't become vengeful, bitter & resentful & unconsciously wound others. Otherwise we will continue the cycle & unconsciously bite others. If we instead seek to understand our own wounds & imbalance that is being reflected back to us we become grateful for what each experience is teaching us.

⚕ The Caduceus

Awakening the Twin Serpents of Healing

The caduceus is one of the most widely recognized esoteric symbols. It depicts two serpents coiled around a central rod with wings extending out from the top of the staff. In ancient Greek mythology, Hermes (the messenger God) was said to have come across two snakes fighting. When he threw his staff down, they both entwined their bodies around it & stayed in that position, ending the dispute. Simply by having a central pillar, (a structure) they spiraled upward like a growing vine instead of outwardly directing their energy at each other.

So too, when we have a structure that assists us to focus on our own self growth we stop creating 'karma drama' by looking to others to fulfill us & then blaming them for not fulfilling us. Iris, the Rainbow Goddess who features in the Tarot card, 'The Star' & was another messenger Goddess who was said to have carried this staff.

The Royal Couple

In ancient Egypt, the pharaohs wore two entwined serpents on their headpiece to signify they had raised their kundalini to become self-realized beings. This level of self mastery is what earned one the title of being a king or queen in ancient Eastern civilizations such as Babylon & Mesopotamia. This is why it was considered so powerful for the High Priestess of the temple to lie with the King of the land each Spring. This union of the spiritual leader & the secular leader ensured harmony & abundance for every facet of their civilization as both aspects were valued equally. This was not some superstitious attempt to 'please the Gods' with a fertility rite as history scholars have interpreted it based on their own hubris, but rather a conscious raising of kundalini by the royal couple who literally embodied the God & Goddess in form because they had fully unveiled & awakened their Divine Feminine & Masculine channels of energy known as the twin serpents. These energy meridians are known in Sanskrit as Ida & Pingala. (N.B. More about the royal couple in the chapter, 'Preparing for Heiros Gamos' in Volume Two.)

Through the suppression of kundalini raising practices & their significance, we culturally have come to rely upon an individual's bloodline as the sole indicator of royalty. Similarly, our political leaders are nowadays puppets sponsored by corrupt corporations. So we have self serving tyrants ruling the people & destroying the land rather than enlightened masters in positions of leadership & we have the audacity to consider our civilization more advanced. In the ancient societies which incorporated the esoteric sciences introduced by visiting star nations a king was not considered fit to rule if he would not join with the representative of the Goddess. He however was a High Priest in his own right & she a Queen as the temple was the largest money lender, illustrating both had developed feminine mysticism & masculine strategy to steward a way forward that was in the best interests of the people.

Ida & Pingala

In Tantra, the inner twin serpents are known as Ida & Pingala. They are 'nadis' the Sanskrit word for energy channels which direct the life force up the central channel known as Sushumna. It is through these channels that the electric currents of prana (life force) & mana (mental force) flow.

Sushumna: This nadi is the central column which connects the base chakra to the crown. When one has awakened this channel they experience 'kriyas'. These are seen as physical spasms as energy moves up the central channel of their subtle body. These movements indicate the flow of prana. (N.B. If you are like me & have an S bend in your spine like a toilet these kriyas can become a source of amusement as they shock unsuspecting onlookers with their severity, like my dentist!)

Pingala: This nadi is the masculine energy channel which corresponds to the left hemisphere of the brain. Being solar in nature, it heats as it pulses energy from the left side of the base chakra to the right nostril. It is often seen as red in color.

Ida: This nadi is the feminine energy channel which corresponds to the right hemisphere of the brain. Being lunar in nature it cools as it pulses energy from the right side of the base chakra to the left nostril. The two paths cross in the optical chiasma. Ida is often seen as blue in color.

The White Wedding

Starting at the base chakra, both Ida & Pingala alternate directions at each chakra until they join at the brow chakra, bowing in humility creating an inner unity of opposites. (Hence it was Hermes, the God of Wisdom who was gifted this sacred symbol as he is the male archetype that governs the third eye.) The meeting of these three pillars (the holy trinity) is known in Sanskrit as 'mukta' meaning liberated. This threefold energy then rises into the crown creating the white wedding (known in Sanskrit as Sandhya) which is a meditative state of inner union between the sun & moon where the breath & mind are one & joy permeates one's being. As energy is always in a constant state of flux, this is a temporary state of being which is experienced before the energy descends back down through Ida & Pingala into the base. My experience is that the energy vortex of Spring Equinox, also referred to as 'The White Wedding' is the optimal time to experience this unity of inner feminine & masculine with Spirit (although one can experience it anytime, anywhere.)

Balancing the Energy Flow of Ida & Pingala

When we breathe through either nostril, the chi in either Ida or Pingala is activated. Unless we consciously breathe through both nostrils simultaneously, we automatically breathe through one nostril at a time. Usually we favor one nostril which indicates the gender polarity we are operating out of as our dominant mode of self-expression. In a person who is balanced, they automatically experience a change from one nostril to the other every 90 minutes & during the transition time they feel calm, centered & meditative. We can assist the balancing of our left brain / right brain functioning by doing the yogic technique known as alternate nostril breathing which is a practice to balance the two energy meridians of Ida & Pingala. It works by stimulating the even flow of energy to both the left & right sides of the physical & subtle bodies & regulates the nervous system. (See the 'Celebrating The Holy Hermaphrodite' chapter later in this volume for more details).

Identifying Meridian Imbalances

Those who favor left nostril breathing will often create what is known in traditional Chinese medicine as 'inner damp' which is due to an excess of cool, yin energy. This manifests as phlegm in the physical body, culminating in symptoms such as sinus, asthma & tonsillitis, making one prone to low energy. Those who favor right nostril breathing will alternatively create 'inner heat' due an excess build up of yang energy which can manifest as high blood pressure, skin irritations & a hot temper along with a highly ambitious outlook. When we breathe equally through both channels we access the positives of both genders so our demeanor is calm, centered & self-assured. Knowing this, when we feel impatient & hot-headed we can cover our right nostril & breathe through our left to calm down & if we are feeling sluggish or slipping into victim consciousness we can breathe through our right nostril to re-balance. Hatha Yoga which literally translates to mean 'ha' - sun & 'tha' - moon is a breath based form of beginner's yoga which aligns the breath & mind & is another helpful practice in balancing these meridians. The more self-aware we become of these breathing patterns the more we can consciously harness these energies by doing outward activities when energy is being drawn in through the right nostril & inward activities when energy is being drawn in through the left nostril. Similarly, when our right side is active (which reaches its zenith at midday as it is ruled by the sun) this is the optimal time for the main meal of the day as this channel aids our digestion when open. Similarly, when our left side is active we better absorb fluids into the body.

The simplest way to raise your inner Ida & Pingala twin serpents is to understand & express the masculine & feminine energies at each of the seven gates. When we do this we uncover our inner jewels (soul gifts) to become truly abundant in every way & attain self mastery by activating our energetic crown. The following chapter will assist you in finding a harmonic balance of opposites at each of the seven gates. This will support the flow of energy spiraling upwards which will improve all of your relationships as you won't feel susceptible to being hooked into old ego power struggles, as symbolized by the fighting snakes. Best of all, when both your inner masculine & feminine serpents stand tall in their empowerment & self expression, you will energetically embody the 11 frequency Master being so your Higher Self can fully anchor into your physical temple, which will shift you into the 5th dimensional consciousness to receive the bounty of Divine providence that is your birth rite.

⚕ Seven Brides For Seven Brothers

Marrying & Balancing the Inner Gods & Goddesses

Just as in the musical 'Seven Brides for Seven Brothers' each of our inner feminine archetypes which govern the seven major chakras has a masculine counterpart. By understanding the interplay of opposing aspects at each of the seven gates we create inner unity, balance & harmony which enables us to then experience balance & harmony externally in relationship with another.

If there is a particular archetype (masculine or feminine) that we have denied we will be attracted to another who has this as a dominant archetype. By spending time with them we can consciously observe & learn how to express this aspect more in our own life, so we may create greater balance rather than unconsciously expecting them to express it for us which creates dependency.

When we awaken both our masculine & feminine expression at each of these seven gates we then awaken the master being or whole self. By seeing & understanding each of these feminine & masculine selves within us we automatically relate more consciously & compassionately to other men & women. So rather than viewing them competitively we adopt an attitude of brother / sister which allows for greater authenticity, vulnerability & emotional intimacy with both men & women in a spirit of conscious community.

So, let's meet the happy couples...

Base Chakra (Red)

Pan, the Wild Man & Lilith, the Wild Woman

This is the physical gate where we need to balance truth with survival. If we are run by unconscious fears of not surviving we won't be able to live an authentic life & we will lose our passion for life. This means facing our fears of rejection & change.

To Recap...

Pan has been deeply shamed as the ugly faun who can't control his lusty desires, by monotheistic religions which only honored one aspect - the distant Sky Father as Divine. As a result they vilified the nature God, Pan as the devil & viewed his natural urges as evil. The irony with this one-eyed perspective is that 'evil' is simply the opposite of 'live' so when we suppress a natural part of us we are unconsciously creating depravity & shame as our secret obsessions unconsciously seek covert expression. Alternatively, when a man has his inner Pan 'on board' he is comfortable in his own skin, content to walk around the house in his underwear & simply be his natural self like a free range animal rather than an angry caged tiger. He is also a great camper who comes alive in the great outdoors & loves watching nature docos to learn about his natural world.

Our inner Pan's greatest challenge is to own the areas of our life where we tend toward irresponsibility. So when this inner couple is anchored consciously we can examine our behavior & take responsibility for it without shame or suppression, which keeps it real & the spark alive! If our inner Pan is empowered we will also honor our need for the wild by instigating a 'getaway' by going camping, fishing or hunting regularly. We will also learn about the wild by watchings nature docos, learning about weather, bush foods, survival techniques & the elements.

His counterpart is **Lilith**, the wild woman who is also comfortable with her nudity & bodily functions & honors the power of her lunar menstrual cycle which enables her to shed that which doesn't serve her so she may continually grow into her authentic power & wisdom. Lilith's challenge is to take responsibility for her own anger (particularly prior to dark moon or prior to menstruating.) For if our inner Lilith is empowered we honor how the lunar cycle affects us. This includes acknowledging any frustration or anger as it arises & discharging intense emotions through active meditation so we can then take action or discuss our need for change & our underlying fears without destroying those around us by unconsciously acting out. Equally when our inner Lilith is empowered we won't suppress our truth to keep the peace as this self deceit then manifests as illness in the body & destroys true intimacy with others. We also appreciate ourself & others for their natural self, never shaming or ridiculing ourself or others for their bodily functions & natural appearance.

Working Together

When both of these aspects are whole & healed we revel in our natural selves, accepting & loving the animal part of our humanity without suppression or judgement. This means we can then accept & adore it in others. This also makes for great, liberated sexual expression - as both of these aspects enjoy earthy, lusty primal sex where their inner animal can be let off the leash to smell, lick, growl, suck & fornicate with wild abandon. The key to these aspects getting along is their ability to look at the truth of a situation & take action accordingly.

Once our inner Lilith becomes consciously aware of a truth about herself or a situation that requires action, our inner Pan must face the truth instead of running away or disassociating like an immature 'Peter Pan'. If we can face our inner truth each month with the assistance of a brotherhood or sisterhood circle, it won't be so threatening to hear someone close to us speak their truth, even if that means naming our shadow. In fact, we will probably feel grateful for their assistance rather than shooting the messenger down in cold blood, spewing molten lava over them or withdrawing into frigidity!

Whilst it may sound like a lot of work; navel gazing & owning your crap in a circle every month, the pay off is spontaneous lusty orgasms the rest of the month. For those of you in conscious partnerships, this means your inner Pan can confidently pounce on your mate from around corners & in wardrobes knowing you won't be told off or coldly rebuked by a woman who refuses to submit to a man she doesn't respect. For if Pan owns his shadow he can confidently pursue his sexual prey knowing he is free to enjoy the thrill of the chase as he is sure in the knowledge that his ambush is always welcome. For as much as our inner Lilith fantasies about a wild man who is confident enough to claim her sexually, no man will risk tearing off a woman's undergarments with his teeth if he fears there's a chance she might scream, 'Rape!' & kick him in his furry nut sack. (And when Pan knows he is welcome to hunt & pounce he doesn't need to fantasize about the thrill of the chase outside the union.) For the inner Lilith's, this means a thawing out of your libido because you no longer have to put your anger on ice to get through another day with painkillers. This means the inner wild cat can simmer in a state of sexual anticipation knowing her mate is enough of a man (in every sense) to handle a hot Tammale woman. She can relax instead of being a cat on a hot tin roof because she can trust her man to honor the power & wisdom of her wild self in & out of the fur lined mattress!

So express your frustration, speak your truth & make the changes that are necessary so you don't need to scapegoat your crap onto others or run away from reality.

Sacral Chakra (Orange)

Ares, the Warrior & Aphrodite, the Beautiful Muse

So this is the emotional gate where we need to learn to balance love & war as our inner Ares wants to assert his independence & identity by proving his might to win victory & glory while our inner Aphrodite wants to be truly seen, appreciated & embraced in order to feel truly loved. You may sense the tug of war that this can provoke.

Both aspects have big emotions as together they govern the sacral chakra which is the access point for our emotional body. Because this gate is where our inner child sits, our childhood wounds are often re-wounded here by these inner & outer aspects until they become conscious through self awareness & emotional maturity.

To Recap...

Our inner **Ares**, (the God of War) often unconsciously carries a chip on his shoulder because he is angry his father hasn't truly seen his strengths & assisted him to achieve some measure of glory. This creates within us inner conflict because we want to show up those who doubted us (like an underdog with something to prove.) This is why the film, 'Rocky' with the hero achieving a victory that seemed impossible due to his apparent lack of paternal support struck such a public chord. His unhealed anger toward the father can make us overreact aggressively to those who doubt us as our inner child's sense of self is threatened. So when we grow into our adult stature & physical power our inner child's reactive explosions of frustration (tantrums) become threatening & dangerous to those around us & their property. This leads many Ares dominant folk to feel like an unlovable beast like 'The Incredible Hulk' whose dark side is always going to be rejected which adds salt to the original wound of rejection from the father.

As for our inner **Aphrodite**, we just want someone to truly see our soul's beauty & in doing so 'know' our true self. This is why the words, 'I see you' as the customary greeting of the nature beings who worshipped the 'Tree of Life' in the film, 'Avatar' was so powerful. (This is a custom I hope more of us adopt both as a greeting & in our courtship / sacred union rites.) Many of our inner children didn't feel truly seen by our parents, nor by the wider community. This is because the unconscious culture that raised us conditioned us to only behave in socially acceptable ways to gain the acceptance of the group rather than encouraging us to express our uniqueness, trusting it would be seen, understood & honored.

Working Together

So before we can express our true self out in the world to receive the praise & glory that our inner Ares craves we must first see our own inner beauty. We can do this by spending time developing our creative potential. Because art is the language of the soul as we express our true self artfully, like Narcissus we look deep within to see, meet, explore & appreciate our true selves. This is the process of falling in love with ourself so we can then share our innocent & playful soul self with another & know we deserve to be seen & loved for who we are. If we fail to do this inner work our inner Aphrodite constantly seeks out partners who don't truly see or get us but like the idea of us or our external appearance. This can create a painful dynamic where the inner child is still trying to gain the love of the parent we have unconsciously projected on to our partner. Developing an emotionally mature Aphrodite will also help our shadow Ares to mature. For when Aphrodite develops self love by learning to fill her own cup he doesn't need to act out his frustration through aggressive & self-centered childish behavior.

Similarly, when our inner Aphrodite is in shadow, we often try to gain external love by being superhuman since Ares is the quintessential superhero. We might try to be a super partner / athlete / parent /wage earner or rock star to impress the opposite sex or our partner & then be quick to anger if our efforts to be superhuman aren't acknowledged or appreciated. If we regularly make time to do that which gives us joy & pleases our inner child we unconsciously don't feel the need to win our affections by impressing someone else with our looks or abilities.

By also finding a regular outlet for our inner warrior to vent excess pent up frustrations we learn to harness our strength & move our energy so our inner Aphrodite doesn't slump from receptivity to passivity, which puts her in victim wanting to be rescued like a princess. Equally our inner Aphrodite needs to use her inspired creativity to generate fun & romance without waiting for someone else to surprise her. Likewise, Ares needs to take the initiative for creating opportunities to shine rather than living through others such as sports stars. N.B. If you find yourself in partnership with a destructive Ares who lashes out verbally or physically it's a wake up call that your shadow Aphrodite needs to enroll in a course of self love for unless we have an unhealed Aphrodite aspect we wouldn't even enter into a dance with a disempowered Ares.

Solar Plexus Chakra (Yellow)

Apollo, the Golden Hero & Athena, the Golden Heroine

This is the mental gate where we learn to balance being a team player with asserting our own ideas. For Apollo is great at doing whatever is needed competently for the good of the whole & Athena can shine as a leader, inspiring others & enlisting their support by providing them with clear guidelines & objectives.

To Recap...

Our inner **Apollo** needs to get out from his Father's shadow by finding out who he really is when he's not being what he thinks others want him to be. One of the ways to accelerate this process is to travel, especially on his own (not just with his private school brat pack) to cultures that are completely opposite to the one that shaped him & his values. If Apollo is not developed we will tend to settle for the safe career option rather than risk doing something we'd really like to do. This can be because we're so used to playing the role of obedient child that we have no idea of who we are or what we really want. By developing the inner counterpart Athena, we start to invest time trying new hobbies or studying something because we're genuinely interested in it rather than seeing it as a means to an end. When our inner Apollo takes the time to hone & develop his true talents & interests together they find the courage to follow their life purpose, even if it meets with disapproval from one's parents or society or if it takes longer to yield measurable results that could validate our choice to others.

If out inner **Athena** isn't developed we will be quite ambitious & competitive in our approach to work (& games) which will alienate peers, authority figures & potentially sabotage our opportunities for advancement. Travel is also helpful for one's inner Athena as it will arouse her awareness of the inequity of global resources & spark how she can rise to make a difference so her ambition can be channelled for a greater cause other than just her own achievement. Her ultimate lesson is to view her perceived failures as the necessary apprenticeship for long-term success.

Working Together

When our inner Apollo has found his true worth as a human being, which is not dependent on how well he performs & Athena has found a cause greater than proving she's just as smart as her Father, these aspects can then work together to create a vision that utilizes their skills to create a career that is deeply satisfying.

So when both of these aspects are functioning well, we are proud of who we are & what we do, regardless of whether others value it or not. This frees us up to never feel the need to earn anyone's approval or respect, whether that's socially, with family members or public recognition. This takes a huge weight of unconscious pressure off so we are able to truly enjoy what we do without the crippling expectation of perfection to try & win external validation. With both

Athena & Apollo traveling well, you will enjoy sharing your ideas & insights with others, expanding your mind with research & study, pitting your wits against another's in strategy games & relaxing with a good book. All in equal measure!

Heart Chakra (Green)

The Green Man & Demeter, the Earth Empress

The fourth gate is that of feeling. When our inner Demeter can acknowledge & accept what we are feeling, we can truly be with the self without seeking distraction. Our inner Green Man can then attend to fulfilling our authentic needs in order for us to grow unimpeded.

To Recap...

Demeter's greatest challenge is to individuate emotionally, mentally, physically & energetically from our Mother so we outgrow the tendency to be like a teenager rebelling against our parental conditioning by doing the opposite of what our Mum would do. Only when we activate the inner Mother by acknowledging the destructive effect our rebellious behavior has on us can we live our lives in a way that is personally sustainable by finding a balance between nurturing others & attending to our own needs.

Our inner **Green Man** has a similar challenge; to individuate from our Father's view of the world. He does this by cultivating his own relationship with nature; the cycles, seasons & cosmos so he can be a true custodian of Eden rather than a mere consumer of it. This leads us to make more conscious choices that promote a sustainable relationship with our environment.

Working Together

Just as in the old relationship paradigm where her domain was the house & his was the shed, when these two aspects are working in tandem you will spend time in both your house & garden to create a balance of harmony between the two. Similarly, if you have children you will find a balance between nurturing activities such as bedtime stories, cuddles, cooking together & crafts & more paternal activities such as teaching them entrepreneurial skills with a lemonade stall, self protection with jiu jitsu (using their opponent's force against them), building a tree swing, making a garden or going fishing. Our inner Father is also the aspect we draw upon to provide a much needed structure. These include providing & enforcing household chores, outlining expectations of behavior by setting clear guidelines & following through with consequences if boundaries are dishonored. Similarly, our inner Mother is the part of us that provides routines that sustain our needs such as baths, meals & shopping.

There will also be awareness in terms of what you are rebelling against in either your father or mother so you are not unconsciously projecting mother / father on to your partners, friends or family members. For example, if you run from the thought of having children (unconsciously fearing you would recreate your parent's behaviors or because your inner child is still unresolved & wounded so you feel overwhelmed at the thought of bearing such responsibility) then consider offering to take a friend or family member's child on a play date. Going to see an animated film at the movies is a great way to hang out with your own inner child which is very healing & equally empowering for your inner parent. (Please note: I am not inferring that those who consciously choose not to procreate are also running away from this possible outcome!)

Similarly, if even the temporary responsibility of a child is too uncomfortable to consider, start with minding or rearing an animal or even a pot plant! When we don't trust ourselves to foster the growth of another it's a pretty good mirror of how much we unconsciously want others to parent us, even if we pride ourselves on our independent spirit. (Which can be in itself a rebellion as if to say, 'Look, I don't need you Mum & Dad!) By allowing our heart to get close to another living thing & delighting in the small steps forward it takes as it grows & develops, you will also create deeper patience, acceptance & gratitude in your own small steps, rather than unconsciously judging yourself for making mistakes. If these heart chakra aspects are undeveloped we have usually been reared by a dominant rational ego who negated the relevance of a more heart centered perspective & approach, seeing it as lesser. Unfortunately, this leads us to then internalize the judgmental parent as our 'inner critic', making it difficult for us to grow into our potential as we expect instant perfection rather than incremental improvement.

When these aspects are anchored you will attract more family friendly events into your life, realizing that it takes a village to raise a child so you will value the opportunity to interact with people of all ages & derive a deep sense of connectedness through conscious community, such as regular shared dinners. You will also understand & revere each stage of growth as equally important: conception, gestation, birth, growth, harvest, decay & death - seeing each phase in every part of your life, from work projects, to the seasonal wheel so you can make respective allowances for each of these stages.

Throat Chakra (Blue)

Chiron, the Wounded Healer & Artemis, the Medicine Woman

This gate represents our etheric body, the subtle body that senses so it asks that we learn to honor & trust our sensitivity as a guide. Chiron invites us to acknowledge our wound & Artemis heals us by expressing our past pain & setting boundaries. Then Chiron can share what we have learnt to help others.

To Recap...

Chiron is the part of us that seeks higher understanding so we can make sense of our wound & how it has served us. When this aspect is unconscious we feel victimized & disempowered as we are self-conscious & ashamed of our deep vulnerability & afraid our weakness will be used against us, should we let it out to be seen.

Artemis is the inner aspect who senses the pain of others, especially animals so can work tirelessly as an advocate for those she feels don't have a voice. Whilst this is noble & necessary we need to ensure we don't use our causes to avoid dealing with our own pain. For when we release our past hurt we increase our personal power & our gifts as a healer. Similarly if we avoid spending time alone it is usually because we are fearful of confronting our past hurts & deep insecurities.

Working Together

When these aspects are healed & integrated we are comfortable with being alone so we don't need to find a partner out of neediness. Those who haven't spent time alone to really focus on their relationship with themselves, by attending to their past wounds & finding their own identity will slip back into co-dependency faster than you can say the word. this is because if we fail to understand & heal our past wounds, we inadvertently replay them & often stay in a wounding situation rather than face our fear of being alone. Alternatively, we may isolate ourself as a means of protection, surrogating our need for intimacy with pets or hoarding 'stuff'. The stronger our opinions & indignation about injustice, the stronger the indicator that we are operating more from our head than our heart to avoid feeling. This is a self protection mechanism which prevents us from healing. For when we armor up by distancing ourselves energetically we become increasingly unapproachable & unavailable to new love.

When these aspects are traveling well, we regularly sit in circle to journey deeper into emotional intimacy with the self & others, realizing it is a process of continual unfoldment rather than a goal to be reached & the greatest foundation for honoring partnerships. The other huge benefit for these archetypes through monthly sharing circles is the deepening of sisterhood / brotherhood friendships. Whether one is in a monogamous relationship or not, nothing feeds these aspects like the trust & support these connections offer. This helps us to feel stronger & more resilient to possible hurts, knowing we have a loving network around us.

When these aspects are empowered we develop friendships with the opposite sex which are not based upon anything else but true companionship. (For those in homo-erotic unions this obviously means having friendships with those of your own gender without any other agenda.) This further helps to heal our own gender issues & broadens the sphere from which we draw our need for emotional connection.

When these aspects are being expressed positively we also make regular time for one on one healing sessions which are needed to maintain our personal energetic well being. This includes being responsible for honoring the health of all parts of ourselves so we may seek out a variety of different healing modalities which address each of the seven bodies governed by the chakras. For instance:

Base chakra: chiropractic or osteopathic care, Core Energetics
Sacral chakra: Watsu water therapy, art therapy
Solar Plexus chakra: counseling, archetypal chart reading
Heart chakra: massage, rebirthing or Reiki
Throat chakra: acupuncture, sound therapy, TRE (trauma release exercises)
Third Eye chakra: hypnotherapy, divination, Matrix Energetics
Crown chakra: Tantric healing, Aura Soma, crystal healing

You will know if your inner Artemis & Chiron are functioning well as you will have a good balance between alone time & time with others & you will know what types of healing work best for you. If these aspects are particularly empowered, you will share your own gifts for mentoring or healing others by holding circles, giving healings or intuitive counsel, whether it is professionally or on a volunteer basis.

Those who have cleared this chakra will have a gift for communicating with & earning the trust of animals, the challenge is then whether you can apply the same gentleness to humans. Those who have these archetypes at the symbolic (conscious) level of awareness will have no problem sharing their truth & hearing the truth of others with mutual respect. They will be comfortable with others expressing their vulnerability, (so will not persuade them to 'snap out of it', ply them with substances or tell them they're no fun to be around.) They will treat other's vulnerability with deep respect, knowing that it takes courage to stay open & feel what is painful when one is feeling hurt. This gives one the ability to hold the space & truly be there, present & attentive when someone is experiencing their human frailty, knowing ultimately they don't need to fix them, they just need to provide a safe space for the hurt to be released. This gifts one great tools for partnership as one can truly listen & hold the other emotionally when needed.

Finally, when one has found their own truth & understood how their past woundings occurred they know the importance of setting appropriate boundaries as needed & have the courage to speak up on their own behalf to communicate & enforce them. This is critical as a foundation for intimate partnerships as this ensures one partner doesn't unconsciously dominate the other, verbally, energetically, emotionally, sexually & so forth.

Third Eye Chakra (Indigo)

Hermes, the Magician & Hecate, the Wise Mystic

This gate is the doorway to the inner realms beyond space & time. These inner aspects that govern this gate ask us to retreat from the everyday world to consider who we are in relation to the big picture. Hecate assists us to do this by alerting us to Higher Will through recurrent synchronicity, symbols & dream messages. When we have stopped to reflect upon the insight being offered by Great Mystery, Hermes then assists us in transforming our life to match our inner intent through conscious manifestation.

To Recap...

Hecate is the part of us that helps us to make sense of the unknowable, the unexplainable & the unthinkable. If we don't develop this part of our psyche, when we get exposed to the dark side of life, either directly (or even via the 6 o'clock news) we retract like a frightened child, fearing the chaos of the world. Alternatively, we unconsciously fragment mentally, shutting down the parts of our mind that haven't been able to integrate what we experienced, which is how unresolved trauma creates long-term mental illness.

Hermes on the other hand is the part of us that unconsciously seeks out experiences with the dark in order to develop his understanding of the psyche, which is why he is the patron God of criminals - as he recognizes & honors the value of journeying experientially to the Underworld to learn about the shadowy side of human nature as a way of exploring his own shadow. So if your inner Hermes is seeking out shadowy types for excitement but you aren't allowing your inner Hecate the time & access to esoteric tools to make sense of it, you're gonna end up with problems!

Working Together

For Hermes to mature he must seek out a wise mentor, one who he respects because they have been to the Underworld & returned to tell the tale as a way shower for others. Hecate is the inner wise mentor we access through dreams & our intuitive interpretation of the signs that affirm our highest choices. Until we develop this inner aspect an external guide is a great help. The more we develop our inner Hecate, the less we fear change as we come to accept the cyclic nature of life. (She is the inner wise woman who, in addition to her own experience has observed & reflected upon the choices of others so she can offer wise counsel for others during their life transitions.) So too, she assists our rational mind to let go

& surrender to Highest Wisdom as she trusts in the unknowable wisdom of the Divine Plan.

Hermes on the other hand is gifted at manifestation, using his third eye to consciously focus upon that which he chooses to create. When both of these aspects are developed he can focus on creating that which is aligned with Highest Will by setting an intention but still surrendering it's ultimate creation to a Higher Power so no harm is ever done. In empowering Hecate he becomes humble & wise, so he no longer uses his quick wits to wangle his way out of trouble or see what he can get away with. Equally he stops using his enchanting persona, sparkling wit, clever arguments & enticing gifts to deceive others into doing his bidding.

When both of these two aspects are mature, we mentor others through wise counsel, helping lost souls to navigate the dark recesses of their labyrinth mind. We also understand & respect that regular descents into our own depths of depression are part of the course in our own journey to become wise so we no longer fear them. We instead embrace them, which enables us to move through our periodical black moods more efficiently & gracefully, having developed the tools to climb back out of the well.

When these two are working as a team, we often move from doing to teaching, as having distilled our knowledge we recognize the value of all that we have to pass on & are confident to share it. This may manifest as a writing a blog or book or teaching classes at a community house or creating for ourselves a new professional role as a trainer. Hermes is inventive & imaginative so this means we can create our dream job by drawing upon our inner gifts & packaging them into a way that ensures we can worker smarter, not harder. This suits Hecate who having developed her extrasensory perceptions needs ample time away from the hurly burly of life to honor her increased sensitivity. Our inner Hermes loves the mental stimulation of others so his proficiency in the cyber world means our inner Hecate can have her solitude without Hermes being isolated from like-minded folk thanks to the internet & social media.

Both of these aspects specialize in different areas of the occult. Hermes is great with alchemy, sacred geometry, astrology & numerology & Hecate is gifted at herbalism, dream analysis, sacred ceremony & divination. When both of these aspects are developed, we are able to channel increased esoteric truths through a broad range of structures. This means we attract other wise men & women into our world who are humble & nonjudgmental, thanks to their own Underworld descents so they are stimulating company to exchange insights with.

Wisdom can only be reached through direct experience, which forges us in the fire of transmutation transforming us from a dense 3D being to a 5D lightbeing. When Hermes is immature, we seek knowledge as a badge of honor to impress but when he is balanced by Hecate who takes him down to the point of breaking, he matures into one who knows that death is the ultimate teacher so his arrogance dissolves as he accepts he can rationally never know the unknowable mind of Great Mystery. When these aspects are fully developed we value wisdom & look for a partner who has also suffered & made sense of their journey through the dark.

Tantra teacher, David Deida says there are three levels of relationship we typically journey through. The first stage relationship is focused on sex, the second stage relationship focuses on amassing resources (such as children & assets) & the third stage relationship focuses on self-actualization.

Source: 'Intimate Communion' by David Deida.

This makes perfect sense if you consider we explore physical & emotional intimacy primarily in our initial partnerships, reflecting our need to enact, understand & heal our dysfunctional stories in our base & sacral chakras. We then form partnerships through study or work & create a home & security to birth our creative & physical children as we revise the dysfunctional stories we have carried in our solar plexus & heart chakras. And finally, we seek out the companionship of one who truly understands our inner worlds as we form mature partnerships based on our exploration of the upper three chakras; the throat, third eye & crown.

I also like his summation as it echoes the final level of self mastery & maturity in the Tarot depicted by 'The World' card. This is the image of the 'Holy Hermaphrodite' who is the perfect marriage of Hermes, the God of Wisdom & Aphrodite, the Goddess of Love who together indicate wholeness & self mastery. Only when we have moved beyond our own arrogant & self serving ego, which is what the maturation of these two aspects, Hermes & Hecate embody, can we truly open our heart to love. This is why the twin serpents are shown meeting in the third eye chakra bowing humbly to their opposite. I see this as significant as the ultimate lesson of the masculine is right action & the ultimate lesson of the feminine is right intent. So whilst Hermes can move as fast as quicksilver (mercury) he will repeatedly manifest disaster through unconscious thought, word & deed if he hasn't learnt to balance himself by developing his counterpart, Hecate who provides him with the stillness to reflect. Similarly, these are the aspects that champion the liberation of the magical child so unless we can learn to genuinely love ourselves through every choice we make we will remain stuck in the Underworld, unable to manifest our intent as it will not be in alignment with Highest Will, which is love.

Crown Chakra (White)

Dionysus, the God of Ecstacy & Ishtar, the High Priestess

This is the gate to Galactic consciousness so these inner aspects ask us to be the embodiment of our true selves, as multi-dimensional star beings. Dionysus invites us to journey with him beyond the stars through plant allies that induce altered states of awareness that release us from reality as we knew it & Ishtar invites us to anchor that awareness into form through sacred practices.

To Recap...

When our inner **Dionysus** is immature we seek altered states through gluttony of hedonistic pleasures. In these altered states we then wreak havoc but have no memory of what we've done. When our inner **Ishtar** is immature we prostitute ourselves by valuing the material world over the spiritual world, which leads us to compromise our truth by doing activities which drain our energy for the short term gratification that they offer us. This refusal to let go & let God & trust the Divine plan blocks our crown chakra so we are completely closed off from receiving our highest guidance. This then makes us prone to seeking quick temporary highs which drain us rather than seeking out devotional practices which would raise our frequency naturally for extended periods of time.

Often, when this chakra is blocked we are unconsciously trying to 'be good' to live up to some moral code that has been instilled in us. This straightjacket of enforced behavior makes 'bad' rebellious behaviors seem very attractive as it is forbidden, offering us a sense of temporary freedom. This is most often seen in those who haven't psychologically individuated from their tribe of origin. For example, Catholic or Orthodox school girls who indulge in really risky behavior with their friends whilst continuing to play the role of 'pious girl' at home. (The film, 'Footloose' comes to mind with Lori Singer playing this double life as the preacher's daughter.)

This split within the psyche can cause many to seek out substances so they have an excuse for not taking responsibility for their actions. This alibi enables them to act out a 'bad girl/naughty boy' taboo side of their nature & then later blame it on their intoxicated state. Typically this results in teens & twenty-somethings getting drunk & having sex with strangers. This is because these inner aspects of Ishtar & Dionysus govern our portal to ecstasy. So those who haven't learnt other paths to directly access ecstatic states of oneness with the Divine on their own will unconsciously use substances & then ride other people as their escalators to Heaven. To avoid your kids indulging in this sexually reckless behavior which can lead to unwanted pregnancies, STD's, public humiliation & deep shame encourage them to self pleasure with the mastery of a Tantrika & explore other paths to ecstasy such as dance meditation, African drumming or boogie boarding as well as encouraging the safe exploration of mind altering herbs!

In the myth, Dionysius swung between desiring & destroying women as he unconsciously enacted his split feelings about his mother. So too, if we have not seen our Mother in ourselves & learnt to accept her traits as human, we swing between honoring & destroying our inner feminine. Our feminine is our emotional / spiritual soul self, so healing this perception of our mother is crucial if we are to not commit self abuse through our choices.

Working Together

When our inner Dionysus & Ishtar are empowered we accept all the colorful aspects of both our masculine & feminine self, making us dynamic to be around as our self expression is truly liberated (which liberates others to release their inhibitions when in our presence). This attracts equally vibrant people into our midst who have a light hearted approach to life because they have found their own authentic multi-faceted self expression & their own unique connection with the Divine. Having made our self actualization a priority, we are self aware & Zen in our outlook so see & accept everything in existence as an act of God, regardless of societal conventions or moralistic doctrines. When this pair are actively on board, sensual hedonism & devotional disciplines are experienced regularly & in equal measure so our life becomes truly sacred & blissful!

This pair of inner archetypes are the king & queen kundalini cobras of the Royal family, so when these aspects are awake & activated, sex is an act of communion with all of existence. This means we are easily swept into transcendent exulted states of rapture both on our own or with a partner. There is no expectation of sexual performance as our consciousness has expanded well beyond ego. Partnership is viewed as a path of mutual soul growth & as a pathway which accelerates consciousness. When these aspects are fully realized we are capable of truly interdependent unions as our first devotion is to Spirit, freeing us from needing another to fulfill our small selves agenda.

When these archetypes are conscious we choose partners who mutually raise our energy up rather than those who we need to teach or initiate which ultimately drains our energy & drags us down. This means we are quick to identify those who are vampiric in nature - those who will attempt to seduce us, (which is the form of mating dance sold to us as romance) by appealing to our base desires such as the glamours of flattery & intoxication. Should one override their intuition & enter into a dance with such a being if you later attempt to assert your will to spiral upwards in a bid to reclaim your personal power & autonomy, they will unconsciously undermine your emotional & psychological well being to keep you around for them to feed upon energetically. By contrast, those who uplift us do so by inspiring us to expand our vision of ourselves & our purpose, so our energy continues to spiral upwards unimpeded.

Becoming a 12 Chakra Cosmic Being

The Activation of our 12 Strand DNA

When we have awakened the twin serpents who climb the inner Trees of Life & Knowledge our lightbody can expand to hold more light. So when fully awakened we appear like a lit Christmas Tree! This is because there are more than the seven major chakras (or wheels of light) in our energy system. In fact, there are thousands of chakras throughout our lightbody, small star gates through which we perceive subtle information as sensations. So when we have plugged back into the energy grid of Gaia & the energy station of the central sun we have the wattage to power up to full throttle! Fortunately we are being supported through this energetic upgrade by the larger cosmic dance & the hundredth monkey phenomena* making it more possible than ever before to activate our twelve chakra system. (*The hundredth monkey refers to how a new learned behavior if adopted by a critical mass is instantly incorporated into the group mind of a species. It is based upon an unofficial study of macaque monkeys.)

Since the year 2000, we have been experiencing an emotional clearing of each of our major chakras to prepare for our internal re-wiring of our lightbodies for the shift into the photon belt on the 21.12.2012 (the Solstice). This has been necessary as beings who operate only out of their lower three chakras will not be able to integrate the intensified light frequencies of the photon particles upon entry into the increased radiance of the Photon Belt. Given the perfection of the Divine plan, our Sun is already in the Photon Belt so it is playing a vital role in activating us with more light via coronial flares & solar storms to assist in the transformation of our energetic bodies. Our misunderstanding of this phenomena due to a fear campaign propagated by the elite has lead many to fear global warming rather than see it as part of a natural cycle. (N.B. The ice caps on Mars have also been melting due to our entire solar system moving into the Photon Belt.)

This natural phenomena can be likened to how physical matter changes its form to liquid when additional heat is applied. For example, ice when heated melts to become water. When more heat is applied, it transforms again to become steam. So too, our lightbodies are being heated by the increased coronial flares & solar storms changing our eternal soul fire from orange to blue, the hottest flame known as plasma.* (This makes sense when you consider we come from the blue planet & brings to mind the images of Shiva, the God of fire who is blue, as well as all the blue beings currently surfacing in our pop culture; Avatar, Smurfs, Megamind.) Regardless of whether a blue tan is in our future the additional heat & light we are experiencing as we approach our full time entry into the Photon Belt is lightening us up in every way. We are eating less dense foods, indulging less in lower emotions & making less fear based choices. (Earth was said to enter into the Photon Belt during the Northern hemisphere's Autumn Equinox in 1987, an event celebrated as 'Harmonic Convergence' by hippies all over the planet in small sacred ceremonies. This 'Galactic

Day' lasted two weeks & then Earth continued her orbit out of the Photon Belt, casting us back into a 'Galactic Night.' She then returned each year for a subsequent 'Galactic Day' which each time was extended by a further two weeks either side of her initial entry date. The date: 21.12.2012 is when she will commence her 2000 year 'Galactic Day' bathed in the light frequency of the 'The Force' known as the Age of Light. This sequence of events is well documented in 'The Pleidian Agenda' by Mayan elder, Barbara Hand Clow.)

*On You Tube Drunvalo Mechizeldek recounts his inner journeys with the 'plasma beings' who currently reside within the Earth under Mexico & France who are surfacing at this time to offer insight into making this transition as they once did from dense matter to light during a previous shift. In his book, 'The Serpent of Light' he explains that the crown chakra of the Rainbow Serpent has moved from Tibet to Peru (which I've noted as an increased desire for Mexican food) but which also offers further insight into why Ecuador (situated next to Peru) was the country to offer refuge to truth teller, Julian Assange when the elite upped the stakes of their witch hunt. As always, it is darkest before the dawn so many have feared that life on our planet was ultimately doomed due to the destruction of our natural resources but fortunately, there is a much bigger picture which literally sheds light on a new way forward. For enlightenment is merely the illumination of a greater truth.

How Will That Affect Me?

So, each one of our twelve chakras corresponds to the activation of our twelve strand DNA. When our twelve strand

DNA are activated we will function as fifth dimensional cosmic beings rather than three dimensional human beings.

'Medical science has established that we have two strands of DNA and claimed the ten strands we don't seem to use are merely 'junk DNA'. They simply have not understood the purpose of that DNA so have dismissed it as 'junk'.' (Lucky we haven't had a garage sale!) **'Recent information has fortunately revealed its higher purpose; that being to support the emergence of our multidimensional consciousness, which is our natural state. Realigning, reconnecting and activating our ten strands of additional DNA is the process by which we attain that state. When we are multidimensional, our physic abilities are reawakened as we have developed a second neural network at the etheric level. This second neural network is what allows us to live in multiple dimensions at once. Then we can hear, see and communicate with others in these dimensions.'** Trey Abernathy http://www.in5d.com/12-strand-dna-photon-belt.html

As many have already documented in their writings about the generation of crystal children, some babies are now being born with twelve strand DNA which is why their more sensitive frequency often has such a severe reaction to the mercury poisoning they receive when exposed to the triple antigen shot for measles, mumps & rubella. This herd mentality vaccination results in a complete shut down of their subtle bodies & distorts their sensory perceptions (usually within 24 hrs of it being administered). The child is then diagnosed as being on the 'autism spectrum' & medicated further while the drug companies continue to avoid being held accountable for this global epidemic.

The 12 Chakras Which Activate the 12 Strand DNA

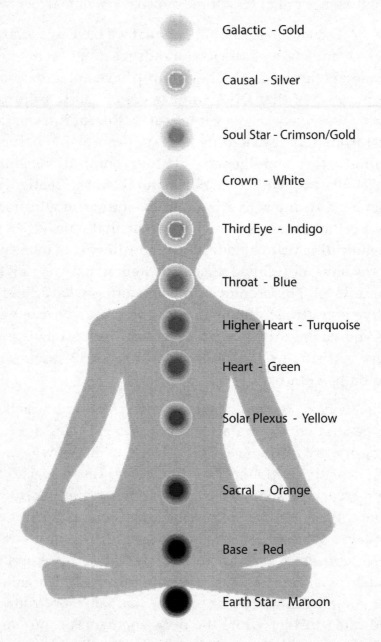

Galactic - Gold

Causal - Silver

Soul Star - Crimson/Gold

Crown - White

Third Eye - Indigo

Throat - Blue

Higher Heart - Turquoise

Heart - Green

Solar Plexus - Yellow

Sacral - Orange

Base - Red

Earth Star - Maroon

N.B. Many people have depicted the 12 chakra system & each varies considerably. I can only share it as I experience it but encourage you to attune to your own energy field (& your clients if you work as a healer) & work with what you perceive.

Earth Star Chakra   Colour: Maroon

Located about a foot beneath our physical body, this chakra connects us to the heart of Gaia, Mother Earth. The crystal, Serpentine is helpful in bringing the essence of the Rainbow Serpent up through her ley lines (energy meridians) & into our personal chakra system via our earth star. This helps us attune to our spiritual home, which is the land that most resonates with our soul. When we re-locate to this landscape we then connect with our monad, our soul family to establish conscious community living in harmony with Gaia & her natural cycles. I see this chakra as maroon. When this chakra is blocked we feel ungrounded & prone to mania such as workaholism. We can also have trouble committing to living in the one place. Reconnecting with this energy center helps us to feel one with the Earth. The crystal, Rosophia helps us to anchor our personal Magdalene codes within this chakra & the Earth.

Base Chakra   Colour: Red

The Base or Root chakra is the energy center of our primal energy. Located in the base of the spinal cord. Specifically in men, it can be found one finger's width up from the perineum (between the anus & scrotum) & in women, at the rear of the opening of the cervix, where the uterus & vagina meet. (That's why internal examinations feel so invasive...they're poking around in our primal fears!) Whilst most established schools of thought attribute the element of Earth to the base chakra I perceive it's ruling element as Volcanic Fire. For when we activate our Earth Star chakra we open a portal at the base to receive the fire from within the core of Gaia which is 'Shakti.' This 'Shaktipat' initiation activates the kundalini like molten lava spouting up a volcano (our central nervous system along the spine). I do still see the base as governing the physical body as by receiving her energetic life blood we then have the power to transform physically, just as this power literally can move mountains in Gaia's body! Like the ancient Chinese proverb, **'When sleeping women wake, mountains move!'**; The Base governs our ability to create what we want in the physical world, our physical body, our passion & base security issues. Stimulating this chakra heightens our sense of smell. Physically it promotes health of our colon, genitals & menstrual cycle. The masculine current of this energy spirals clockwise & the feminine current spirals anti-clockwise. When blocked: we don't trust nature, we focus on acquiring material possessions & fulfilling own desires. When open: We are down to earth, dynamic, practical, innovative & energized. In meditation it's visualized as a red lotus with 4 petals representing the 4 elements of creation. It governs the skin so eruptions in the form of rashes, boils, pimples indicate something has made our blood boil but in sitting on it emotionally it's coming out through our largest organ.

Sacral Chakra   Colour: Orange

Also known as the emotional centre, the sacral is located in the sacrum (along the spine), two inches below the navel. It's ruling element is water so by consciously connecting to this energy center we strengthen & empower our emotional well being. I see this energy center as the entry point for our inner child's connection to Luna, Grandmother Moon. The sacral governs our ability to love ourselves through increased self honoring choices. This creates more emotional balance & increases our receptivity to experience greater sensate awareness & pleasure. Stimulating this chakra heightens our sense of taste. Physically it also promotes reproductive health, healing of genetically inherited dysfunction & kidney & bladder function. Structurally it enhances strength in our lower back, pelvis & hips. When blocked: we are unstable emotionally, unable to express feelings leading to overwhelm & overindulgence. When open: We feel creative & sensual with a sense of spontaneity & fun, possessing the ability to see beauty in ourselves & others. In meditation it is visualized as an orange lotus with 6 petals. (So if you have a stiff lower back - do something fun!)

Solar Plexus Chakra   Color: Yellow

Located two inches above the navel it governs the lower mental plane (rational mind). I perceive it's ruling element as air since it governs thought so by consciously connecting to this energy centre we enhance our psychological well being. The suit of swords in the Tarot rules the mental plane & is symbolized by the element of air. (However ancient texts attribute the ruling element of the solar plexus as fire as it is known as the 'inner sun'). I see this energy center as the entry point for Grandfather Sun's personal connection to us which inspires us to reach for the inspired thoughts of the higher mind. The solar plexus governs our ability to know & value our self-worth so we can feel the confidence to assert our personal identity. As we learn to exercise our personal will we increase our courage & develop an optimistic mental attitude about ourselves, our abilities & our life. Stimulating this chakra heightens our sense of sight. Physically it promotes a healthy nervous system, liver, spleen, gallbladder & improved digestion. When blocked: We unconsciously seek to control & dominate in an effort to appease the constant doubts of the rational mind to feel secure. We can also seek out security by conforming to the status quo to receive approval from external authority figures if our own connection with the Heavenly Father (Grandfather Sun) is not experientially strong within us. (The Tree of Life Meditation is a good way to increase this connection. The link is in the next chapter.) When open: We can think clearly & are organized with a sense of purpose. We also have the confidence to take calculated risks & follow through a step-by-step plan to achieve our goals. In meditation it is visualized as a gold lotus with 10 petals.

Heart Chakra   Color: Green

Located behind the sternum in the center of the chest. It governs our feelings & sense of well being. I perceive the heart's ruling element as Earth (despite the traditional view attributing it the element of Air). This is however the external garden of Earth which has a different quality to the volcanic fire within the Earth which governs the Base or the deep energy of Middle Earth which governs the Earth Star chakras. This is the soft, lush green energy of Mother Nature so by consciously connecting to this energy center we enhance our growth by strengthening our sense of abundance & support. The heart governs our ability to be in the present moment & respond lovingly from our heart's truth. Stimulating this chakra heightens our sense of touch. Physically it promotes healthy circulation, as well as a healthy heart, chest & upper back. When blocked: what we give has an agenda - giving in the hope of getting something back. When blocked we do not give enough to the self so habitually negate our needs. When open: we give to others but not to the point of exhaustion so we maintain a sense of calm centeredness & patience. This enables us to speak & act from the heart. In meditation it is usually visualized as a green lotus with 12 petals. I see green in the center with pink as the outer rim of this energy center. I often see clients needing to find a balance between the pink & green frequencies of the heart. If one is attracted to wearing green clothes & crystals they are being supported by their soul to enhance their ability to give to the self (through self care & nurturing) which promotes self growth. When our needs are met this automatically extends outward as a pink unconditional love light to others. The crystal, Watermelon Tourmaline is helpful in addressing this balance between giving & receiving or alternatively you can carry aventurine (green) & rose quartz (pink) in each of your pockets or bra cups. This balance helps to promote the sustained growth of our Garden of Eden within.

Higher Heart Chakra   Color: Turquoise

Located between the heart & the throat, it's color is turquoise. It governs the highest frequency of love which is compassion, for self & others. Chrysocolla has been chosen by my clients in nearly every session for the past five years ever since this center was collectively activated. I see it as particularly important for women seeking to heal their shadow Aphrodite wounds which is why when one meditates upon this mermaid archetype they will often see turquoise (like her home, the ocean) instead of orange, the color of the sacral chakra which Aphrodite governs. When one has transcended the lower emotions, this Higher Heart chakra opens symbolizing that we have learnt to 'go with the flow' & swim in our emotions rather than drowning in the undertow of our past childhood pain. Primarily we open this center through compassion for the self which we can extend to all beings. This center feels like the new emotional center if the heart is the new 'base' chakra that we operate from in the new consciousness. When blocked: we judge ourselves for our lower emotions & desires. When open: we love ourselves completely & unconditionally seeing every aspect of our emotional journey as necessary. This leads us to live in a state of grace blessing every experience. I see this as the twin heart of the Higher Self which when activated emits the color ray of the blue flame (plasma) which acts as a beacon calling in one's twin flame to join & merge in the physical realm. This is why bluebirds have long been associated with true love.

Throat Chakra   Color: Blue

Located in the throat it governs communication. It's ruling element is ether which I experience as the connection point to Father Sky which gives us a sense of expansion & explains why so many boys love the color blue & why Artemis women retreat to the clear blue skies in the mountains until they learn to protect themselves. By consciously connecting to this energy center we enhance our etheric (energetic) well being. The throat governs our ability to speak up on our own behalf so our truth can set us free like a bird to fly. Stimulating this chakra heightens our sense of hearing. Physically it promotes healthy vocal chords, throat, lungs, thyroid, jaw & neck. When blocked: we feel fearful of being judged or shamed so feel unable to share our deepest truth & vulnerability with others. This results in physical ailments such as a tense jaw, sore throat or a persistent cough. Our psychic armoring makes it hard for others to approach us due to our aloof demeanor which is an unconscious way of keeping others at arm's length to protect our vulnerability. When open: we can attune to our inner voice so we can always sense when to speak & when to remain silent. This chakra also gives us the ability to express our sensitivity without shame. When clear we are very clairsentient (clear sensing) which makes us gifted as healers as we can sense where to place our hands, what to say or what notes to tone. When the Higher Heart is open the frequency of tone we emit through our Throat chakra can instantaneously clear etheric blocks in others & be a channel for Divine Truth. Our demeanor is both peaceful & compassionate, engendering trust from sensitive beings such as animals & young children. In meditation it is visualized as a blue lotus with 16 petals.

Third Eye Chakra   Color: Indigo

Located behind the forehead between the eyes. It's ruling element is space so I perceive this as our connection point to the black hole at the center of our Milky Way. This is the void of pure potential & all that is unmanifest so it's Sanskrit tone is 'Om' the vibration of this dimension. This is the place of death, surrender & stillness - the stage preceding birth. By consciously connecting to this energy centre we enhance our trust in the unknown. The Third Eye chakra governs our ability to see what is hidden - the underlying intentions of external circumstances. Stimulating this energy centre strengthens our subtle senses of clairvoyance (clear inner seeing), clairaudience (clear inner hearing) & intuition (inner knowing). Physically it promotes clear sinuses, healthy eyes & ears. (So when your ears or sinuses are blocked consider what messages you have been ignoring!) When blocked: we reject extrasensory perceptions which can't be physically substantiated by the five lower senses. Should we experience phenomena through our subtle senses we become fearful that we are going mad. Given that these subtle senses open with age to prepare us for our time of crossing over, there is often an unconscious fear of aging. If this center remains blocked in one's elder years, we become more prone to migraines & senility. When open: we trust our inner senses & act upon them, embracing the cycle of life with grace which enables us to trust ourselves to intuitively navigate using our inner guidance during times of chaos. In meditation it is visualized as an indigo lotus with 96 petals.

Crown Chakra   Color: Violet

Located at the top & center of the head it governs our connection to our Higher Self. It's ruling element is light which is the essence of the cosmic creation. This is the center where we experience the union of opposites so by connecting to this energy center we enhance our sense of interconnectedness with all things. The crown governs our ability to open to an expanded view of ourselves & life. It is our first experience of ourselves as multi-dimensional beings. Stimulating this energy center strengthens our ability to perceive other frequencies of Higher Intelligence like varying bandwidth on a radio. This enables us to serve as a scribe, channelling Divine truths from higher realms of existence. Physically it promotes healthy brain function. When blocked: we tend to swing between anxiety & depression as we feel separate & unable to imagine cosmic unity. This makes us susceptible to addictions to grasp a temporary sense of bliss & connectedness. When open: we live with a sense of unity, seeing the Divine in ourselves & others so we feel called to serve the collective 'World Soul' rather than our individual ego. This state of 'oneness' is maintained by incorporating devotional practices into daily life. In meditation it is visualized as a violet, white & gold lotus with 1000 petals.

Soul Star Chakra: **Color: Magenta / Gold**

This chakra is the seat of the God/dess head. I see it as magenta (deep crimson pink) with gold emanating around the outside like royal robes! This level of awareness is when we awaken to our own embodiment of the Divine essence & begin to honor ourselves accordingly. Opening this gateway often corresponds with a change of one's name to reflect their soul's identity rather than identifying with their ego. This resonance assists the recollection of one's soul gifts, which are the skills & abilities we have honed in alternate lifetimes. Opening this star gate gives one a special glow which attracts others seeking their true self. This means we must learn to be very discerning with how we use our energy so our personal energy field is not depleted or compromised. Maintaining a regular sacred energy practice is essential to energetically recharge as is spending regular amounts of time in sacred high vibrational spaces of intent. Selenite which anchors the light into the physical temple assists one at this gateway to anchor the Higher Self into one's body.

Causal Chakra: **Color: Silver**

I see this chakra as luminous silver which awakens our link to the celestial feminine. I also see the silver cord that connects us to our body when we astral travel like a celestial umbilical cord linking us to the Cosmic Mother. Connecting with this chakra enhances our ability to realize & utilize our spiritual abilities through the activation of the inner merkabah (6 pointed multi-dimensional star) so we may evolve past the limiting perception of linear time & space. This includes the awakening of phenomena such as teleportation, bi-location & instantaneous manifestation. The ascended master, Metatron channels this energy to those who call upon him for assistance in opening this gateway.

Galactic Chakra: **Color: Gold**

I see this chakra as brilliant gold, as it is the portal to the mind of God. It connects us with our universal consciousness, a state of 'oneness' with the all. It is the frequency of Source. It is beyond all rational description & is simply the frequency of 'I Am'.

12 Chakra Crystal Grid

As we are changing the molecular structure of our bodies from carbon based (dense matter) to crystalline (lightbeings), working with crystals - which are different emanations or healing rays of light crystallized into form assists our bodies in this transformation. Below are a list of crystals that support the opening of all 12 star gates. You can buy these as small tumble stones, (it is not a case of bigger is better.) You may wish to start by purchasing the ones you feel drawn to the most to stagger the cost as these are the ones your body knows it needs & then you can add the others later as required. You may wish to add one per month, as I recommend with the 7 chakra crystal grids I created for those activating their kundalini using my earlier book, 'The Inner Goddess Makeover' as their workbook. I recommend always starting with the Earth Star & Base chakra so you are grounded before adding the higher frequency crystals to avoid a kundalini emergence crises.

To Program The Grid

Place the healing stones up to your Third Eye & state telepathically your healing intention for the grid, (that being to clear & activate your 12 chakras, linking your 12 strand DNA to your Higher Self). N.B. My understanding is that the Pleiadians (the star beings from the 7 star constellation, the Pleides) are assisting us to clear our 7 star system within so the Sirians (the star beings from the constellation of Sirius can assist us with the configuring of our 12 strand DNA.) Regardless of how, who & when trust all is well, now & always & we are deeply loved & supported by those who resonate at higher frequencies.(Yes, we have some nice Galactic neighbors!)

To Activate The Grid

To create your own ascension grid, simply place 6 terminator (pointed) clear quartz crystals, (with their points facing inwards) in the formation of the 6 pointed star. The clear quartz crystals are generators of light which emit a laser of white light out of each point so when you place the 12 chakra crystals in the center, their healing properties will be amplified. (Clear quartz are literally the batteries that power our wireless radios & computers.) N.B. I always like to include smoky quartz terminators in my sacred geometric layout as they dispel negative (fear based energies) & ground the intention of the grid. In terms of location, I suggest placing them on a shelf or altar table in your bedroom to create a crystalline healing temple in which to sleep so your energetic transformation is as graceful as possible. Alternatively, if you want a grid that will support the energetics of your whole family, set the grid up in a more central area or simply ask that the grid encases your home & all who enter, creating a 5D temple space which anchors the Higher Self for all in accordance with free will & for the Highest Good of all. (This ensures if it's not appropriate their Higher Self can intervene so they don't blow a gasket.) Once you have laid the stones, I start by telepathically thanking the lightbeings (healing stones) for their service & then use my finger as a wand as I visualize the sacred geometric symbol of the 6 pointed star to connect the terminator quartz with white light, I then visualize this amping up the wattage of the central healing stones & as I send a beam of light out of my third eye to expand it from a 2D energetic diagram to a multi-dimensional crystalline temple of light which surrounds me & fills the room, containing all the colors of the stones contained within the grid. (I often see pillars of crystal in the place of the clear quartz.)

To Cleanse The Grid

Just like us, crystals absorb negative energies so they need to go to nature to discharge their toxicity & recharge their life force. Full moon is an ideal time to collect your stones & place them outside in the elements for at least 24 hours when the light of the moon is at her fullest as she reflects the light of the sun. Given this grid is intended to anchor sacred union within, having both the solar (masculine) & lunar (feminine) energies is ideal but if you've missed full moon get them out in any case no matter what time of the month it is.

12 Chakra Healing Crystals

I have tried to put a few options down for the crystals which may not be so readily available. Trust that what is available is exactly what you need. When selecting crystals, allow them to choose you - one may call out to you by making itself more magnetizing than the others around it. Please respect the service these lightbeings gift us by using them for the healing purpose for which they were intended. If you have crystals sitting around your home as mere decorations, gathering dust please return them to Gaia (Mother Earth) or gift them intuitively to someone who needs a particular stone for their healing journey.

Earth Star Chakra: Rainbow Magnetic Hematite, Magnetite (lodestone), Vanadinite, Smoky Herkimer Diamond, Serpentine, Rosophia

Base Chakra: Garnet, Ruby, Red Jaspar, Smoky Quartz

Sacral Chakra: Carnelian, Orange Fluorite

Solar Plexus Chakra: Tiger Eye, Citrine, Clear Quartz

Heart Chakra: Petalite, Aventurine, Rose Quartz

Higher Heart Chakra: Chysocolla, Aqua Aura

Throat Chakra: Kyanite, Aquamarine, Lapis Lazuli, Blue Lace Agate

Brow Chakra: Iolite, Moonstone, Amethyst

Crown Chakra: Charoite, Herkimer Diamond, Opal

Soul Star Chakra: Selenite

Causal Chakra: Phenacite

Stellar Gateway Chakra: Golden Calcite

☤ Celebrating the Holy Hermaphrodite

Practices to Create Yin / Yang Wholeness & Balance

It is one thing to grasp a concept mentally, but it is yet another to put it into practice as this is what really anchors our understanding into one of embodiment. Keeping that in mind, what follows in this chapter are practical processes to anchor sacred union within. This is done primarily by opening the seven major stargates so one's energy may flow freely promoting the full awakening of one's consciousness. These processes are collectively known as Kundalini Rising practices. N.B. The awakening of the 12 chakra system can only be done when the major 7 gates are clear & spinning evenly so these processes mainly focus on the 7 chakra system. Trust that when the 7 gates are open the full set of 12 will open automatically in one's sleep state which can be assisted by use of the previously mentioned crystal grid.

Kundalini Raising practices date back to the 5th Century BC as they are recorded in the Upanishads, Hindu's sacred scriptures practiced by Yogi's, (devotees of Yoga). Kundalini Yogic practices are a sacred science which remained hidden for thousands of years & were privately passed down via the oral tradition from teacher to student. Spiritual teachers from the East have disseminated these practices to Westerners who have visited their ashrams & now many Westerners teach these practices.

The Benefits of Kundalini Raising Practices

Raising one's kundalini through Yogic practices increases longevity of life, vitality, immunity, relaxes the nervous system & calms the rational mind. In addition, they create personal awareness, empowerment & promote health of inner organs as well as strengthening & generating suppleness of muscles.

Examples of kundalini raising practices include:

- dancing
- chanting
- mudras (hand positions that activate chi meridians)
- mantras (affirmations)
- asanas (yoga poses)
- yantras (creating mandalas for each of the chakras)

(For the Australians who remember the VB beer ad, 'You can get it chanting, you can get it dancing...matter of fact I think I've got it now.)

Why Kundalini Practices Are Relevant Today

As mentioned earlier, the resonance of our Earth (known as the Schumann Resonance) has been 7.8 Hz for thousands of years. Since 1980 it has risen to over 12 Hz. This means that 16 hours now equates to a 24 hr day. Yes! Time has literally sped up & there's scientific data to prove it, (for those who can't believe how fast Christmas arrives each year!) This phenomena is colloquially known as 'the Quickening'. This acceleration, coupled with technological advances have created an increased epidemic in nervous stress & mental exhaustion as we unconsciously expect ourselves to do more in less time, treating ourselves more like machines that human beings. Some of the reported symptoms of this change in frequency include:

- Mania / insomnia / interrupted sleeping patterns
- Loss of appetite / nausea / anxiety
- Electrical sensations (pins & needles) in the limbs, extremities & spinal column
- Muscular cramps (including more severe menstrual cramps) & stress pains
- Extreme tiredness, scattered thinking & restless energy

Kundalini practices assist the nervous system, energy body & rational mind to integrate these changes in the Earth's resonance, lessening these side effects. Yoga also releases the hormone melatonin from the pineal gland which helps maintain the sleep / wake cycle lessening insomnia symptoms. This also maintains the immune system & is an anti-aging & anti-cancer agent. N.B. These symptoms may be experienced more acutely during full moons, eclipses & the seasonal star gates (Solstices, Equinoxes & Cross-Quarter Vortexes) as this is when the energy shifts up a gear!

Raising Kundalini Safely

Whilst raising one's kundalini progressively up through the chakras enhances one's health & well being, there have also been many cases of people who have experienced an energetic healing crises because they raised their kundalini suddenly without sufficient grounding. This can occur through an ecstatic energetic experience such as devotional chanting, dancing or participating in the heightened energetic field of a sacred ceremony without being adequately grounded. So whilst it is customary to fast before entering into an altered state it is essential to eat afterwards. Ensuring yourself or your ceremony participants are not hung over or overtired is also good practice as is placing your third eye on the ground to send excess energies raised down into the Earth after any work between the worlds. The likelihood of a kundalini emergence episode occurring is considerably increased if one is a regular drug user, as recreational drugs are powerful in opening doorways of perception but if not managed properly under the guidance of an experienced shaman, can compromise the energetic integrity of one's subtle bodies. This makes one susceptible to erratic energetic states. Hence there are many studies which show links between drugs & mental illness, as severe swings energetically then create equally severe mood swings & mental instability. This is why the symptoms of a sudden kundalini emergence are identical to what is labelled a 'Bi polar psychotic episode' by Western health professionals.

Ultimately we are all essentially Bi polar, just as our bodies are a microcosm of the Earth & the stars, which all have a south pole & a north pole with magnetic forcefields that run between them. The more we are polarized, preferring to reside in the energy of one pole over another (such as head over heart, or Spirit over matter) the more chance we have of our energy swinging suddenly to the other extreme, like a see saw. For example, we may work late repeatedly as we are consistently fueled by the high of what we're achieving & then when our project, assignment or creation is complete collapse energetically & spiral emotionally into a depression. Growing up doing performing arts it was widely acknowledged that the second night performance was often flat following the high of opening night. Similarly after a season of a show ended one would often experience an emotional low.

Dealing with Kundalini Emergence

For those who witness a loved one in psychosis, due to an event which triggers their kundalini to spike without conscious integration this can be a very challenging time. It is vital that there is more than one person to take turns supporting & midwifing the person through their altered state as their energy is so intense that they will literally fry the nervous system of those around them by demanding their heightened attention 24/7! So time & space to center, rest & replenish the support team's energy levels is essential.

To assist one in stabilizing their kundalini, the first response is to ground them. This can be done by getting them to take their shoes off, lie on the ground, be in nature, eat root vegetables, meat, proteins & red foods such as kidney beans at regular intervals. Physical activity is great to get them back in their body as is massage, in particular foot massage.

The key is to avoid over stimulating them even further so herbal teas such as chamomile tea with honey is helpful to calm their overactive mind, especially before the lunar energies rise each night. Attune their bodies to the natural light cycle by using only candlelight after dusk & drawing the curtains to avoid the lunar energy of the moon arousing them further. Where possible, avoid the use of fluorescent lighting & stimulants such as TV, computers, sugar, artificial flavors & colors, chocolate & caffeine as these will continue to arouse & spike their energy. Some gentle yoga is also great for helping to regulate their sleep cycle.

For long-term drug users & those who have experienced trauma early in life there is a heightened chance of experiencing a kundalini emergence episode (psychosis) as the Earth's kundalini continues to rise. If you are exposed to such an episode, use your intuition to gauge how stable the person is & whether they are receptive to pro-actively taking steps to stabilize their own energy. Importante! If they persist in behaviors that generate the high of mania it is essential you exercise self-care & notify their family or mental health authorities as you cannot help someone if they are not helping themselves & their continued high will exhaust your own coping reserves. If they are actively participating in their own breakthrough rather than spiraling out of control which will lead to an inevitable breakdown then it is a great honor to midwife them through this process, viewing it as a shamanic vision quest. Unfortunately, because of our societal lack of understanding of our energy system we are taught to fear such emergence symptoms by locking people up & medicating them as a first response rather than viewing these energetic shifts as an opportunity for a psychological death & expansion of consciousness. Which is how these events were once viewed & honored in indigenous cultures.

Whilst our personal kundalini is being raised by the rising of the Earth's kundalini, it is helpful to use crystals & vibrational essences in conjunction with Yogic chakra practices so this process is as graceful & well integrated as possible. Similarly, just as electricity is dangerous if it's not grounded, so too are we if our personal electrical current, our kundalini is erratic, swinging between ecstatic joy, delusional paranoia or rage which happens if our energy spikes without us remaining grounded.

N.B. How unearthed we are as a society is a subject of a recent book, 'Earthing' which highlights all the modern health epidemics which can be attributed to the fact that we carry unnecessary inflammation in the body as we insulate ourselves with rubber soled shoes which interrupts our kidney chi (our major immune meridian) accessing the Earth. The authors, Clinton Ober, Stephen T Sinatra & martin Zucker recommend standing barefoot on damp ground to strengthen one's Earth connection for ten minutes each day.

For more info visit: http://www.earthinginstitute.net/

So during this amplification of our wattage I recommend eating, exercising & sleeping regularly to create a stable physical foundation, indulging salt cravings (the alchemical element of earth) & drinking adequate water. In addition, taking the mineral, magnesium as a supplement will assist your energetic body to assimilate the frequency shifts & the physical body in lessening the emergence symptoms listed earlier. Magnesium also strengthens the nervous system against electro-magnetic field pollution (EMF's) which are generated by all of our electrical devices as well as the manmade sound waves generated by the multi-national project known as HAARP. HAARP is a sinister project which consists of antenna farms in numerous locations around the globe emitting sound waves which disrupt weather patterns & cloud formation. These experiments have resulted in countless birds dropping dead out of the sky, as their inner guidance is compromised. They then encounter an energetic wall of sound flying at full speed & fall to their deaths. On Nov 6, 2010 I saw this phenomena with my own eyes as my daughter & I visited a back beach on the Mornington Peninsula in Victoria (Australia). It was an eerie sight as we saw hundreds of dead birds all over the beach. Whilst I had heard of HAARP & seen footage & articles about it on the Internet I didn't put the two together. Then in 2011 I went to see a woman by the name of 'Little Grandmother' speak & she spoke briefly about the HAARP project & asked the audience how many had seen dead birds en masse. Close to a hundred people raised their hands! It is claimed that this project is targeted at high density areas in a futile attempt to keep the masses in an unconscious consumer sleep state.

Sacred Practices

1. Meditation

There are two types of meditation; ergotropic (active) & subatropic (passive). Active meditation involves expressing all of the noise, thoughts, pent up emotions within through free form movement, sound & breath to clear energetic blocks in one's channel. By expressing all that you've stored in your tube you climb the 'Stairway to Heaven' & feel blissfully ecstatic & one with the Divine. This method is often favored by women as it activates the Shakti, (the Sacred Feminine energy) actively up one's spine by first clearing unexpressed emotions which rule the feminine.

Passive meditation involves becoming receptive by becoming still physically, emotionally & mentally so you can become focused as pure consciousness which is the essence of Shiva, (the Sacred Masculine). This is why this method is preferred by masculine based philosophies such as Buddhism as it assists in stilling the mind which rules the masculine. (This is why men like to zone into a TV whereas women prefer to go to a class.)

Religion has been polarized for a long time with people swearing an allegiance to the group mind of a particular philosophy (Eastern or Western) & adopting it as part of their personal identity. Personally, when I conduct sacred ceremony I like to include both polarities with a yin (ergotropic) meditation such as chanting, dancing or breath work with a yang (subatropic) meditation to provide a balance of polarities. So, below I have provided processes in these two categories. N.B. Recorded copies of these meditations are available as MP3 downloads on my website: www.starofishtar.com Teachers are welcome to use these meditation scripts in their classes but please respect the copyright of this work by not recording them.

Subatropic Meditations

Tree of Knowledge Merkabah Activation.

Aim: To ground & access additional energy from both Mother Earth (below) & Father Sun (above) & balance all polarities within.

Best Time to Practice: Daily as a morning meditation.

Author's Note: As explained by an aboriginal elder Bilawarra Lee at a recent Goddess Conference here in Australia, elders would sneak up behind the children & attempt to push them over from behind to see whether they had done their grounding exercise to connect them to the Mother. If they fell over they would know that they hadn't & send them off to ground their energy. As a mother, I do this for my daughter when I notice she is scattered & tired & starting to bump into things! The Tree Meditation is in many traditions & connects us energetically to both polarities of Mother Earth & Father Sun, helping us to balance right / left brain functioning by balancing our yin (feminine) & yang (masculine) polarities.

Meditation

Find somewhere comfortable to sit where you won't be disturbed. Make sure your spine is straight so the chi (energy) can flow freely up your spinal cord. Close your eyes & allow the tip of your tongue (which connects to your heart) to rest just behind your upper teeth on your hard palette.

Take your awareness down to the base of your spine & sense or visualize energetic roots emerging & going all the way down to the center of the Earth.

(N.B. If you are particularly ungrounded visualize a skirt of roots & if feeling vulnerable or assisting someone through trauma get them to stay in the center of the Earth feeling held within the Mother.)

When you're ready, breathe up red revitalizing energy from the heart of Gaia - see it spiraling up your spine opening up your crown as energetic branches emerge & extend up to the Sun.

(N.B. If you've been feeling dark mentally or depressed, stay in this golden light of Source a while.)

When you're ready bring this golden light down through your crown & feel both energies of the Divine Mother & Father meeting in the center. This activates the 6 pointed star as a multi-dimensional temple of crystalline light in your heart center which refracts rainbow light through all your bodies & balances all of your polarities: spirit & matter, light & shadow, feminine & masculine.

Rainbow Serpent Activation

Aim: This meditation brings the Shakti (Divine Feminine) energy up through the 7 major chakras, to cleanse & balance these energy centers.

Best Time to Practice: Monthly at new moon to cleanse the whole energy field. May do more often as needed.

Authors Note: This meditation is for both men & women to awaken & strengthen the Divine Feminine essence within. It is also great for practitioners & facilitators to do before holding sacred space or ceremony.

Meditation

Close your eyes & sense or visualize energetic roots going down into the crystalline matrix of Gaia's womb. They spiral in the vortex of her power, in deep reverence for the creatrix that is our Divine Mother. Now take a deep inhalation & receive up through your roots, into your soul star chakra a foot beneath you the holographic Rainbow Serpent. As her energy enters into your Soul Star, she turns maroon & spirals clockwise opening this energy gate, activating your connection with the inner light of the Great Mother so you feel energetically held by this umbilical cord to her loving support as her Divine child.

Now allow the energy of the Serpent of Light to rise up into the base chakra (at the base of the spine) as it transforms into red light & spirals anti-clockwise, opening, clearing & recalibrating the base chakra so it shines as a sphere of brilliant red light. When you're ready, allow the energy to rise up into the sacral chakra located in the belly as the serpent changes to orange & spirals clockwise, opening, cleansing & recalibrating the sacral chakra so it shines brightly as a sphere of orange light. When you're ready allow the energy to rise again into the solar plexus chakra located between the belly & the heart - as the serpent now changes to yellow light it begins spiralling anti-clockwise, opening, cleansing & recalibrating the solar plexus so it glows as a brilliant yellow sphere of light. When you're ready, allow the energy to rise again into the heart chakra as the serpent changes to emerald green light & spirals clockwise, opening, cleansing & recalibrating the heart center so it emanates a magnificent bright green light from a central sphere. The energy now rises up into the throat as the serpent changes to electric blue & spiral to open, cleanse & recalibrate the throat center so blue light shines brightly in the throat. The energy continues to rise now into the third eye just between your brows as the serpent changes to a deep bluish purple, opening the third eye, cleansing the third eye & recalibrating the third eye so this sphere emits a ray of indigo light. The energy now rises up into the crown chakra as it changes to refract all the colors of the rainbow as if it's scales were diamonds refracting light as she moves into the crown, opening this star gate, awakening the

crystalline matrix of your soul as it moves up to the Soul Star &
activates your halo of stars that anchor your Soul Self within your
physical temple. As you look down you see all of your spheres of light
glowing brightly, each the same size illuminating thousands of small
chakras all over your lightbody so you emanate the light of your true
Divine essence.

Lightning Bolt Activation

Aim: This meditation brings 'the Force' (Divine Masculine)
energy down through the Sephirot in the three pillars of the
Kabbalistic Tree, to cleanse & balance these energy centers.

Best Time to Practice: Monthly, when the sun moves into a new
sign.

Authors Note: This meditation is for both men & women to
awaken & strengthen the Divine Masculine essence within. It is
also great for those seeking new ideas, insight, creative
inspiration or innovative visions to illuminate their soul's
purpose.

Meditation

Close your eyes & visualize branches emanating from the top of
your head all the way up to the temple of the Great Central Sun.
Feel the filaments of light at the top of your branches enter into the
warmth of Father Sun & bask in the rapture of his unending love.
Now feel a ray of his golden light entering in through your Soul
Star chakra, one foot above your head, bringing new awareness
down through your crown. Clearing the neural pathways of your
mind with golden light.

This golden ray of light moves down through the crown & into the
left shoulder, across to the right shoulder, down into your left
waist, across to your right waist, down into your left hip, across to

your right hip then into your belly & down through your genitals & into the Earth Star chakra a foot beneath you & all the way down to the center of the Earth. Now sit silently & notice any inspired thoughts, ideas or revelations.

Twin Serpent Meditation.

Aim: Activates Ida & Pingala, the yin & yang energy meridians, promoting health, vitality & wholeness by marrying the God & Goddess at each gate.

Best Time to Practice: Great to do monthly at Full Moon.

Author's Note: Helpful when letting go of a lover to heal feelings of separation.

Meditation

Close your eyes & take your awareness into your Base chakra. See or sense a beautiful red lotus of light unfurling to reveal a central red jewel. Spiraling around this jewel are two serpents. One glows red, one glows white with a bluish hue. The white serpent spirals anti-clockwise & the red serpent spirals clockwise opening up this vortex to reveal the energies of Pan, the Wild Man & Lilith, the Wild Woman naked in an erotic embrace.

Your awareness moves up into the sacral chakra where you see or sense a lotus of orange light unfurling to reveal a central orange jewel. The serpents spiral upwards into this lotus, alternating directions so the white serpent, Ida is spiraling clockwise & the red serpent, Pingala is spiraling anti-clockwise opening up this vortex to reveal the energies of Ares, the Warrior & Aphrodite, the Beautiful Muse playing & laughing together in the ocean.

Your awareness moves up into the solar plexus chakra where you see or sense a lotus of yellow light unfurling to reveal a central yellow jewel. The serpents spiral upwards into this yellow lotus, alternating directions so the white serpent is spiraling anti-clockwise & the red serpent is spiraling clockwise opening up this vortex to reveal the energies of Apollo, the Statesman & Athena, the Golden Heroine shaking hands & nodding heads in agreeance as they look each other in the eyes.

Your awareness moves up into the heart chakra where you see or sense a lotus of green light unfurling to reveal a central green jewel. The serpents spiral upwards into this lotus, alternating directions so the white serpent, Ida is spiraling clockwise & the red serpent, Pingala is spiraling anti-clockwise opening up this vortex to reveal the energies of The Green Man & Demeter, the Earth Empress hugging each other in a heart filled embrace in their garden.

Your awareness moves up into the throat chakra where you see or sense a lotus of blue light unfurling to reveal a central blue jewel. The serpents spiral upwards into this blue lotus, alternating directions so the white serpent is spiraling anti-clockwise & the red serpent is spiraling clockwise opening up this vortex to reveal the energies of Chiron, the Spiritual Teacher & Artemis, the Medicine Woman who are toning together in a forest.

Your awareness moves up into the third eye chakra where you see or sense a lotus of indigo light unfurling to reveal a central indigo jewel. The serpents spiral upwards into this lotus, alternating directions so the white serpent, Ida is spiraling clockwise & the red serpent, Pingala is spiraling anti-clockwise opening up this vortex to reveal the energies of Hermes, the Wise Sage & Hecate, the Wise Mystic who are doing sacred ceremony together in a cave deep within.

Your awareness moves up into the crown chakra where you see or sense a lotus of white light unfurling to reveal a central clear diamond. The serpents spiral upwards into this diamond lotus, alternating directions so the white serpent is spiraling anti-

clockwise & the red serpent is spiraling clockwise opening up this vortex to reveal the energies of Dionysus, the Zen Master & Ishtar, the High Priestess who are spiraling up out of the crown as beings of starlight entwining in ecstatic rapture as they soar higher & higher into the heavens as the Holy Couple. They transform into holographic serpents of light spiraling all the way back into your physical temple, illuminating all 7 Divine Couples embracing at the 7 gates.

When you're ready take 3 deep breaths & sense all your inner archetypes within the 7 temples of light with the infinity sign running electric light in all the colors of the rainbow balancing the polarities at each of the 7 gates.

Ergotropic Meditations

Active Chakra Meditations

There are many different forms of dance meditation which can be done either in the privacy of your own home with a CD or MP3 download or at a public event which is held by a facilitator. (For a further understanding of dance meditation check out the film, 'Dances of Ecstasy' by Michelle Mahrer.)

Dance meditation works on the premise that if we attune to the innate wisdom of our body & allow it to intuitively move to music that evokes different emotional states without seeking to control our body with rational thought then it will instinctively free itself of energetic blocks. Energy's natural state is to be in a constant state of movement. This is why babies express themselves freely, moving from one emotional state to another without judgement, without getting caught up in creating beliefs or stories about their emotions. This way of being is Zen, completely in the moment, accepting what is & trusting it will pass.

When we don't allow ourselves to express our emotions freely for fear of judgement from self or others, this 'e-motion' (energy in motion) is literally swallowed back down, becoming trapped in the body. In fact, often our habitual postures enable us to unconsciously store suppressed uncomfortable feelings in favored parts of the body. If left long enough without being freed, they will eventually cause chronic physical dis-ease in our bodies alerting us to focus on healing that part of our bodies to free them of the pain they have been holding.

So whether you put together your own playlist to shake, moan, boogie, leap & scream to at home or access one of the recommended suggestions below, dancing is a great way to free yourself of old emotional pain which inhibits open-hearted being & relating with others. Below are a list of recommended Dance Meditation CD's / MP3's, most of which are available on itunes:

- Dynamic Meditation, Kundalini Meditation, Chakra Sounds & Chakra Breathing by Osho
- 5 Rhythms by Gabrielle Roth
- Chakra Dance Natalie Southgate & Douglas Channing
- Chakra Trancen-dance by Antara Decker
- Kundalini Dance by Leyola Antara

Chakra Yantras

A Yantra is a mandala created to open the inner energetic stargates, (chakras). The word, 'Yantra' means 'instrument' as it is a practical tool used for this purpose like a visual recorder or flute. In the Tantric tradition one will often see wall hangings depicting a mandala for each of the 7 major chakras. Wearing these is also said to assist one in opening energetically but the act of drawing or crafting your own is even more powerful.

When I used to facilitate women through a 9 month journey to open their chakras by unveiling their inner Goddess archetypes, as homework each month they were asked to create a mandala for the chakra they were working with. (This practice is also recommended for those undertaking this journey in my book, 'The Inner Goddess Makeover'.) The range of mediums & artistry shared each month in our 'show & tell' segment were mind blowing. Some crafted them out of natural objects as huge wall hangings, others painted or drew them, others collected images to create collages, jewelry out of beads & felt, food mandalas & even arial shots of medicine wheel altars, creating powerful photographic mandalas. When I intuitively asked the women to complete this monthly 'Act of Beauty' to anchor the strengths of each archetype I had no idea this was in fact an ancient tradition dating back 2000 years. Then one of the women sponsored me to attend a Goddess exhibition where I was delighted to find Tantric Yantras on display which explained this ancient practice.

I later came to find even deeper reverence for this practice when one of my priestess graduates was diagnosed with cervical cancer & she shared how she had felt a strong inner calling to re-work her base & sacral Yantras that she had created during the course to clear blockages in those energy centers. When she had completed these Yantras she invited me to see them & they were so full of vitality & power. She passed a year later inspiring us all with a fully conscious crossing as all her energetic gates were open, allowing her soul to leave unimpeded through her crown.

Creating a mandala is about the journey, not the end result. It is one of the oldest forms of art therapy. I was fortunate enough to be midwifed through my 'Sacred Union' mandala by world renowned mandala artist, Karen Scott who emphasizes the importance of the transition phase to all her students before they commence collecting symbols & colors they feel drawn to include. She explains it is inevitable one encounters a stage of frustration, self criticism, overwhelm or defeat as you confront your inner blocks but as you resolve your mandala, so too your inner blocks shift & heal. For more info about Karen's work visit: www.mandalamagic.com.au (Pictured below is my mandala.)

Another wonderful tool I have encountered is a DVD called 'Chakra Vidra' which offers teachings on the 7 major chakras but then invites viewers to focus upon the Sanskrit mandala for each chakra on screen & then close their eyes to visualize a mandala at the location of each of the 7 major chakras which they then draw.

For fans of sacred geometry I recommend checking out the multi-dimensional mandalas created by the Dutch artist, Janosh. He has created a set of oracle cards called, 'Keys of the Arcturians' which offer not just a divinatory meaning but an energetic activation. By holding the selected card 20 cm from one's face & allowing your eyes to go out of focus whilst focusing on the central point of the mandala you receive a kundalini kriya (energetic surge) which assists in opening a particular stargate. (Many of his mandalas are also crop circle images, keys gifted to us by our galactic friends to assist us in our awakening.) In addition, he has teamed up with an animator & composer to create a kaleidoscopic video where each mandala transforms into the next, creating a healing symphony of light, colour & sound. Inspiring to see a video clip that raises consciousness when so much money is poured into pop music videos which embed deliberately dark images of Baphomet & the Rain Man showering money on to subservient female sex slaves, to anchor the worship of money & the denigration of the feminine. A deliberate attempt to undermine the rising feminine as an agent of change. For further info watch: http://www.youtube.com/watch?v=DikoLMfnEgE To find out more about Janosh's work visit: www.the-arcturians.com

Chakra Mudras & Sanskrit Toning

By placing our hands in certain positions we create energy circuits that amplify our energy. When we combine this by attuning our focus to a certain energy gate & tone the sound that opens that stargate we promote the flow of chi to that area which in turn creates health in the organs & muscles governed by that energy center. Doing the sequence of 7 mudras & Sanskrit toning is recommended before commencing yoga asanas (poses) or before devotional chanting. N.B. These are best done sitting crossed legged in lotus with a straight spine, if that isn't possible sit upright in a straight backed chair so the chi can flow freely up the spine.

Base Chakra: Open your hands, allowing the tips of your thumb & index finger to touch while focusing on the base chakra. to intensify the activation you may wish to contract your anus & perineum (the muscle between your anus & genitals) as you inhale. Tone the sound, 'Lam' (pronounced L-AH-M).

Sacral Chakra: Place your hands, palms up in your lap with the left hand underneath the right with the tips of your thumbs gently touching while focusing on the sacral chakra located in the belly. To intensify the activation you may wish to contract your anus & perineum (the muscle between your anus & genitals) as you inhale. Tone the sound, 'Vam' (pronounced V-AH-M).

Solar Plexus Chakra: Place your hands together, pointing outwards from your navel so the fingers are outstretched but touching at the tips the same finger of the opposite hand & cross your thumbs at the top. Focus on the solar plexus chakra. To intensify the activation you may wish to contract your anus & perineum (the muscle between your anus & genitals) as you inhale. Tone the sound, 'Ram' (pronounced R-AH-M).

Heart Chakra: Place your right hand pointing toward your heart so the thumb & index finger are touching & resting against your heart center. Place your left hand on your left knee. Focus on the heart chakra. To intensify the activation you may wish to contract your anus & perineum (the muscle between your anus & genitals) as you inhale. Tone the sound, 'Yam' (pronounced Y-AH-M).

Throat Chakra: Rest your hands on your lap, interlacing your fingers with your palms facing upwards with the thumbs raised so they form a circle with the tips of the thumbs touching. Focus on the throat chakra. To intensify the activation you may wish to contract your anus & perineum (the muscle between your anus & genitals) as you inhale. Tone the sound, 'Ham' (pronounced H-AH-M)

Third Eye Chakra: Place your hands opposite your heart with the middle fingers straightened & touching at the tips. The remaining three fingers bow to the corresponding fingers on the opposite hand so they touch at the knuckles. The thumbs are outstretched pointing toward you & joined at the tips. Focus on the third eye chakra. To intensify the activation you may wish to contract your anus & perineum (the muscle between your anus & genitals) as you inhale. Tone the sound, 'OM'

Crown Chakra: Place your hands across your stomach with the ring fingers straightened & touching at the tips. The remaining fingers cross, alternating with the corresponding fingers on the opposite hand, clasping each other. The left thumb rests underneath the right thumb. Focus on the crown chakra. To intensify the activation you may wish to contract your anus & perineum (the muscle between your anus & genitals) as you inhale. Tone the sound, 'AUM' To watch a demonstration of this visit: www.youtube.com/watch?v=Kyz59DO5Nss

N.B. In Kundalini Yoga instead of ending each tone with the sound 'Mm' they tone the sound, 'Ng'. This is said to embody the Divine whereas the sound, 'Mm' is the sound of the Divine unmanifest in form as in the tone, 'Om'. Experiment with both!

Chakra Mantras

Mantras are words of power which are affirmations of truth. I received these when I did an Osho 'Chakra Sounds' active meditation alone at home. After clearing each of my inner stargates these are the mantras that came through. You may wish to affirm them as a daily practice or when healing a specific chakra. Like a Yantra, you may find it healing to write one or all of these mantras on a T-shirt in fabric paint & wear it!

Opening The 7 Eyes of God: Chakra Mantras

When I came back down through from the crown to the base, ready to start the final cycle of 'Chakra Sounds', I spontaneously affirmed the following at each of the gates:

Crown: I opened the eye of God/dess & affirmed, **'I am One, I am the I AM'** & white light shone out of this gate.

Brow: I opened my third eye & received, **'I am Divine Wisdom'** as indigo light shone in through the back of this center & I affirmed, **'I am Divine Wisdom'** & indigo light shone out the front into the world,

Throat: I opened the blue eye of God/dess & received in through the back, **'I am Divine Truth'** & blue light shone out the front of the eye as I stated, **'I am Divine Truth'**

Heart: I opened the green eye of God/dess & received in through the back, **'I am Divine Love'** & green light shone out the front of the heart's eye as I proclaimed, **'I am Divine Love'.**

Solar Plexus: I opened the yellow eye of God/dess & received in through the back, **'I am Divine Will'** & yellow light shone out the front of the yellow eye as I spoke, **'I am Divine Will'.**

Sacral: I opened the orange eye of God/dess & received in through the back, **'I am Divine Joy'** & orange light emanated out the front as I spoke, **'I am Divine Joy'**

Base: I opened the red eye of God/dess & received in through the back, **'I am Divine Passion'** & red light emanated out the front as I declared, **'I am Divine Life'**.

N.B. For those of you who facilitate sacred ceremonies I recommend taking participants through the Twin Serpent meditation as an active dance meditation then having them stand still in the grounding position, (legs parallel, knees slack & arms down by each side) & taking them through these mantras. This is particularly powerful at each of the gates around the Wheel of Eight (Sabbats) of seasonal chakras.

Alternate Nostril Breathing

There are many combinations of alternate nostril breathing, though one of the simplest is to breathe three exhalations and inhalations from one nostril, and then three from the other. This is called one round of alternate nostril breathing. Three rounds is generally done to complete the practice. This is a great daily practice to balance the Ida & Pingala twin serpents. My yoga teacher, Alison introduced me to a beautiful way of doing this practice. As you breathe in through the left, visualize the energy moving from the base up the spine into the sinuses & into the third eye, then as you exhale visualize the energy moving down the right side from the third eye to the base. Then breathe in through the right, visualizing the energy traveling from the base to the third eye. Then exhale as you move the energy from the third eye down the left side into the base. You may want to try extending this down into the Earth & up into the Sun.

Yoga Asanas

As stated earlier, Yoga releases the hormone, melatonin from the pineal gland which helps to maintain the sleep-wake cycle, making it an ideal way to reduce insomnia. Yoga which means 'union' of mind, body, heart & soul & stimulates the correct functioning of our inner organs as well as strengthening & toning our outer muscles. Yoga helps to maintain a healthy immune system & is an anti-aging & anti-cancer agent as it awakens kundalini (life force).

N.B. I cannot include images of Yoga Asanas for the 7 major chakras without infringing copyright but recommend you look on You Tube or ask your Yoga teacher.

Sacred Tools

In addition to the practices mentioned, it is also helpful to further support your lightbody through this energetic transition from 2 strand DNA beings to 12 strand DNA beings with any of the following you feel intuitively drawn to.

Acupuncture: to open energetic meridians & clear blocks, optimizing health

Vibrational Essences: distilled during precise frequencies in accordance with lunar, solar, seasonal & planetary transits these energetic healing tinctures use crystals, shells & flowers to create an energetic attunement. N.B. I have created chakra crystal essences & a Sacred Union crystal, shell & flower essence, which combines numerological gateways, astrological transits, sacred geometry, Sanskrit toning, color therapy & affirmation. Avail at www.starofishtar.com

Crystals: Crystals are literally crystallized light which act as batteries, charging & amplifying anything & anyone within a 3 meter radius with their healing benefits.

Altar Making: 'As I create externally, so too I create internally' So consider creating an altar for each chakra, perhaps one a month as my 8 year old daughter suggested we do for each month of 2012 to activate the 12 chakras & celebrate with a community lunch! These are sacred circles in nature using natural objects such as crystals or on a designated table or shelf inside, incorporating images, candles, colored altar cloths, talismans & statues for each chakra. You may want to include a Jewish Menorah, a seven stick candelabra to honor the light in each of your 7 stargates with taper candles in the 7 color rays.

How to Self Pleasure Like a Hermaphrodite

Understanding The Pathways of Ecstasy

'Sacred sexuality is our most potent tool in our quest for enlightenment & the evolution of our species'

Tanishka

Some of you may read that & think to yourselves, 'when my glands are swollen & pulsating with blood I'm not able to think, let alone evolve.' So permit me to explain...

The Western world is under the greatest illusion of all. We think we are sexually liberated. We are not.

- We manicure our appearance, repressing all trace of our primal, wild erotic selves.

- We focus on sexual performance rather than on exchanging a deep connection.

- We seek to control the experience by 'making the other person come' to prove to ourselves 'how good we are in bed' rather than spontaneously dancing with our lover's lightbody, trusting our physical selves will follow.

- We try to perfect techniques which keep us in our mind rather than open & feeling with our hearts.

- We use battery operated toys which overstimulate & numb our subtle sensate responsiveness.

- We watch films that associate sex with violence.

- We watch people dishonor themselves & fake orgasms because we don't how to become multi-orgasmic on our own.

- We don't object to the bombardment of paedophilic images & products being sold & advertised*.

- It is commonplace for people to use another person's body to relieve their pent up stress through sex without honoring them as a whole being.

- We do not introduce our youth to the concept of sacred sexuality through educational programs & rite of passage initiations.

(Please support the campaign to eradicate pedophilia on Facebook http://stopchildpornonfacebook.com/)

Just because our culture is highly sexualized does not mean we are sexually empowered, aware or free. For the images we are sold as 'sexy' are manipulated. They are not authentic representations of human sexuality. The degree to which we are hung up culturally about our appearance provides a telling indication of how far away we are from truly understanding, honoring & exploring the full spectrum of our authentic sexual self expression.

The Yang (Masculine) Orgasm

Most people in our society think they know what an orgasm is. What they are referring to is the yang orgasm as it is the only one our society acknowledges. A yang orgasm is what we create through friction based sex, like rubbing two sticks together when we build the energy up & then it spouts out as a release. Depending on how far we raise the energy it will either spout out of our crowns as a showering of energy or we will simply experience an emission (ejaculation) which is not technically an orgasm. It is a spasm of tension releasing the built up energy but is not necessarily accompanied by ecstatic bliss. This is because ejaculation is controlled by the parasympathetic nervous system whereas orgasm is controlled by the sympathetic nervous system. An orgasm is the result of deepening our state of pleasure & opening to feel the waves of sensation sweeping through our body whereas an ejaculation is the result of tension building up in the body which is then released in a series of jerking movements, along with a bodily secretion. Men & women can ejaculate without climaxing & both can climax without ejaculating. There are also many ways to experience a yang orgasm. (Listed later in this chapter.)

The Yin (Feminine) Orgasm

The yin orgasm is the opposite to the yang orgasm. Where the yang orgasm is a raising of inner fire & heat, the yin orgasm is the lowering of cooling energy. This is the state of being we enter into immediately after the yang orgasm is experienced. Unfortunately, many miss the window to enter into a yin orgasm as they mistakenly think the main event is over - so they collapse, dissolve into social space, roll over & go to sleep, disconnect energetically or go outside & have a cigarette! If however we stay in the moment & bring all of our presence into the subtle energies & sensations we are feeling we will move into a very deep, altered state. This is the yin orgasm. It is a sublime form of meditation. It is an opportunity to expand our consciousness & experience ourself as pure consciousness, the Buddha. The yin orgasm is when, after the frenetic raising of energy we enter into supreme stillness where everything is magnified. Kind of like scuba diving in a great deep abyss when the ocean floor beneath you falls away revealing a whole new wonderland of oceanic bliss to explore. Here's the real secret: the deeper we go here by prolonging this state which is done by staying with ourselves or even better with our lover if they are still 'with us' energetically on every level...the higher we will then soar together or alone when the energy completes its circle & starts to build again in the base. Just as the Tree of Life is often shown inside ever-expanding rings, each time we complete the circuit the circle gets bigger & our pleasure more sustained, both the height of the yang flight & the depth of the yin glide!

The Art of Self Pleasure

Self Pleasuring is viewed in our 3D culture as something pathetic you do out of desperation because you can't 'get laid'. (Proof that the teachings of The Magdalene weren't delivered at the pulpit on Sundays!) Just like a pilot, the more flying hours you put in here learning how to fly your starship the less dependent you are on others (either in person or in cyberspace) to get you off the ground. This is how one becomes a skilled & artful lover. By attuning to their own sensitivity - sensually, mentally, visually, energetically, aurally & orally. For the more you know how to generate pleasure through sensate arousal the more you will be able to open to deeper states of intimacy & pleasure with yourself which you will then be able to share with a lover.

Imagine my joy when 'Oprah' had a sex therapist give Middle America the recommended sex talk for girls & heard her primary focus was on encouraging our daughters to self pleasure! For it is an essential part of any teens empowerment (male or female) to know they have the power to gift themselves pleasure & not be dependent on anyone else to give them that arousal & joy. This equips our kids with their birthrite of sovereignty so they can make an informed choice to only lie with someone ONLY if they have earned the right to be their lover by demonstrating their character & values are honoring & compatible. What's more, if we become adept at exploring the many ways of experiencing deep pleasure when we are young as a natural part of growing up, inspired by exposure & training in the love arts such as erotic literature, art, burlesque cabaret, wine appreciation & culinary aphrodisiacs we are less likely to need battery operated stimuli such as vibrators when we are older to get out of our heads & into our bodies.

In addition, self pleasuring gifts us the following benefits:

- relaxation
- self awareness
- emotional release of pent up emotions
- increased health & vitality
- anti-aging raising of kundalini

Let it be said however that one should not focus on the genitals just as one would get bored with a lover who ignored the rest of our body! Initially, yes massaging the yoni or lingum is a great place to start just to unwind & bring awareness & blood into the most concentrated area of nerve endings. However, after the first orgasm do 'make love' to yourself by exploring & stimulating every bit of yourself as this literally turns more of you on so the release can be more rejuvenating for more of your body.

It is Not the Size of Your *** That Makes You Hot!**

When we are regularly gifting ourselves this kind of deep pleasure we fully inhabit our body which is what makes us attractive, regardless of our shape or features. Many of us will self pleasure long before puberty just as infants discover the nerve endings in their genitals offer pleasurable sensations when touched. There is even evidence of foetuses self pleasuring in utero! This is a natural sensate arousal & exploration which is our right to enjoy without anyone inferring it is dirty, suggestive, sexually provocative or wrong. N.B. The amulets of Ishtar show her with a big booty & my observance is that bottom heavy women often have a lot of base chakra (Lilith) energy whereas women with large breasts (naturally) often have a big helping of heart (Demeter energy). Equally men with large penises often have a good helping of Pan energy. I have been told that traditionally Tantrikas preferred lovers with more body mass as this assisted them to generate more energy in lovemaking. That said, the lightbody can be large even if the physical body isn't.

So Why Aren't We Encouraged To Do It?

Due to the repression of our natural sensuality & sexual self expression as a culture many parents find it confronting to see their children pleasuring themselves so will discourage them from doing it, which can create feelings of shame & embarrassment. Fortunately more parents today are affirming their children's right to explore their own bodies & experience pleasure whilst emphasizing the importance of honoring the appropriate time & place, such as only when they are alone in the privacy of their own bedroom or in the bath.

Beauty Comes From Within

Self Love is our inner Aphrodite's beauty secret. So this is what gives us an inner glow. In addition, when you gift yourself regular pleasure you will be less inclined to compare your appearance with others or be susceptible to the marketing campaign of cosmetic & fashion brands who trade on manufacturing insecurity to create a demand for their products & increase their profits.

Tantra For One

When embraced consciously as a path of deep communion with the self, self pleasuring is a meditative practice which expands one's experience of the inner world, which in turn increases one's sense of inner fulfillment & selfhood which then manifests as confidence in the outer world.

Self Pleasuring For Women

There are three main types of orgasm women experience. Ideally, women will explore all three on their own, opening their intimate flower layer by layer to become more transcendent & fulfilled with each subsequent journey within. This is what is meant by the term, a multi-orgasmic woman. A woman who can completely give in to the physical & energetic sensations she is experiencing within her body, enabling them to build into a magical mystery tour which is different every time she makes love - either to herself or with a partner.

Clitoral.

There are more nerve endings in the clitoris than anywhere else in our bodies so by rubbing the clitoris, known in Tantra as 'polishing the pearl' the sensation is so intense that it's easy to focus on nothing else but the feelings of arousal. This allows those feelings to build until one reaches a climactic point where the energy is raised & no more pleasure can be contained so we surrender to a brief state of complete ecstasy along with physical spasms as the muscles contract enabling us to collapse into a relaxed state. This type of orgasm is the quickest to bring about but also the quickest to end & the most shallow in terms of full body pleasure. It is the initial orgasm in lovemaking that gets us out of our head & into our bodies. Unfortunately many in the West stop at this point as they think that is all there is. To explore deeper states of pleasure, I recommend completely allowing this first wave to carry you into a meditative state after the first climax. Then when your energy starts to return, begin the next stage. N.B. If we overindulge the clitoris, (such as relying on battery operated toys) we increase the likelihood of only having shallow orgasms.

Vaginal

The second type of orgasm is when one begins to explore the lips or petals of the labia with one's fingers. This increases the amount of fluid produced, opening one's flower so the muscles relax & open & your vulva feels receptive to the gentle penetration of a soft, warm finger gently massaging with circular strokes inside the entrance to your temple. This awakens the body consciousness of the vulva, like a hungry mouth wanting to be fed a phallus on which to suck. Ideally one's finger is preferable to a synthetic dildo as it emits the life force out of the tip of the finger. What's more, if one is opening to feelings of self love, heart energy streams down from the heart chakra along the heart meridians down the arms automatically - which is something an object, (no matter how well it is crafted) will ever have. The waves of pleasure then build as one involuntarily begins increasing the speed &

intensity of the penetrations of one's finger inside. You may find that as you ride the waves of pleasure, you alternate between stimulating the clitoris & feeding the vulva's desire for pleasure, becoming increasingly wet. The focus must simply be on pleasure & not on 'coming' as this puts one back into the head, disassociating from the body which disconnects you from your trance state as the kundalini (surges of energy) awaken more forcefully through your senses. It is important not to feel rushed, as this deeper orgasm may take many peaks & troughs of intensity & relaxation before you surrender once again into complete loss of all bodily control. When this happens, again allow time to enter into a meditative state for as long as you feel before continuing on to the next stage.

Cervical

The third orgasm is the deepest as usually it is after you have been satiated sexually & so could easily just roll over & go to sleep, content, deeply relaxed & happy. But this is akin to missing out on dessert! This is when one's vulva begins to awaken again & crave deeper pleasure as the energy returns to the base chakra & begins once again to gather. (This is when a patient lover will know to really take & claim his woman by gently & patiently awakening her sensate pleasure by stroking & kissing her all over but especially her thighs, bottom, breasts & lips before introducing his phallus for the first time to her temple.) For women who are self pleasuring this is when I recommend visualizing a man doing exactly that (or a woman with a strap on if you are homo-erotic). Or you may wish to try invoking the presence of deities, such as Pan or Shiva to have energetic sex with at this point. (Having been a single mother for many years I came up with this recipe card in my self pleasuring file long before discovering it was an ancient practice for Tantrikas.) This is when you may want to have a dildo handy. Whilst physically, this orgasm is brought about through the deep penetration into the cervix, for me it is about the deepest of feelings it elicits emotionally for the lover I am fantasizing about. These are feelings that stir my soul's deepest passion & even grief if that is what needs to be released emotionally. Because it is the most internal this is the most profound (& often noisiest) release. it is therefore followed by a yin state so deep that you may feel unable to move, speak or open your eyes for a very long time afterwards as you enter into a state of complete Zen (communion with the all, devoid of any mental chatter.) For more info about the three states of orgasm I recommend reading, ' The Enlightened Sex Manual' by David Deida.

Self Pleasuring For Men

Exploring these three types of orgasm will assist men to become multi-orgasmic. When men focus on ejaculation, mistaking it for orgasm the opportunity for multiple-orgasms is missed. Because the male orgasm & ejaculation are usually experienced so closely together they are confused as being the one phenomena. However the orgasm starts just prior to ejaculating & then ends shortly afterwards. You may want to check out these links for more info:

http://www.whitelotuseast.com/MultipleOrgasm.htm

http://tantraecstasy.blogspot.com.au/2010/01/7-types-of-male-orgasm.html

Glans (Head) Orgasm

The nerve endings are most concentrated at the tip of the penis which provides intense sensations similar to those experienced in the female clitoris. The most sensitive part is the frenulum, the 'love heart' shaped line where the head joins the shaft on the underside of the penis. (N.B. It is also referred to as the crown or corona.) By encasing the head with one's warm, lubricated hand & stimulating by rhythmically rubbing this area the intensity builds until the pelvis involuntarily thrusts & a man reaches what is known as 'the point of no return'. This is when he can feel ejaculation is inevitable which shortly follows. If however, a man builds the fire of pleasure but stops stimulating regularly, visualizing the fire spreading into other parts of his body he can contain more pleasurable sensations within the totality of his being rather than only building the fire in his base chakra & blowing his stack physically. (If self pleasuring with a partner they can assist by using deliberate hand strokes to lovingly move the energy away from his genitals & down his legs, up his torso, down his arms etc.) N.B. The slower & more gentle one begins rubbing the frenulum the more sensitivity one can build. (So don't impatiently start beating yourself senseless or you'll plateau, get exhausted & no doubt frustrated as well!) Stimulating your own nipples with the other hand (which connects to the heart chakra) or placing the other hand on your heart is another way of connecting your base chakra sensations to your central feeling center which will engage your soul essence & lessen the chance of experiencing just a localized release. Another technique is to put your other hand behind your neck & massage your neck which directs the sexual energy up through the chakras. This can be assisted through intent & visualization. Clenching the pelvic floor (PC muscle) also assists one to halt the unconscious spurting of yang energy. In Sanskrit this action is known as 'mula banda'. It works by creating an energetic lock in the base chakra, preventing any more energy leaking out & directs the energy already generated in the base to flow up the central channel known as 'Sushumna'. Alternating between stimulus of the base chakra & holding & spreading the energy will produce micro orgasms & an orgasmic state. (For more info see below for definitions.)

The more one releases on sound the less chance of ejaculation as the energy is being released gently & evenly on moans, groans, grunts, exclamations, words & sighs so it doesn't build to the point of physically exploding out of you. This can be confronting since culturally men have been conditioned to be the strong, silent type like John Wayne (which some believe comes from self preservation as you can't make a lot of noise on a hunting expedition or you'll get eaten!) This is another reason why it's good to devote time to experimenting with conscious self pleasuring in private so you can be completely relaxed, undisturbed & unself-conscious. (So not a quick hand job in the shower before work!) For the more we anchor this quick ejaculatory release as an experience of male orgasm the more likely it will eventuate each time, whether we want it to or not. This is why it is preferable to honestly encourage your sons to take time pleasuring themselves rather than stealing away in their room trying to get it over with quickly for fear of being caught out as this leads to premature ejaculation & shallow orgasms.

Perineum Orgasm

The perineum is the patch of skin between the testicles & the anus. It is the muscular floor of the base chakra, which when stimulated through rubbing can create deeper & more intense orgasms than those experienced through rubbing the head. (This is why sitting on a bus can apply continued rhythmic pressure to this area, producing an erection.) One may wish to combine rubbing the head while stimulating this area to deepen the pleasure after building the waves of intensity several times through rubbing the top of the penis without ejaculating. It is nice to alternate the sensations so experiment by holding your testes (balls) with a warm hand while you continue to apply rhythmic strokes to your perineum & then ever so delicately, lightly fondle your balls while continuing to stroke. Don't be afraid to spontaneously alternate your position, flipping over on to your knees & rubbing your perineum from behind, this will also help to mobilize pockets of stuck energy rather than lying in the one position like a plank. Alternatively, don't be afraid to draw your knees up or splay your legs open for fear of being overly feminine. Receiving pleasure is not about performance or how you appear. Being receptive does mean experiencing yourself in the feminine polarity & this position allows for a seamless transition into the next, deeper stage of male orgasm. Again, during this phase when you find yourself nearing the point of no return, stop & breathe deeply releasing on moans & sighs to disperse the energy. Run your fingers through your hair & caress other parts of your body to awaken more subtle sensations which cause lighter energies to ripple through your body. These are kundalini kriyas which occur when your lightbody is electrified with voltage, allowing the spasms of pleasure to be felt all over the body & not just in the pelvis. These act as valves releasing just enough pressure to allow you to remain fully charged without blowing a fuse...Flash Gordon eat your heart out!

Prostate Orgasm

The prostate is located inside the wall of the rectum & is generally about the size of a walnut. It is also known as the male G-Spot. It can be touched by inserting a finger approximately three centimeters inside the anus & it feels spongy & warm to touch. Usually stimulating this area produces intense pleasure if the mind can relax & focus purely on the sensations being experienced within the body. Closing the eyes can help with this. However in some men, especially if they have been sexually abused or shamed this area can hold unexpressed emotional pain making it tender to touch. Alternatively it may produce a sensation of needing to urinate as a fear response from the kidneys. Breathing deeply & releasing on sighs while gently massaging this area will help to release trauma, the same as massaging the female G-spot. N.B. It is worth loving this area back to full vitality & freedom as stimulating this region will produce the most deep, vulnerable & intense orgasms a male can experience. (Personally I believe this stored shame & trauma held in sexually neglected prostates is what contributes to prostate cancer.)

The more one has 'turned on' their entire lightbody by cyclically building & holding pleasure within their whole being (including all their subtle bodies) the more mind blowing this final orgasm will be (& yes! you can ejaculate if you wish.) This process is the 'blow by blow' ('scuse the pun) description of a multi-orgasmic man. Again, social stigmatism about homosexuality can prevent men from exploring this pleasure zone both alone & with a partner but a true Love God will not limit his potential for pleasure because of such a fear based prejudice. (Obviously ensure your nails are cut short & your bowels empty. Some men like to flush their colon prior to lovemaking with a home enema kit so they can feel more relaxed about opening up to experiencing love & pleasure in their anus.) As always I recommend using one's finger as the warm fleshy digit emits love light from your heart out of the tip is far superior to a battery operated butt plug. That said, a butt plug can be initially very helpful in awakening the chi in this area & relaxing it. Just don't overindulge or you'll numb your sensitivity. The anus is a muscle that can contract just like the female cervix so one can feel seismic waves of energy involuntarily generated by this muscle causing a major release of energy akin to a tidal wave. Then allow yourself to dissolve into a yin orgasm as described above!

To Ejaculate or Not Ejaculate...That is the Question

Male Ejaculation

There is so much debate about this which seems to polarize a lot of men. So here's my take on it...yes, ejaculation does deplete one's life force, notably the chi from the kidneys. However, if one learns to become a multi orgasmic man by deepening his states of pleasure as outlined above so he builds an excess of chi in both his etheric & physical body I can see no harm with ejaculating. If, on the other hand a man only generates chi in his base chakra before habitually ejaculating then yes, he is going to compromise his longevity & vitality. This is a very personal decision which no man should make because he feels pressured by another either way. For the austere Yogis who view lack of ejaculation control as a personal failure this sense of shame is more toxic than any emission & to the base dominant men who don't feel they've had sex unless they ejaculate I suggest exploring other ways to affirm your masculinity so you don't send yourself into an early grave!

I, as you know am an advocate of 'The Golden Mean' so I recommend a combination of both paths. I also suggest sexually active men doing daily Qi Gong to build up their kidney chi as well as acupuncture & taking Ginseng. This supports the energetic body so it can maintain the health of the physical body. Ejaculation also reduces the likelihood of 'Blue Balls'. Blue Balls is a condition caused by a build up of seminary fluid in the prostate & testes. It is not experienced universally by all men & is relieved through ejaculation or applying coolness to a man's crutch. Hence the recommendation of a cold shower for men who feel sexually frustrated. When you consider that each testes produces nearly 150 million sperm every 24 hours (which lessens over time) one can understand why teenage boys are continually 'milking' their prostate or experiencing nocturnal emissions known as 'wet dreams' to drain the excess fluid. Symptoms include tenderness in the testes which can last between one to forty-eight hours & can sometimes be reduced by lying down. (For women who have breast fed this would be akin to the pain of milk engorged breasts & no baby to relieve them!)

'War is Over if You Want it' John Lennon

Ejaculation 'jump-starts' the sympathetic nervous system which governs the 'fight or flight' response. Whereas orgasm is governed by the parasympathetic nervous system which produces feelings of relaxation & bliss. So my theory is that the more men become multi-orgasmic the less they will unconsciously feel the need to assert their manhood by dominating nature (the feminine). This manifests in a myriad of ways such as the competitive pursuit of property, assets, resources & wealth, unsustainable industry practices & acts of war & violence against the feminine (in men as well as women.)

The personal pay-off is that men will live longer & their quality of life will be more relaxed & pleasurable. Perhaps I should get a bumper sticker made up, 'Give Peace a Chance,

Become Multi-Orgasmic!' Worth a try when you consider that men currently die on average seven years earlier than women in our ejaculation obsessed culture. Ultimately, sex that focuses on ejaculation as the goal is as Neanderthal as spilling your seed quickly with the unconscious intent to procreate before a saber tooth tiger comes along. If we are to evolve into beings governed by love rather than fear we will instead take our time & indulge all of our senses, both physical & subtle. So yes! We need to rethink our image of what's sexy. Rather than dominating men spurting their seed all over subservient women - men with their fingers in their anuses gurgling with delirium incapable of having a war based thought. My kinda sex symbol!

Female Ejaculation

There is so much misinformation about this that I am going to share with you a site that seems to offer the most accurate & comprehensive info about it:

'There are two types of female sexual fluids. The most commonly known is called leukorrhea and is what lubricates the vaginal walls. It is a thicker fluid and is slightly acidic in order to prevent infections. Female ejaculation is a thin fluid that originates in the Gspot and is pushed out the urethra (where your urine comes out). The Gspot is comprised of the Skenes / Paraurethral glands and is what makes this fluid.' http://www.holisticwisdom.com/services_female-ejaculation_what-is-it.htm

Just as with male ejaculation, female ejaculation is completely separate from an orgasm, although it can occur at the same time. Whilst the fluid is not fertile it does deplete one energetically with many women falling into a deep sleep shortly afterwards. Most women are capable of ejaculating (doctors assert that about 3% of women are physically incapable) but most don't as they are unaware of the cues to follow. Basically when the urethral sponge (female Gspot) is stimulated it fills with a salty fluid which can cause a woman to have the sensation like she needs to urinate. Most women contract the Kegel (pelvic floor or PC muscle) instinctually which prevents this from occurring. However by pressing down & forcing one's energy outward this fluid is then released out of the urethra. (Just like a man's ejaculation is released out through the urethra & neither are urine.) In terms of health, it is said to have a cleansing effect on the urethra as between 1.5-2 cups of fluid are generally released. Toys which feature a dual stimulus for the interior & exterior of the female G-spot are one of the most popular ways to generate them. I find it curious that just as men are discovering the feminine art of deep pleasure by focusing on becoming multi-orgasmic, women are discovering the masculine joy of physical release. The concept of female ejaculation can be as confronting for a woman to experiment with as a man lying on his back being penetrated in his anus. Trust & honoring is essential as we explore ourselves as Hermaphrodite beings.

Other Types of Orgasm

N.B. All of these examples are yang orgasms, except for the multi-orgasmic state. All of these can be followed by a yin orgasm simply by staying present.

Micro Orgasm - this is one of the smaller waves of energy one experiences as the sexual energy starts to build to a crescendo. Usually it is recognized by the tightening of one's pelvis & legs. Both men & women experience them. In fact one of my lovers had observed that if he kept his legs relaxed he could maintain his erection indefinitely without ejaculating but as soon as he allowed his legs to constrict he ejaculated soon afterwards. For women who question their ability to orgasm it is helpful to focus on these waves as energy flows where attention goes. So the more we can give over to each of these sensations the more we allow them to build until they completely take us over.

Energetic Orgasm - kriyas (electric spasms) up the spine or within a particular chakra occur when our body has become so charged with kundalini that it continues to spark without external stimuli. That said, if the lightbody of your lover or someone who lights you up walks into the room they can set you off with kriyas. I have had this occur even when I have been fast asleep & the strength of the kriya has woken me up.

Breath Orgasm - Any repetitive open mouthed breathing where our jaw is completely relaxed allows the energy to pulse in our genitals as the jaw corresponds to the base chakra. Building up the life force by inhaling deeply & fully & releasing on the sound 'Ah' will allow the rhythm to naturally increase until waves of energy overtake you in a loop. This is great to do with a partner, sitting opposite each other in lotus (crossed-legged.) A good tip for orgasmic birth! There is an example of this in the film, 'Sacred Sex' which was released in the early 1990's.

Sonic Orgasm - I have experienced this whenever I do a sound or movement meditation & end up involuntarily expressing sounds through a repetitive pulsing movement. For example: Osho's 'Chakra Sounds' meditation. I also remember witnessing in college a married couple who were music lecturers & whenever they played on stage in their quartet they would both become completely orgasmic in a totally unselfconscious way. (This was compounded by their merged energy fields, passionate pieces & the fact they were in a religion that forbade sex unless it was for procreation.)

Mantra Orgasm - Again, this is another form of non-touching orgasm that is popular amongst puritanical cults. This is the raising of energy through speaking in tongues or vocalizing one's praise to a Higher power repeatedly. Pagans have their own form of it which is to constantly recite an incantation invoking a Higher power as a pathway into an altered state charged with the cone of fire (breath). The Yogis use sacred invocations which are spoken or chanted to invoke a Higher power, again expanding the energy field & relaxing the mind so devotees become taken over by the energy of the intent & experience ecstatic fervor & joy. I recommend trying these as part of a group by attending an ashram or congregation as the group energy will amplify the energy being raised. If, however you do want to try alone at home or with a lover I recommend doing it in a body of water, such as a bath. This is because water is a conduit which will amplify your personal electric current. So too, awaken the senses by lighting candles, playing a background of rhythmic repetitive music & anoint your crown with spikenard oil to promote the simultaneous spinning of your chakras & consider setting up a crystal grid in the space with serpentine to support the rising of your kundalini. A sample mantra is, 'I am Divine.'

Anal Orgasm - the anal sphincter can contract just like the cervix & prostate so one can experience waves of intensifying energy building within the anus (whether male or female) which are really liberating given how much shame we can store in this part of the body due to societal conditioning. Because it governs the base stimulating the anus can produce the most primal, guttural & animalistic release.

Relaxation Orgasm - this is the kind of spontaneous release one has when they get into a thermal spring & they experience a rush of energy throughout their body that brings any unexpressed tensions to the surface to be instantaneously released, usually on a deep & vocal sigh from the bottom of one's being.

Emotional Orgasm - this is a spontaneous expression of tears being brought uncontrollably to the surface & then released. More common for women than men, especially after the birth of a child which opens the heart chakra so one is moved to tears more easily. Feels deeply cleansing & renewing rather than sad.

Smell Orgasm - consider if you will removing the cap on a bottle of 100% pure rose oil & the intoxicating scent sending you into a heady euphoria as it bewitches your nose, travel all the way up to your crown followed by waves of dissolving heat as the effect ripples down into every part of your body, before you jam your nose back into the stopper desperate for another hit. That's an orgasm recognized by your olfactory sense as it recognizes the vibration of pure love. Love is what brings us all undone, unraveling our demeanor & reducing us to one humbled by the presence of Divine truth.

'A human being has a frequency of 66mhz. When the frequency lowers, by pollution, depression, negativity, we enter the frequency ranges of illness and dis-ease. A Rose has a frequency of 320mhz, 5x more then a human. By adding a high frequency to a low frequency, the low frequency actually raises. It is said rose oil will begin repairing DNA within 21 minutes.' Young Living Oils

Taste Orgasm - it has long been a source of amusement amongst my friends that I murmur when I eat. For me food has always been a state of communion as it is for most babies when they are introduced to solid foods they like for the first time.

They completely become one with the substance like manna from Heaven. They revel in its texture, smear it through their hair, delight in the color & marvel at how many ways they can eat it. You will hear them gurgle, squeal, laugh & sigh spontaneously as they interact with their food. We then introduce them to the concept of table manners. This list of social rules they must adhere to or face painful consequences which takes them out of their bodies & into their heads, imposing a state of separation (or 3D Hell). We then have the audacity to take them to church & ask them to be silent, get down on their knees & take a tasteless wafer into their mouth & tell them 'That's Holy Communion'. Personally, I think the best way to enter into a state of 'Holy Communion' is to thank the Earth, elements, animals (if not Vegan) & everyone in the food chain by losing yourself so completely in reverence & appreciation that you allow yourself to fully express the waves of pleasure that wash over you with every mouthful. (Needless to say I have not been a good role model for table manners in our house, rolling around murmuring like a hippo in mud with my face so close to the plate the mandala of food blocks out all peripheral vision.) So whilst you may want to teach your kids 'appropriateness' so they know how to eat when meeting their partner's parents for the first time you may also consider having a regular finger food 'floor picnic' or 'food play' night to bring some of the joy back to your gastronomical communion. For those who think I've lost the plot suggesting they can have orgasms while eating, instead of thinking about the baked beans in the cupboard, think back to the most amazing chocolate you've ever put in your mouth or the meal you never wanted to end... 'mmmm, donuts!' (One final thought, consider how we are sold the image of a skeletal woman as sexy. Sex is largely about exploring & consuming the textures, tastes, smells & sights of your lover's flesh. So show me someone who knows how to eat themselves into delirium & I'll show you a good lover! This is yet another way the feminine has been separated from it's natural state. For if you're counting calories & chewing every mouthful a hundred times you're in Hell & our natural state is ecstasy (Heaven).

Fantasy Orgasm - a fantasy orgasm is when we feel flushed with heat & feelings of arousal simply from the power of suggestion. Women have long accessed this type of arousal through erotic literature. As the biggest consumers of romance novels like 'Mills & Boon' & more recent successes, 'The Naked Bride' & 'Fifty Shades of Gray' many women have returned time & time again for this titillation without realizing what they were experiencing was a prolonged state of anticipation, stimulation & waves of heat infused pleasure. Just because we're conditioned to think the only kind of orgasm is when we're arching our back & biting the pillow don't invalidate this as another type of orgasm. Women are governed by the upper chakras so their clairvoyant ability (imagination) is often more developed whereas men on average prefer to enter into this fantasy orgasmic state via hard copy images of erotica. So I recommend indulging in some really exquisite & artful erotic images rather than porn which has a lower vibration.

Multi-Orgasmic - this is simply when we allow the full circle of energy to return & build after having a yang orgasm so the energy can gather in the base & rise again. I recommend doing this without a partner first if you haven't experienced it so you can really attune to the subtleties of your own body & energy before expecting yourself to share this experience with a lover. The more orgasmic you become pleasuring yourself regularly the more easily you will relax into that state with a partner.

Orgasmic State - this is when your body is so electrified that every little sensation & movement sends jolts of ecstasy through your body. This is not a state someone should strive for as a goal with their mind. It is a natural by-product if our sole concern is on worship (giving) & pleasure (receiving). This means not rushing or being concerned with who's turn it is to give but allowing yourself to become so enraptured in both states that you experience both as equally orgasmic until everything is overwhelmingly filled with erotic sensation - even making lunch & urinating afterwards can be ridiculously orgasmic as this state can last for hours! (Funny to experience & watch.)

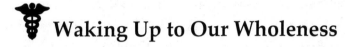 Waking Up to Our Wholeness

Understanding What it Is To Be Sovereign

How Mother Nature Is Helping Us To Wake Up & Transform

We are all currently experiencing a huge evolutionary leap. A fact made evident by the rapid developments being made in the fields of science & technology, which are mirroring the quantum leap in consciousness that we are experiencing as a species. This evolutionary shift can be attributed to the acceleration of the Earth's vibration or heartbeat (known as Schumann's resonance) which has risen from 7.8 hertz to 12 hertz since 1980. This quickening vibration at the center of our home planet is in turn quickening our personal vibration & frequency, accelerating our conscious understanding of ourselves, each other & life itself. This is quite simply why our relationships are literally busting at the seams, as we have outgrown the old model of relating.

For example, the 1950's version of 'wedlock' which confines one to operating out of traditional gender roles seems to many like wearing a straightjacket now as it isn't balanced & the 1960's 'free love' approach which rebelled against this paradigm also feels unfulfilling as it failed to acknowledge the emotional ramifications of transient partners, unexpected pregnancies & STD's. So during the past thirty years, (the cusp period of the emerging Aquarian Age, where the new energies have been expressed through the old forms), many have simply swung internally between wanting these two paradigms, finding neither of them to be truly sustainable.

We entered into gates of Eden on 11:11:11, having completed on October 28, 2011 the nine waves of consciousness acceleration as mapped out by the Mayan calendar, so we are now ready to create a new form of relating, befitting our new awareness. This new relationship model will reflect this shift by honoring our soul's true values as it's primary function. To do this we must first each take full responsibility for our ego's fears which create the old dance of relating. That being to revert to one of the following default behaviors in response to our fear of true intimacy:

a) avoid the true self by seeking an unconscious external relationship as a form of security & distraction which will not challenge us to grow or...

b) engage in polyamorous partnerships as a way of avoiding the deep exploration of shadow aspects intimate monogamy reveals or...

c) avoid the fear of rejection altogether by forming surrogate relationships with pets or inanimate objects such as collectables which distract from one's need for true intimacy with both self & other.

Only when we fully commit to having a truly intimate relationship with the Self are these impulses, 'to fuse, run or hide' understood, making it possible for us to create an interdependent conscious partnership where both parties operate with a high degree of self-awareness & responsibility so each can witness & communicate their inner landscape rather than project it upon or reject it in the other.

Committing to the Self: Becoming A Sovereign Being

When I turned thirty I married myself in front of all my guests at my birthday party. Some, I suspect thought this a desperate act by a woman who, according to my patriarchal dictionary was, by definition a 'spinster' as an unwed woman over the age of thirty. Regardless of how unconventional it seemed at the time, I just felt an inner need to do it. In the three years leading up to this I had felt inspired to create & facilitate 'Tantric Bridal Showers' which offered an alternative to the degrading pub crawl in a tulle veil & hen badge. In these 'Secret Women's Business' nights I would veil the bride-to-be & ask her to take three vows to herself. These included agreeing to uphold her personal values, educating her partner & children as to the gifts of the feminine & honoring the needs of her body, mind, emotions, & spirit in every choice she made. This commitment to Self was witnessed by her inner circle of soul sisters in the Red Tent who would then support her in married life to uphold her vows. The idea behind this was that I questioned how we could truly take vows to commit to another when we hadn't first made that commitment to ourselves! For it seemed to me a precarious act to make vows of intent to another if we didn't start from such a solid commitment to self to back them up! Formally stating that we can count on ourself to not compromise our truth is an act of self-love that I see as a necessary condition of entering into conscious partnership. When we consider that people treat us according to the standards & boundaries we set as acceptable, this simple but profound act of power ensured a mutually honoring union one could commit to whole-heartedly without hesitation or fear of commitment.

The Art of Being Consciously Single

Growing up in a largely unconscious culture that ostracized people who were single as 'wallflowers & losers', it is ironic that what makes someone a truly good partner is how much time they have invested in knowing, understanding & healing themselves, (which is undoubtedly easier without the demands of a relationship or family responsibilities). That said, there are certain lessons that can only be learnt through relationship with others, so ultimately it's about finding a balance between what we learn from both time with self & time with others.

When we consider the nature of our universe is holographic, meaning everything we create in our subjective experience of reality is a mirror of our conscious thoughts & unconscious expectations, it makes sense that to create a truly committed & loving partnership we must first make a deep commitment to love & honor ourselves & since love is a verb that means making loving choices & actions. How we feel about & treat ourselves will be mirrored back to us in those who we attract into our reality. In addition, the greater the capacity we develop to truly love & honor ourselves through conscious choice, the greater our capacity for truly loving & honoring others without fear based agendas.

Commiting to 'The One'

Before we can commit to another with the best of intentions, we must also make a commitment to that which is greater than us alone (the ego) & for the highest good of all. Call it what you will - Spirit, Source, God, the Universe, the Force or whatever 'Tupperware label' sits comfortably with you. Making this commitment to serve our collective, 'Oneness' marks the shift from ego to soul. This is the second birth, when one is 'born again' not into a specific doctrine but to the realization they are here to serve the greater or true self, the Soul which is part of the one 'World Soul'. For unless we have made this decision to serve the Divine plan by fulfilling our potential in service to the greater good, we will look to our partner as 'The One' & expect them to save us, by being the center of our world & fulfilling the infinite abyss within us which is not a fair expectation of a fellow human being & one which only creates such a clingy dependency that one's mate soon feels cramped by their overwhelming need.

When we make this commitment to embark on a path of spiritual growth, seeing every experience as a lesson, we make the transition from the child who blames others & feels sorry for themselves whilst unwittingly hurting others into a conscious adult. I see this as one who examines their thoughts & actions so they become wise & humble through self-reflection & the seeking of a higher truth. It is important to add here, that it doesn't matter what path you take so long as it deeply resonates with your own soul. Personally I'm not a fan of 'off the shelf' doctrines, groups or philosophies that claim to have the only exclusive path. As our truth is ultimately dictated by our own conscience if we take the time to listen & is reflected in all paths just as the Divine is. It doesn't matter what practice you adopt, whether it's a traditional sacred path like Tai Chi or just sitting by a lake or talking to the Higher Mind by reading the symbology of the clouds - all that really matters is that you make regular time to do it. I like to take inspiration from a wide range of spiritual paths, just like I enjoy cooking & eating foods from various cuisines. It is all Divine in essence so it's not as if you're a naughty child disobeying your parents by honoring the Divine in a form that is different from the standard Judeo / Christian meat & three veg equivalent you perhaps were fed growing up. So if you feel like creating a meditating Buddha & lotus water feature in your garden to create a serene sanctuary where beauty can uplift your soul or if you were raised Hindu, there's no reason you can't sing your heart out to Aretha Franklin's Gospel CD for a DIY Spiritual high!

A Solid Foundation for Soul Mate Union

Both of these marriages to Self & to Spirit are the essential building blocks for the new paradigm of Sacred Union, a conscious partnership that honors the holy trinity of self, other & the all. This creates a pyramid energetically, a temple of mutual growth so the union fosters an upward spiral of evolution, rather than a downward spiral of entropy which is what occurs despite our best intentions when we only focus on the other as a way of getting our needs met.

In the Tarot, this level of co-dependent partnership is illustrated in 'The Devil' card which portrays a couple who are operating unconsciously from their lower selves, outwardly pursuing that which they desire rather than developing those qualities within themselves. This is indicated by them focusing only on each other, a level of awareness which keeps them shackled as they unconsciously expect their partner to fulfill them & then resent them when they don't. This anchors a dynamic of dependence & need as the wounded child within each seeks to be unconsciously parented by the other.

THE DEVIL.

In the card, 'The Lovers' the same couple are featured but the woman is instead focusing on Spirit...this symbolizes that the feminine aspect is now fulfilling her soul's potential rather than looking outside herself for someone to save her from her misery & sense of separation.

THE LOVERS.

This dynamic occurs both internally & externally in partnerships. For example, externally it is often the woman or more feminine partner who will pursue a relationship with Source in order to explore her inner self & connection to the All. She will then try to inspire her more masculine partner to do the same. If they awaken their own inner feminine the partnership will grow to the next level by ascending the Tree of Knowledge. If they however, reject her feminine inspiration to grow she will either suppress or compromise her inner truth & need for growth at a cost to herself or eventually leave the partnership to be in alignment with her core values. Internally this dynamic also occurs within us, with the feminine part of us seeking out greater inspiration & meaning. This increases our receptivity to intuitive guidance so our rational ego (our masculine self) may then externally act upon it. For women or feminine dominant males who lack confidence in the external world they may first need to awaken the courage to act upon their convictions before they can empower their inner masculine to take action.

So unless we reawaken our connection to the Divine & honor ourselves accordingly by creating harmony & balance of the sacred feminine & masculine through the embracing of teachings & practices which foster our upward spiral of wholeness & reconnection, our relationships will spiral down the toilet into Hell. (That being the mindset of fear based reality we have been living, based only on the thoughts & perceptions of the lower senses.) To do that, we need to replace the subconscious programming that has kept us focusing on our fears, perpetuating an experience of Hell. For when we focus on the Divine, an eternal source of love & see ourselves as reflections of the Divine by delighting in our archetypal Gods & Goddesses, we become filled & inspired with love which fuels us to create situations that reflect this. Then it is possible for us to live Heaven on Earth in every aspect of our lives, as in this card we are the embodiment of love so we attract a reflection of this in every moment.

To find out how to share this with a lover I recommend reading, **'Volume Two: Creating Sacred Union In Partnership'**

Blessings, Tanishka

References to astrology

=> Uranus opposition + Chiron return: P. 61

=> Uranus square + return: P. 60